HOW TO WIN
THE WORLD CUP

SECRETS AND INSIGHTS
FROM INTERNATIONAL
FOOTBALL'S TOP MANAGERS

CHRIS EVANS

BLOOMSBURY SPORT
LONDON · OXFORD · NEW YORK · NEW DELHI · SYDNEY

BLOOMSBURY SPORT
Bloomsbury Publishing Plc
50 Bedford Square, London, WC1B 3DP, UK
29 Earlsfort Terrace, Dublin 2, Ireland

First published in Great Britain 2022

A catalogue record for this book is available from the British Library

Library of Congress Cataloguing-in-Publication data has been applied for

ISBN: HB: 978-14729-9079-2; eBook: 978-14729-9075-4; ePdf: 9781472990761

2 4 6 8 10 9 7 5 3 1

Typeset in Adobe Garamond Pro by Deanta Global Publishing Services, Chennai, India
Printed and bound in Great Britain by CPI Group (UK) Ltd, Croydon, CR0 4YY

MIX
Paper from
responsible sources
FSC
www.fsc.org   FSC® C171272

To find out more about our authors and books visit www.bloomsbury.com
and sign up for our newsletters

CONTENTS

PROLOGUE

'This has become a desire, a tremendous desire to win the World Cup competition,' said Sir Alf Ramsey as he stood in the Wembley tunnel less than an hour after his England side had lifted the Jules Rimet Trophy.

The Three Lions' first and, as yet, only World Cup-winning manager was the stereotype of an English gentleman in 1966 – principled, fiercely proud and guarded to the point of sometimes seeming cold in times of great emotion.

Ramsey's typically understated response to the BBC reporter's question about what it meant to win the World Cup on home soil does little to diverge from that perception. '[The desire] had rubbed off on to the players to some great extent and it leaves you a little flat at the same time. You have this tremendous feeling of satisfaction,' Ramsey continued.

In a moment when even the sternest of masters could have been forgiven for letting their hair down, Ramsey's words may suggest an indifference about the achievement. But anyone who came across the England manager during his time in the Wembley hot seat knows that impression couldn't be further from the truth.

The reality was that Ramsey had been bitten by the World Cup bug, just as many of his fellow international managers had been previously, and since. He had a clear plan of how he was going to lead England to glory in their home tournament and started putting it into action before he'd even agreed to take the job.

Ramsey's predecessor Walter Winterbottom had been little more than a coach. A committee of selectors not only chose his squad, but often voted to decide on the starting line-ups, leaving Winterbottom with little chance to impart his tactical wisdom.

But Ramsey wanted full control. If he was going to be England manager, he knew he had to row his own boat in order to get the best possible results. He'd built a blueprint for glory in eight successful years as Ipswich Town manager and wanted to bring his own methods to the job. And it worked, as England's single World Cup star from 1966 attests.

Football may have changed a lot since England's victory, but the concept of a manager needing to put a plan in place in order to get anywhere near their ambition of leading a nation to a World Cup win remains. As Roberto Martínez, Belgium's manager as they reached the semi-finals in 2018 said, 'You'll never find a national team that wins a World Cup by coincidence or by accident and that's the work of a national team manager.' It might seem like an obvious statement, but formulating a winning strategy is easier said than done.

There are countless issues to tackle – such as getting the right balance in squad selections, handling big stars, and achieving the best possible atmosphere for a tournament camp under extreme pressure – as well as managing scenarios specific to taking a national team to a World Cup. And, yes, that includes negotiating a penalty shoot-out.

Throughout the decades, more than 350 managers have taken charge of a team in a World Cup, with thousands more entering in the qualification phase, each one of them with their own masterplan. Yet only 20 men have managed to get their hands on the trophy and there's only a couple of dozen more who can claim to have truly become immortalised in the countries they've managed on the back of their World Cup exploits.

There are plenty of pieces that need to fall perfectly into place for a nation to be on top of the world. And this is what *How to Win a World Cup* explores: how coaches have successfully jumped the myriad hurdles that stand in the way of their dreams, and the lessons learned from the ones who have fallen flat on their faces.

When we romanticise over past World Cups and the great moments from them, it's normally the players we remember. We think about Pelé's boyish genius, Marco Tardelli's celebration, Diego Maradona's impudence and many more flashes of brilliance from decades gone by. But we rarely consider the man who's made it all possible. The guy standing in the dugout. The boss.

Without a manager providing a platform or environment for the world's best talents, none of those moments would be possible. Sure, there's nobody in world football who could have choreographed Maradona's inspired performances for Argentina in 1986, but history doesn't remember that it was only at the insistence of La Albiceleste manager, Carlos Bilardo, that El Diego was made the focal point of his team. If Bilardo had bowed to national pressure, Maradona may not have been selected at all.

Throughout the following pages, I speak to managers and players from different nations and eras to discover if there really is a winning formula, or at least a common thread of dos and don'ts, when it comes to negotiating the pitfalls of a World Cup.

One thing's for sure, with international football such a unique arena to compete in, if teams are going to come out on top, desire is the bare minimum they need to succeed. Just ask Sir Alf.

CHAPTER 1

A DIFFERENT WORLD: INTERNATIONAL MANAGEMENT

The pinnacle of the game. The most-coveted job in football. A vocation reserved only for the very best. That was how an international manager's role was viewed for decades. And the World Cup was where the globe's most-skilled coaches would go head-to-head in the dugout, just as the best players were doing out on the pitch.

While the advent of super-rich clubs and the growing importance of domestic leagues and the UEFA Champions League has curbed international football's reputation in the 21st century, there remains a special enchantment to leading a national team to glory. The opportunity to unite a nation across club boundaries remains a unique one. There's no other sporting job in any football-mad country that gives a manager the chance to bring such unbridled joy to so many people.

The impact international football success has had on national morale, politics and even economies shows the influence coaches can have. But the pressure of such an influential job isn't for everyone. Neither are the different challenges and styles that need to be adapted to. For while some of football's greatest club managers and former players have had a go at replicating their exploits on the international stage, it takes a distinct character to get it right. This has created a band of international specialists, experts whose temperament and approach suits a different type of football. One that culminates with the chance to write their name in history at the World Cup every four years.

So what type of manager suits international football and how can those leaving the club game adapt?

* * *

If somebody had asked Roberto Martínez three months before he became Belgium's manager if international football was on his horizon, he'd have given them a straight answer: no. The then-Everton boss was a Premier League mainstay, having taken charge of a side in England's top flight for every match of the past seven seasons. He was the quintessential club manager and while his third campaign in the Goodison Park hot seat hadn't gone to plan, the Spaniard's move to take over the Belgian national team took many people by surprise. Not least Martínez himself.

'It's something you don't plan,' he tells me. 'You always say international football is the start for a coach if you're a former player and it's a first job that's an introduction to management; or at the end of your career if you're a very experienced coach and you don't want to be in the day-to-day anymore. In my case, I was open to another project.'

Aged 43 at the time of his appointment, Martínez says it was the prospect of working with a supremely talented Belgian generation that enticed him to make the switch from the club game. He broke the traditional mould for an international boss as he was a manager who'd established himself at domestic football's top table and appeared to have his best years ahead of him at club level.

Martínez was more prepared than many of his club compatriots, though. His studious nature meant he'd already got an insight into the role of an international manager, but he admits a big readjustment was still necessary to bridge the gap between the two codes.

'It was very difficult and I was constantly fighting the way I'd been working,' Martínez explains. 'Club football is always a 24-hour job and it's always about looking forwards – it's very rare you get the opportunity to look back. Everything is about what you can do to affect the next game. Even the press

Club football is always a 24-hour job and it's always about looking forwards.

conference straight after the 90 minutes is about the next game and the way you can affect the preparation.

'International football is the opposite. It's about a very intense period, after which you don't share any emotions with the players, which does change the strength of relationships and the group – whether you win or lose, the players just leave. At that point it becomes about preparing for the next game by looking back, reassessing, and I enjoy that.'

Moving to a less fast-paced role with greater retrospection isn't for everybody. The lack of regular contact with players, the inability to work on the training pitch each day and the comparatively pedestrian pace of the fixture list has led to some coaches becoming restless.

A recent example is Antonio Conte, who yearned for what he described as the 'cut and thrust' of the club game during his two years in charge of Italy. He was a few years Martínez's senior when he took over the Azzurri after climbing the rungs of the Italian club game, but never felt truly at ease having to adapt to the slower nature of the international game and agreed to join Chelsea before sampling his first tournament at Euro 2016.

It's a feeling Martínez can relate to. The Spaniard had to grapple with those same instincts at first, but soon settled into a new rhythm focusing on analysis and long-term development, leading to him becoming a more well-rounded coach.

'At club level, you have 60 sessions pre-season to prepare for your first game. When you go to international level, you've got three days,' he says. 'It's accepting that I couldn't work in the same manner [as I did at club level], because at international level we have five camps every year, so it's not the same as meeting the players every day. I thought the way to prepare games and try to affect the players would be the same, but I was wrong.

'I had to change my mindset and focus on what was essential in this job and try to learn very quickly how to prepare the players in the best way in a short period of time, which shouldn't be looked at as a disadvantage. I shouldn't compare my role to what I did at club level, I should compare it to the other international managers – and they have exactly the same amount of time as me.

'When you change that mindset, everything becomes a lot easier. It's an impossible job to manage internationally the way you do at club level. When you realise that it's completely different, then you can evolve in many ways.'

Letting go of those preconceptions is a crucial part of a club manager's transition into the international game. It's more hands-off, and patience becomes the buzzword for managers as new ideas swill round and round inside their heads as they watch weekend after weekend of club matches, where the closest they come to a touchline is sitting in the stands.

At a club, managers have the chance to control every aspect of match preparation, and for those who like to run a tight ship, entering an environment where they're on the outside looking in at players can be difficult to accept. International bosses need to check themselves so as not to become an impertinence to their players or their club managers.

'I didn't have too much contact with the players when they were with their clubs as they had to concentrate on their club football,' recalls former Switzerland boss Ottmar Hitzfeld. 'As I was a club coach myself, I knew you shouldn't interfere. When it's the international break again, you have the players and can communicate things to them, but I let them be when they were at their clubs, unless they contacted me.'

Hitzfeld was a club coach of high regard and is one of only five managers to win the European Cup with two different clubs – Borussia Dortmund in 1997 and Bayern Munich in 2001 – but even he admitted the move to international management was a 'big adjustment'. The decades of experience he'd clocked up domestically were still relevant, but this was a new challenge.

The German says it wasn't so much about changing his style when he was with his squad, but says working with a national team did bring different skills to the fore that hadn't quite seemed as crucial previously.

'You see a club team every day and you can better develop the players on a day-to-day basis,' Hitzfeld continues. 'You can have a lot of discussions when possible and you can manage a lot more intensively as you have more influence. With a national team you see the players, have a match and then go off again for three or four weeks. It makes a big difference, of course, as you don't have such a big influence with a national team. You have to communicate openly and be sincere with the players. You have to talk clearly about your aims and discuss them clearly, be very consistent and determined about what you do.'

The crux of a coach being successful at international level seems to rely heavily on his ability to work succinctly with his players. Less time means being more selective about which instructions to give, the focus of training sessions, and the level of detail surrounding certain sequences of play.

But it's not simply about stripping down technical and tactical information. It's also important to make sure the messages a manager does choose to convey are interpreted in the way that's intended, depending on each player's background. There isn't the time for communication to fail.

'When you manage a Seleção [Brazilian national team], everyone comes from different places, they're used to playing in different game situations and they need to adapt to the new environment,' Brazil's 2002 World Cup-winning coach Luiz Felipe Scolari explains. 'You need to be more observant and the tactics need to be very well defined for the whole group because in a club you can work things out daily. In a national team you don't have that time. 'So you need to be a lot more observant, collect more data, take special care with certain players and try to create a game situation that all these players from different clubs around the world can adapt to.'

Explaining a tactical approach is one thing, but any manager knows a winning team also requires emotional strength. Creating a special bond among the squad and with the coaching team is key for any side, so it stands to reason that this, too, will be more difficult in an international setting.

People-management has been one of Scolari's greatest qualities throughout a managerial career that saw him take charge of Brazil and Portugal's national teams, alongside stints at top club sides including Chelsea and Palmeiras. So with little face-to-face contact, other considerations need to be made, too. 'It's a special situation,' Scolari says. 'Every player has next

to them another player who is very different to them. They
have different characteristics, so there needs to be a very big,
general adaptation process. In order for the players to develop
their football, they need to adapt and comprehend their
team-mates.'

It's a challenge every international manager has faced over
the years, so the connection has to be created in different ways.
Technology does mean maintaining contact among the group
and individuals is easier than it was, but there's no substitute for
the spirit created within a team when everyone is together.

That's not to say it's impossible to achieve a tight bond
among a group using other methods, it just means a manager
has to find new ways to leave a positive impression that carries
on during the weeks between meet-ups. That can mean a coach
showing loyalty to a core group of players by selecting them for
every camp or not being as tough on the side as he might have
been in a club environment.

'I'd just say he was very straightforward,' remembers
England's Terry Butcher as he looks back at Bobby Robson's
time as England manager between 1982 and 1990. 'If you did
the business for him, he'd be very happy and he was very loyal
to the players who did that. He'd speak to you in a way that's
very familiar and passionate, but also in a way that's very
structured, ordered and disciplined.'

Butcher was Robson's captain when the two worked
together at Ipswich, so the big centre-half was more familiar
with the inner workings of the much-loved England gaffer than
most. After long briefing sessions, players would ask him if this
was what Robson was like at Ipswich and while Butcher would
joke the meetings were longer, the 77-cap defender says there
were some subtle differences to his manager's approach at
international level.

Robson couldn't abandon the methods that had earned him the success to land him the job in the first place, but made just enough changes to adapt to his new environment. One of his biggest changes was in the way he dealt with the players, to create a fondness that blossomed throughout his tenure. Working with Robson became one of the big appeals for joining up for an England camp.

'The thing I liked about Bobby was that he'd take you to one side, put his arm round you and say "come with me son", then we'd go and speak,' says Butcher. 'Every player likes to be told if you're doing things right or if you're doing things wrong and how you can improve, and he did that very well.

'Particularly for England, he didn't see the international players a lot because there's gaps in between matches, but he'd speak to them in such a way that you felt wanted, loved and as though you'd run through a brick wall for him.

'He was like that at Ipswich, but because it was day-to-day, he was probably more strict and more aggressive in how he spoke to you because he demanded results pretty quickly. He couldn't do that with international players because they weren't the property of England, they were loaned to England from the clubs.'

With all of these different aspects to balance, there's no wonder the international manager has become a specialist position. In more recent years, career national team bosses have become more common within the major nations, with coaches moving up the age groups just as a player would. It means they're institutionalised to the way a federation works and more familiar with what it takes to be successful in a national team role – meaning there are fewer growing pains during the metamorphosis from club to national coach.

'There are certain figures now who become coaches for federations rather than for clubs,' picks up the *Independent*'s chief football writer, Miguel Delaney. 'There's a very distinct strand, the likes of Gareth Southgate, Joachim Löw and Spain – up until Luis Enrique – where they try to make a virtue of bringing in coaches who have come through the ranks. Coaching the junior teams to a point when taking over the full senior team becomes a natural step.

'We're seeing that a lot more and that's to the betterment of international football because it's not like the 70s, 80s, 90s, or even the start of the millennium, because I don't think you can just transpose a manager's abilities from the international [game] to the club game, or vice-versa, so easily.'

With international management jobs seeming to be less appealing than in previous decades when the position was considered the pinnacle of a nation's game, it might seem merely convenient to promote from within. But the idea that managers should have strong knowledge of their players from a young age is very important and it's part of the vision of many federations to have a 'golden thread' running throughout its entire system.

'Different qualities are needed for the job, so it makes sense the federations would look towards a different coaching type and personality,' says Delaney. 'Somebody who is used to, or better disposed to, this job where it's a changing group of players with a one- or three-month break [between matches]. That's before you get to what people like Southgate and Löw exemplify, where they've come through with various players – they know the traits the federations would want.'

* * *

That method of hiring is not how many international sides have appointed managers in the past. Legendary former players have had a habit of going straight from retirement into their national team's managerial post, with their reputation enough to earn them a crack at the big job.

This approach had mixed results as the sink-or-swim nature of football management spat out those not ready for the role, while others grabbed the chance with both hands to show they were just as effective on the touchline as on the pitch.

The impact of having such a strong figurehead at the top of the national team is powerful, just as West Germany found when Franz Beckenbauer replaced Jupp Derwall at the helm in 1984 – a matter of months after Der Kaiser had hung up his boots with New York Cosmos. Beckenbauer was one of the world's biggest stars and appeared in two World Cup finals as a player, winning in 1974 after defeat to England in 1966. He'd been an innovator long before getting his first coaching job, concocting the 'libero' role behind West Germany's defence to make the most of his defensive and ball-playing talents, and lending guidance to his managers in order to maximise the team's potential.

While Beckenbauer's path to West Germany's top job may have seemed obvious, his appointment marked a change compared to his predecessor. Derwall had enjoyed a fine playing career himself and had worked his way up the coaching ranks to get the international job, but his profile wasn't nearly as prestigious as the megastar who, for all intents and purposes, had been installed on reputation.

'They were two very different coaches,' explains winger Pierre Littbarski, who was a member of the Germany sides that reached the 1982 and 1986 finals before finally winning the trophy under Beckenbauer in 1990. 'Derwall was more like a father type, he was a little naïve but very kind and trusting of the players. Whereas Beckenbauer, he knew all the tricks already, so we couldn't cheat him – if we performed badly, he could see it directly.

'We wouldn't embarrass ourselves with our performance. It was a different way we had to approach the games and there was a lot of respect for Beckenbauer in every training session and everybody was very focused.'

Beckenbauer's presence alone appeared to extract that extra performance from his players and while he was quite a hands-off coach in terms of tactics, his experience as a player and strong understanding of the game came to the fore when it was necessary. As a legend of the German game, he maintained a hold over his players in a way many others wouldn't have achieved, and the image of him standing on the touchline was enough to inspire his charges.

'With Beckenbauer, I think everybody had the motivation to deliver 100 per cent in every minute because he was accepted as a football player by the strong personalities in the squad,' adds Littbarski. 'The players had a lot of respect [for him], but also for themselves, and they wanted to show Beckenbauer they could deliver something similar to what he delivered as a player. To perform at a high level, not everyone the best, but in terms of being very strong physically and having a presence – that was maybe different than with Derwall.'

The aura of a national team hero taking over the reins as a manager can undoubtedly provide a boost, although it's rarely sustained across the same length of time as Beckenbauer achieved. But while many stars don't go on to have long legacies in the dugout, the short-term bounce a team can get from a high-profile appointment means longevity isn't always the only barometer for measuring their impact.

If a team is having a bad time, hiring somebody who is a national icon can change the dynamics of the situation entirely, as happened when Diego Maradona was brought in to coach Argentina in 2008 during an ailing World Cup qualification campaign. The prospect of working with a man many of the players had grown up worshipping was an extra incentive for success and created a renewed buzz about Argentina training camps. The balance of influence had changed.

'It was the first time I'd met Maradona and I'd never seen him face to face,' says Jonás Gutiérrez. 'It was something special to be with him because I loved him when I was a child and my parents talked about him – so when he takes charge of the national team, it's a special moment.'

While Maradona's time in charge lasted fewer than two years, his impact was immediate as La Albiceleste won four of their first five matches after he took charge. The only possible drawback was if his status created nerves among his starstruck players.

'I was really nervous,' Gutiérrez continues. 'I remember what time he came into my room. I was with [Ezequiel] Lavezzi and I was in shock, there was a [mental] block and I couldn't say anything. When Maradona left the room, Lavezzi was laughing at how I reacted in that moment. I was sweating a lot, I listened to him but I could say nothing to him. Maradona had something special, he brought something you can't explain in words, you had to feel it. For me it was the first time I had met my hero, he was talking to me like a normal person and it was something I will always remember.'

Maradona's managerial prowess may not have matched up to his talent on the pitch, but the prospect of playing under him and not wanting to let him down was similar to the way Littbarski spoke about Beckenbauer. That prestige alone might not be enough to hang a career in club management on, but in an international environment perhaps there's an argument for a famous profile holding more sway than in a day-to-day role.

That can transcend nationalities too. Just as the promise of working with a big-name manager can be the tipping point for players when moving clubs, so was the reputation of Fabio Capello a key factor in Jamie Carragher agreeing to return to the England fold for the World Cup in 2010. The then-Liverpool defender had turned down overtures to return in the aftermath of his international retirement in 2007, but a trip away with Capello provided the push he needed to make a U-turn.

It's a tangible impact that lesser-known managers can't compete with, with Carragher's vision of what it would be like to work with Capello providing an insight into how a player's psyche can be affected by who's in the dugout.

'I was just imagining what he was doing with Maldini and Baresi [who Capello worked with at AC Milan] and I'm thinking, I want a bit of that,' says Carragher. 'He's Fabio Capello. What you think of Ferguson, Mourinho and Wenger 10 years ago, what you think of Guardiola and Klopp right now, he was the manager of the 1990s and to me he was the [best] manager in world football.'

The trouble with having grand illusions about working with a particular manager is when reality doesn't match up to expectation, meaning managers need to deliver in order to retain their mystique. If they don't deliver, their balloon is quickly punctured. Although Carragher admits he was underwhelmed by Capello while they were away at the 2010 World Cup, it's clear a healthy respect remains.

'I just thought he'd be a lot more hands-on on the training pitch, but I guess he was a lot older then as a manager,' Carragher recalls. 'His toughness, he had a class and an aura, he looked the part even at that age. He looked after himself, he was very strong and stern, he wasn't worried about upsetting players. I loved him. I envisaged working with him on the training pitch with the back four and what he did at AC Milan, but there wasn't so much of that.

'I used to sit with him regularly and watch every game at the World Cup. I'd sit in the TV room in the afternoon and if there was a game on, I'd be watching it. It would normally be me, Steven Gerrard, Fabio Capello and Franco Baldini [Capello's assistant], the other lads weren't interested in watching the other games. We'd always be in there watching football. His English wasn't great, so they'd converse in their own language or he'd make the odd comment about something or throw his arms up.'

... I believe you'd be a much better international manager if you've been a national team player at a World Cup ... It would be so much easier to be accepted by the players.

If the lure of a high-profile manager is so large, then it stands to reason that the task of being successful in an international job is far greater if you don't have previous playing experience. Traditionally, it was always thought that managers needed to be ex-players who have played at the top level, although that view has softened in more recent decades with the emergence of José Mourinho and Julian Nagelsmann at the top of the world game. So does Brazil's 1994 World Cup-winning coach Carlos Alberto Parreira, who never played professionally, agree that having a strong playing CV can help an international boss?

'Speaking openly, I believe you'd be a much better international manager and coach if you've been a national team player at a World Cup,' he reveals. 'It would be so much easier to be accepted by the players, there's no doubt about that.'

Parreira's story of how he made it into the exclusive club of World Cup champions started in 1958 after witnessing Brazil's masseur Mario Americo's role in the Seleção's maiden World Cup triumph. Americo was famous for being sent on the pitch to pass secret messages from manager Vicente Feola to Pelé,

Garrincha et al during matches, and a young Parreira dreamed of one day being the national team's fitness coach as well, rather than being the main man in the dugout. Yet the veteran manager worked his way up to become part of Mario Zagallo's coaching staff as Brazil won the trophy in 1970, before being asked to take the Kuwait job in 1978 after initially going there as Zagallo's assistant.

After leading the Kuwaitis in their first World Cup campaign, Parreira's stock steadily grew until he was asked to end Brazil's 24-year wait for a fourth World Cup trophy. He duly obliged, proving it's possible to succeed at the top level without having played at it. In fact, he makes it sound as though it was easier than if he'd been working at grassroots.

'The players respected me,' Parreira adds. 'I didn't need to teach big players like Rivellino, Romario or Bebeto how to kick or control a ball, I had to organise them as a team – and this was OK because I knew how to do that. My responsibility was to organise them as a team, which is where I was successful and I did this well, especially in 1994.

'I believe if a manager of a national team is a player who played in the World Cup before, I think the hire is more acceptable [to the public] and easier for them to be successful. In my case, I didn't have to fight the system, people pushed me.'

While that might have been the case for Parreira, not everybody with ambitions of reaching a World Cup has had the same luxury.

CHAPTER 2

STARTING FROM THE BOTTOM: MINNOWS

World Cup glory comes in many different forms. While it's the vision of a victorious captain holding aloft the famous gold trophy that most people recognise as football's zenith, the competition's allure means there are often so many more champions than simply one.

With 207 nations eligible to enter qualifying for the 2022 World Cup, the expectations of fans in each corner of the globe vary wildly. Although the major powers will see success as nothing less than stepping on the field to contest the final, for other countries making a tournament appearance or simply scoring a goal in a qualifier is the yardstick they'll measure their campaigns by.

Success changes from nation to nation, team to team, individual to individual. So it's only right the first step of our journey has to consider the little guys. The minnows. The managers who take jobs in places where the prospect of boarding a plane to play at a finals isn't even spoken about seriously. Instead, taking charge of a lower-ranked side is part of a process, a move that managers of these nations hope will one day see them lead a team to take part in a World Cup finals party. It's just that there are several outposts to visit first.

And it's often in these smaller nations, with reduced resources and scant infrastructure, where the true test of a manager lies. Sometimes it means taking over teams so used to losing by heavy margins that damage limitation is the default setting. For others, the goal of upsetting the odds has led to bonkers plans hatched in the name of unlikely glory.

As legendary Serbian coach Bora Milutinović, who holds the joint record with

My real target is to go with a nation to the World Cup... that's the highest you can achieve.

Carlos Alberto Parreira for leading five different countries to tournaments as a manager, says he told more than one national football association when interviewing for the jobs: 'It doesn't matter about anything else, just let me go to the World Cup.'

* * *

Tom Saintfiet has always had a clear plan. The Belgian coach has worked for more than 12 national teams in four different continents, but has always had his compass pointing in the same direction. 'My real target is to go with a nation to the World Cup,' he says without a quiver of self-doubt in his voice. 'For me, that's the highest you can achieve. Higher than the Champions League, because that's a tournament that happens every year and a World Cup is once every four years, where the best of the best from all over the world come together.'

Don't tell that to UEFA, who see the riches on offer at their premier club competition as being the pinnacle of the game for everybody, but few people across world football would quibble with Saintfiet's desire to place the World Cup on a pedestal of its own. Yet only a select number of people go to the lengths the 49-year-old has on a quest to reach the finals.

After being forced to retire from playing at 23 due to a series of cruciate ligament injuries, Saintfiet turned his attention to coaching. And after racking up his coaching badges, a sports psychology qualification and experience managing in the Belgian lower leagues, he started putting his passport to good use – embarking on a two-decade sojourn that has seen him manage the likes of Gambia, Malta, Yemen and Bangladesh.

He now ranks in the top five coaches for the number of national teams ever managed. Yet despite taking charge of two nations that have previously reached World Cups – Togo, and Trinidad and Tobago – he's never come too close to achieving his dream. 'Not every job can be selected on World Cup chances. That's the aim, but sometimes I have to make decisions and accept deals for financial reasons,' Saintfiet explains. 'It was never the aim to manage lots of national teams, but you need to work and be in the business and to take care of your family.

'I accepted a five-month deal in Ethiopia and a three-month deal in Malawi. It didn't always help my CV, so it wasn't always about going to the World Cup. When I signed with Yemen, Bangladesh and Malta, I knew beforehand they weren't countries I could guide to the World Cup. But on the other side, I have to earn money, gain experience and grow as a coach, so I took these decisions.

'The aim is to go to the World Cup, but before a footballer gets there, he starts in the lower leagues and moves up, step by step. You can't sign immediately for the biggest club in the world and I can't sign immediately with the biggest nation in the world.'

There's always the threat of the dream falling flat, of course. But Saintfiet isn't alone in ploughing on towards a goal that may never become reality. Scour the names of the world's national team managers and a startlingly high number of

Europeans – and a dusting of South Americans – jump out, rather than home-grown natives. A host of predominantly British, German, Dutch and French coaches who have dedicated their careers to qualifying for a World Cup.

It's not a wild goose chase, though. Just ask veteran German boss Otto Pfister, whose first international management job began with Rwanda in 1972 at the start of an eye-watering 34-year wait before finally cracking the code when he took Togo to the 2006 World Cup.

The octogenarian describes his coaching career as a 'permanent adventure' and only called time on it in 2018, a few months short of his 81st birthday.

He could have been forgiven for thinking his chance to manage at a World Cup had passed him by. After playing key roles in the development of future African qualifiers Senegal, Ivory Coast and Ghana, Pfister oversaw Saudi Arabia's qualification for the 1998 World Cup, but was moved aside before the tournament kicked off after falling out with Prince Faisal, who was heading up the Saudi Arabian Football Federation at the time.

'Two weeks after qualifying, the Confederations Cup started in Saudi Arabia. In the first game, we lost 3–0 to Brazil and their team full of stars. Afterwards, the president of the federation [Prince Faisal] was not happy with the result,' Pfister says.

'He told me he wasn't happy, but it wasn't a big problem. He said, "Give me a programme for World Cup preparation and I'll give you three weeks to give me the list of players". Three weeks later, I met him and gave him all this information, but he said I had to change one player.

'I told him, "My royal highness, you are my boss, but I'm your coach and I cannot accept that". Twenty-four hours later,

I was put in charge of the Olympic team and Carlos Alberto Parreira was given the job to go to the World Cup.'

Pfister was later offered his job back for the final group match of the tournament after Parreira had himself fallen foul of the Prince following defeats in the first two matches of the World Cup, but the German refused.

A hectic managerial merry-go-round isn't unusual for international coaches trying to make their mark and it was Togo's sacking of Stephen Keshi three months before the 2006 World Cup that presented Pfister with his own 'special story' at the tournament. And the German says handling precarious job security and tumultuous situations are part and parcel of the job of a travelling manager.

'In Africa, in Saudi Arabia, sometimes in Europe, you hear these stories,' he says. 'You need to be strong mentally or you can't work in this area – you have to accept this. It's another world, you need to respect it because you can't change this world.

'I know a lot of German and English coaches who try to bring discipline to Africa, but you cannot do this. You have to accept the status quo and the situation. If you don't accept this, you cannot work in these countries. You have to make compromises and if you're not ready for compromise, you cannot be a coach working in this area. I have experience of this my whole life, but I have no problem with it. If you do, it cannot work.'

Attempting to overhaul long-standing cultures might seem like the obvious first port of call for some national team bosses when starting a new job. And while Pfister warns some of these areas need to be left alone, at least initially, there are certain jobs where the only real remedy is change.

* * *

Scroll all the way down to the very bottom of FIFA's world rankings and you'll find a bloc of countries that have one thing in common: a history of heavy losses. While in leading nations such as England, there's regularly talk about the Three Lions' decades-long years of hurt since they lifted the Jules Rimet trophy in 1966, some of the world's tiniest nations can go for years without simply avoiding defeat. It puts England's woes into sharp perspective.

So what sort of manager accepts these jobs on possibly the furthest rung from a World Cup? One man is former Trinidad and Tobago striker Stern John, who took over FIFA's second-lowest ranked nation, Anguilla, at the end of 2020.

The ex-Birmingham City and Sunderland hotshot knows what it takes to make it to the World Cup after reaching the 2006 tournament with Trinidad and Tobago. But while the Soca Warriors upset the odds to get that far, John would have even further to climb with Anguilla. The island, with a population of only 15,000, is used to getting walloped on the pitch, with two of the five matches prior to John's appointment seeing the team ship double figures, including a 15–0 defeat to the new manager's home nation. A record of conceding 100 goals in their last 17 games before the Trinidadian took charge (that's an average of just under six per game) doesn't sound like a recipe for World Cup glory.

'I didn't kid myself,' John says frankly. 'We had to rebuild a lot of stuff and put it into place. Most of the players here are part-time and we had to adopt a more-professional mentality first before we can think about getting to a World Cup.

'It's a long-term process. When I look at the last couple of fixtures [before John took over], we hadn't won a game in two years so it's baby steps. We had to take all those losses and bring them under control first, then we could look at winning games. It's a process and it takes a while.'

It puts an entirely new spin on the fabled 'project' managers talk about when they start a new job. To motivate yourself to go into a position where your first aim is to simply be competitive in matches takes a special sort of mindset, but one that is appealing to certain managers.

'It's a ladder for both sides,' explains Vin Blaine, who's worked as a director of football and technical director with Jamaica, Grenada and the US Virgin Islands. 'The manager wants to show he is worth the investment in him, but coming in he knows exactly what he's faced with. For him to do well, it's not even by getting to the second round or drawing a game, sometimes it's losing 1–0 instead of getting beaten 6–0, based on the history of the team. To the manager, he wants to prove the team can play good football and that's really the aim. It's about not getting downbeat, because that can happen easily.'

Blaine has witnessed every level of how football develops in the Caribbean with the nations he's worked for, and is familiar with what encourages some of these coaches to take on a job many deem as a thankless task – work your fingers to the bone just to suffer another defeat? No thanks.

But the Jamaican says that while some coaches quickly fall by the wayside when they realise there's no magic wand to wave for instant gratification, that does provide openings for those who can remain optimistic and keep their eyes on the bigger prize.

'They [the mangers] come in at first because it's a good thing on their CV if they can establish themselves and turn things around,' Blaine adds. 'They might not go to a World Cup, but if you move the team up the rankings then you can make your name from that. You come in with a different mindset depending on what the reality is. And the reality can be changed based on how you approach it – if you accept five-, six- or seven-nil losses, then you deserve to go.'

That's what John needed to rally against with Anguilla. On one hand, he understood the need to get to grips with the nation and had to avoid the temptation to rush in with the big-league attitude he was familiar with in his playing days in England, but realised he had to instil some higher standards quickly to arrest the team's wretched record.

'We have to rebuild the whole football infrastructure here, as well as the culture and understanding of playing at a high level, and what it takes,' John says. 'The biggest challenge is having them [the players] buy into the professional environment because most of them go to work in the daytime and train in the afternoon, so we had to speak to the government so the guys can be paid for training.

'There's no better thing than representing your country, so our biggest fight is to understand that we're trying to compete at a high level and we want to get these things in place to go to that level.'

At least John has some heritage to lean on to make that change. In some of the world's youngest – and smallest – nations, football has no foundation to grow from and their managers are expected to act as figureheads for the birth of a national sport right down to grassroots, rather than simply take care of what the seniors are doing on the pitch.

Particularly in underdeveloped parts of the world and those blighted by years of conflict, even the most basic facilities are scarce, making the chances of creating a team to compete much more difficult. So the task of lifting the fortunes of a national team without access to a stadium, an organised league or even a training pitch with grass on it becomes much harder. Yet for some managers, small is beautiful. Despite the paucity of provisions, there are certain benefits to having a blank canvas to create something in their own vision.

'I remember going to a play a tournament in Bangladesh called the Banga Bundle against club and under-23 national teams from different countries,' recalls well-travelled manager Stephen Constantine, who took over Nepal's national side in 1999.

'I was given six weeks with the players in my first camp to prepare. In the lesser-developed countries, the national federations control the clubs not the other way round. In the major Asian nations, like South Korea, you'd never get six weeks because of the league and cup. But in Nepal, the president can stop the league for the national team.'

It's the perfect scenario for a coach to really get to grips with his players. However, while it means a manager can make a lot of progress in a much shorter amount of time with the federation's backing, the base level is much lower to begin with. In fact, sometimes that added advantage may only be in getting back on an even keel with opponents.

'When you get players from professional clubs, you don't need to work on fitness and technique. All you need to do is work on the tactical aspect, or the particular role of a player, or what system you want to use,' Constantine continues. 'That's enough in two or three days [of an international window], but when you take some of the lesser countries where the coaching hasn't been good and players aren't getting a lot of things they should be from their clubs, you have to do it at national-team level. With countries like Nepal or India – where I've also been manager – you have to do the job of the club and the national team.'

This scenario is a breeding ground for innovation. And for a growing number of managers taking jobs at some of the less-developed nations, some of the biggest gains can be made by spending time in the passport office rather than the training pitch. Particularly in the Caribbean islands and some African countries, identifying talent with appropriate heritage is becoming an art form. Over the past two decades, international managers have regularly received pitches from agents representing players who qualify for a certain nation, while some coaches cast the net out themselves.

'I send messages everywhere: Canada, America and all over Europe,' reveals Montserrat boss Willie Donachie. 'Anyone from Montserrat or with Montserratian relatives, I'm happy to go and see play, or get in touch with. Montserrat is in a really unique situation because there's only about 4,500 people on the island, which is less than a borough in London, so it's very difficult to develop our own players there.'

When former Scottish international and Manchester City defender Donachie took over Montserrat in 2018, he knew what he'd be up against at the Caribbean nation – which has one of the smallest populations in the world – and, much like John at island neighbours Anguilla, had to first stop the rot.

With a pool of only 14 players, several of who Donachie says weren't up to scratch, the new manager started recruiting a cluster of players with Montserratian blood from England's non-league clubs. Tapping into the vast Windrush community in and around London, Donachie brought in a host of players and soon started picking up some respectable results – making it an easier sell when contacting new targets.

'We won a couple of games in a row and they couldn't believe it, people on the Montserrat FA were crying, which was emotional to see,' Donachie says. 'Since then we've had a few good results, it's getting better. We're finding more new players who want to play for Montserrat, whereas before they weren't interested and saw us as a Mickey Mouse team.

'The big challenge here is that a lot of the players in the London area are sons or grandsons of Montserratians, so I'm trying to find out what's going to happen with the next generation. Will their children be able to play for Montserrat? At the moment, the rule is only players with parents or grandparents who are from here [are eligible], so the next generation might miss out.'

Donachie has instigated plans to develop teenage players on the island, such as entering them into league systems on nearby islands. But it's another of his former employers, Antigua and Barbuda, that has attempted the most ambitious plan to create a stream of homegrown talent. And it's one they hoped would take them all the way to the World Cup. In 2011, the Antigua and Barbuda Football Association planned to enter their international team into the United Soccer League as a club side, Antigua Barracudas, playing a US league season in the summer and World Cup qualifiers in the winter. The hope was that the togetherness and exposure to better football would carry them all the way to the tournament.

'It was a fantastic idea for the country in that it was a national team playing as a club side,' explains Tom Curtis, who took over the dual managerial role when the initiative began. 'We'd play together and get used to each other, playing against different types of opposition. We'd be able to prepare as best we could for the World Cup games in the winter, which is really what the programme was about.

'As well as qualifying for the World Cup, we were tasked with getting into the world's top 70 nations because that would mean players could get work permits to play in many European countries, so they could go overseas and make a living. It was hoped that would have an implication on tourism by raising awareness and was supported by the government at the time. It was an idea full of innovation and I don't think many nations had done that sort of thing before.'

The idea was so crazy, it almost made sense. And inspired by Curtis's Barracudas clocking up thousands upon thousands of air and road miles, it almost worked, as they cracked FIFA's top 80 and reached the last 12 of CONCACAF World Cup qualifying – heights the Benna Boys hadn't scaled before.

Things were looking good until internal disputes and reality bit regarding the financing needed to keep what Curtis describes as an 'intense but incredible' experience running. Yet Curtis, who now works for England's FA, says he had to adapt quickly to the island's big dreams.

'I remember turning up in St John's, the capital city, when I took the job and tried to get a feel from the president of his expectations and where he thought we could finish,' he adds. 'And he said, "Coach, I want to win the World Cup". He was genuine. He wanted to win the World Cup, he wanted to get there and that was his dream. I love that and everyone should have that passion and dream of getting to the World Cup final. That's what it's all about, wanting to win and achieve. It's very difficult for the smaller nations, but I don't think that'll stop people trying.'

Once you're bitten by the World Cup bug, it's hard to shake off that ambition. The romance of living a dream is why managers keep taking jobs at some of the world's least-fancied nations. But it's a challenge that isn't exclusive to the coaches hell-bent on making a name for themselves in the world game, as was proved when Dutchman Guus Hiddink took charge of Curaçao in 2020. The two-time World Cup semi-finalist may be more familiar with working alongside the globe's biggest stars, but it turns out the prospect of achieving the improbable with a small Caribbean island ranked 80 in the world was too tempting to ignore.

'It may not be obvious, but it was difficult to say no,' the ex-Real Madrid and Chelsea boss said at the time. 'Curaçao had made good steps in recent years. I'd like to help the players and staff to get one step higher on the international ladder.' The island nation, which is a constituency of the Netherlands, has never reached the latter stages of World Cup qualifying, but the prospect of using his experience and contacts to enhance their fortunes was enough to attract Hiddink to the role.

It was difficult to say no... I'd like to help the players to get one step higher on the international ladder.

Even if the reality of making it to the World Cup finals is still a bit far-fetched, it's that glimmer of hope and feeling that you're playing a part in achieving that ultimate dream that provides the motivation for these coaches. Big name or not, it's why they do it.

'Realistically, the countries I've been manager of aren't going to a World Cup and have never been to a World Cup, but as a manager you like to think you can make a difference,' explains Constantine, who has managed India, Malawi, Sudan and Rwanda since starting out in Nepal.

'For that particular country, going to an African Cup of Nations or Asian Cup is like going to a World Cup. But, of course, I want to go to a World Cup, who doesn't? I've been fortunate enough to be at a major tournament with one of the worst teams in Asia [India at the 2019 Asian Cup]. So, can it be done? It can, absolutely. We've done it.'

CHAPTER 3

LOOKING INTO THE ABYSS: QUALIFICATION

Getting a national team job with a country that has a realistic chance of qualifying for a World Cup is only the first hurdle in a manager's quest to make it to the finals. Negotiating qualification can sometimes be more of a trial than it's given credit for, even when managing an elite country.

While some of the smaller nations are celebrated as heroes for getting their name on the list of qualifiers, for many others their progression is taken as a foregone conclusion. A guarantee they will always make it to the World Cup. But as history suggests, that's not always the case. Only two countries have ever made it to the finals of every World Cup they've entered: Brazil and Germany. The rest have fallen short during qualification on at least one occasion. It goes to show that nothing is ever a given and although some nations seem to make light work of qualification on a regular basis, a manager can't ever afford to rest on his laurels.

The ordeal of getting through qualifying has lessened in more recent World Cups as the number of finalists has steadily grown to its current 32-team format. But just try telling Italy bosses Gian Piero Ventura and Roberto Mancini it's easy, after the Azzurri crashed out before the 2018 and 2022 tournaments. With plans to extend the competition to 48 countries for 2026 onwards, though, the odds of major nations missing out are getting slimmer.

The difficulty of qualification also seems to be dictated by which continent a country is in. In Europe, there are significantly more spaces up for grabs than in other regions, with 13 spots on offer for UEFA in the 2022 World Cup in Qatar –

Managing the national team is the highest honour ... that generation of players deserved one more chance at a major tournament.

making up more than a third of the draw. Conversely, it's possible for Oceania to have no representatives at all. Of course, this is all decided by past performances, FIFA World Rankings and the relative strengths of the continents, but there's an almost self-fulfilling prophecy that Europe will continue to dominate when it has so many finalists.

In Africa, where only five of the 54 teams taking part will make it to the finals, qualifying is highly competitive and it's tricky for coaches to build on the momentum a good tournament can bring if a couple of slip-ups mean they miss out in four years' time. It can mean managers are walking a tightrope to maintain their World Cup dreams, long before the big tournament kick-off.

* * *

Failure wasn't an option for Zlatko Dalić. The newly appointed boss had been given only two days and one match to rescue Croatia's ailing qualification campaign, but he was already piling the pressure on himself. As Dalić sat in his first press conference after being unveiled as Ante Čačić's replacement, he told the assembled journalists he'd quit if Croatia failed to qualify for the World Cup. Lose away to Ukraine two days later and that would have been it; avoid defeat and they would merely be booking a play-off spot for Russia 2018.

It could have been one of the quickest qualification disasters an international manager had ever suffered. Although this was no act of hubris, Dalić's bold opening gambit was his way of avoiding such a conclusion.

'That's just how I felt. I believed in myself and I believed in the quality of the team,' Dalić explains. 'I wanted to show the whole team that I was there for them, to help them achieve great things and not for myself, for my contract or for money. Managing the national team is the highest honour for every coach, so money and contracts were not important to me at that point. I just wanted to qualify for the World Cup because that generation of players deserved one more chance of a big result at a major tournament.'

A brace from Andrej Kramarić ensured there were no first-night dramas against Ukraine, before an emphatic 4–1 aggregate victory over Greece in the play-offs meant Dalić's words didn't come back to haunt him.

A combination of positivity and openness had seen Dalić breathe new life into a side that had won only one of the previous four qualifiers to leave the Vatreni's World Cup dreams hanging by a thread under previous coach, Čačić. And while the new boss deserves credit for his role in that, the Croatian federation's decisiveness in making a managerial change at such a late stage – and, unusually, during an international week – tells a fascinating story.

International football rarely witnesses new managers making the instant impact on a side in the same way the club game does, but that's usually due to faltering coaches being given a significant chunk of qualification campaign before meeting their maker. By then, the damage may already be done. Čačić could still have done the business himself with similar results, yet the Croatians showed that hire 'em, fire 'em could work, too.

The night after the Croatian team celebrated victory over Greece, there was a stark reminder of the pitfalls of qualification elsewhere in Europe. About 1,000 miles (1,600km) away from the scene of Croatia's win, Italy were suffering despair in Milan as they missed out on a place at the World Cup for the first time since 1958, after losing in a play-off to Sweden.

This failure was unthinkable for a nation that had come to take its place at the finals for granted. After being drawn in the same qualification group as Spain, Italy had kept faith in coach Ventura and understandably so as, other than a draw against Macedonia, Italy's only dropped points had been against La Roja.

Ventura himself even admitted he was 'amazed people are surprised we're in the play-offs' ahead of the Sweden match. In the pre-match press conference, he said: 'We knew from the moment we picked Spain in the group phase that we'd be heading for the play-offs. Nobody can be surprised we reached this point. We started out with people talking about the apocalypse.'

If Ventura faced the apocalypse then, things were about to get worse as Italy tumbled out of qualifying for the 2022 World Cup after losing 1–0 to North Macedonia in a play-off semi-final at home. By then, Roberto Mancini was in charge, having won Euro 2020 less than nine months earlier – highlighting how easily qualifying mishaps can happen.

'Last summer [the Euros] was the most beautiful joy, now comes the greatest disappointment,' said Mancini in a post-match interview. It's not easy to think of other things, I am very sorry for the boys: I love them much more tonight than in July. I am the coach, I am responsible, the boys are not.'

Despite the defeat, Mancini's prior record helped him avoid the sack. But four years earlier, Ventura paid the price for play-off heartbreak with his job, although there's an argument that

Italy's failure had as much to do with past results as the ones in that qualifying campaign.

For 2018 qualifying, the Azzurri ranked outside of the top nine European nations on UEFA's seedings, below the likes of Wales and Romania, leaving them in the second pot to draw Spain – highlighting how a current manager's job can be made more difficult by his predecessor's misfortunes. The task of qualifying can, in theory, become harder with every failed cycle.

FIFA's ranking system is used to decide on seedings, with past success or failures meaning the weighting of draws could make the path to qualification easier or harder depending on recent results. In the past, some managers and federations would try to use the system for their advantage, carefully selecting opposition for friendlies that were likely to guarantee more ranking points and therefore a higher overall position – earning potentially more favourable draws in the process.

'I've never used the ranking myself, but I know over the years some countries try to use that to have a good draw,' says Denmark's Morten Olsen. 'Nowadays, more and more coaches in the smaller countries are doing it in that way. That is what you have to choose, it's part of the game. Although now with the Nations League, there are fewer friendly games to be able to do that.'

As one of the longest-serving international managers in recent years following 16 years in charge of Denmark, Olsen knows only too well how easy it is to suffer a blip in qualifying and end up with a more difficult draw in the next four-year cycle. It's an occupational hazard and as a non-elite nation with a smaller pool of players to choose from, it's much easier to fall foul of a bad run if the strength in depth isn't available, or if there isn't a conveyor belt of replacements when one group of players gets older.

'You have to be OK with the situation that sometimes you miss key players in some games,' he laments. 'The difference between club football and the national team is that you have maybe eight or 10 games [in a qualification campaign], so there's less room for error.

'For instance, in our last qualification, one of our key players, Christian Eriksen, didn't play because he was injured. You may have one player who makes the difference, but as a small country, you maybe have more key players that are necessary than in Germany or England – the big countries – who have more depth to choose from. In my time, we qualified for four major championships, but if you lose two games in qualification, you are out.'

The most difficult competition in the world is the African qualifiers – it's a nightmare. It's tough and really competitive.

While the idiosyncrasies of seeding can trip up some countries in Europe, UEFA's weight of importance in the world game does mean there are more qualification places available for their nations than in other federations.

In Asia, at the time of writing, there are two group stages to negotiate – not to mention an initial knockout for the lower-ranked sides – followed by play-offs for the sides finishing outside of the automatic qualification spots. While in Africa, the smaller nations contest a first round before the top seeds join in a second group stage. Only the winners of each group then progress to a two-legged knockout to claim the five places on offer. In short, it makes for a long, drawn-out qualification process with plenty of chances for slip-ups along the way.

'Carlos Queiroz once said the most difficult competition in the world is the African qualifiers – it's a nightmare,' says South African journalist Mark Gleeson. 'It's tough and really competitive. There are 15 worthy countries chasing five places and then it becomes a generational thing. South Africa, for example, had a great team in 96 and won the African Nations Cup, we had a tough World Cup qualifying group in 98 and qualified and that extended into 2002, but we haven't qualified since.

'The same is also true of Ghana, who are one of the great African footballing countries, but they took forever to qualify for a World Cup. Ivory Coast first went in 2006, Egypt won three African titles and never got there. It's a very intense qualifying competition.'

As a result, the pressure on managers is immense to build something substantial. The great Egypt side Gleeson mentions epitomises the challenges they face – becoming the first ever nation to win three successive African Cup of Nations, but always failing to reach a World Cup in that time.

It's a quirk that only goes to highlight the tightrope managers are walking to reach a major tournament, especially in regions where away matches can be uncomfortable affairs with several cultural and logistical hurdles to jump along the way.

Sometimes, a bit of local knowledge can go a long way in getting through a difficult qualification campaign. Even if a country is one of the bigger powers on its own continent, understanding the conditions and styles that need to be dealt with is crucial before planning for the finals can be considered.

Trips to certain outposts within that continent can be particularly treacherous for the uninitiated, with hostile crowds, different extremes of weather or even oxygen-sapping high altitudes to contend with. Each are potential pitfalls for the unsuspecting manager.

'There were two really high-quality competitors in CONCACAF (Confederation of North, Central America and Caribbean Association Football) – that was Mexico and Costa Rica – the others were manageable,' says Steve Sampson, as he looks back at his time as USA boss in the late 90s. 'No foreign coach who has come in to be in charge of the US national team, like Jürgen Klinsmann, understands how difficult it is to play in

Honduras or in El Salvador, or in Guatemala or in Costa Rica, with the conditions they have there.'

Knowing what's in store with certain fixtures is only half the battle. The second is coming up with a plan to deal with those specific circumstances, which is a tall order when international breaks are so brief. Luckily for Sampson, he had a little bit more flexibility to work with before a do-or-die qualifier against Mexico to reach the 1998 finals.

'When we were preparing to play Mexico in Mexico City, it's 10,000 feet (3,000m) up and its noon when we play games in the Azteca Stadium. You're in front of 120,000 people and it's one of the most contaminated cities in the world from an air pollution standpoint,' he says. 'You're playing at one of the of the highest-altitude venues in the world outside of La Paz in Bolivia and Quito in Ecuador.

'[Ahead of the game], I said to the federation, "I need 10 days to prepare this team for altitude acclimatisation". They agreed and we took a team into the mountains in Southern California, a place called Big Bear, and we prepared for 10 days.'

For all the familiarity home and away matches across a continent can provide, the World Cup's qualifying structure can still throw up some more unusual fixtures. While the vast majority of matches are kept between recognised regions, there's normally at least one inter-confederation play-off – providing completely new challenges across two legs.

That can mean coaches need to quickly adapt their style, or hurriedly scout out unknown opposition, just as Republic of Ireland boss Mick McCarthy had to do before a 2002 play-off against Iran.

'That was a culture shock to say the least,' McCarthy remembers. 'It's just a vastly different culture, I'd never seen so many Hillman Hunters (the cars) in my life. We stayed in a hotel, went to the game to do our scouting – I think we'd been in UAE to watch them first, then they went back to Iran. My picture was flashed up on one these big screens in the stadium with all these fans in there and I'm stood beneath. I thought, "I could do without that". We sat on plastic picnic chairs in the stand. It was nothing like if you turned up in Dublin and you'd be in the directors' box.'

Ireland took care of the first leg with a 2–0 win, but McCarthy's job ahead of the return trip was to prepare his players for a very different atmosphere in Iran. The Irish manager recognised it was the psychological side of things that were going to make or break their trip to Tehran.

'There were certain things we had to be aware of. Prior to the game there was this prayer-like noise and it boomed out of these big speakers,' he says. 'They're all fellas in the ground, so there's this huge baritone noise, singing or chanting – it was quite intimidating – then they had their national anthems.

'We told the players what would happen and said, "that baritone noise is not the national anthem, stay where you are". But, of course, they were all so geed up beforehand, so after the Iranians had that big baritone effect, all our players disbanded and started running around the pitch, but it wasn't time.

'When we won [Ireland lost 1–0 on the night, but progressed 2–1 on aggregate], the Iranian fans started railing against the authorities and there were loads of glass windows smashed, and anything they could set fire to in the stadium, they did. But as I walked through them, they applauded me. Their reaction wasn't actually against us. The atmosphere the Iranians created there was eerie and intimidating, I have to be honest.'

* * *

Bolivia's Estadio Hernando Siles has long been a graveyard for opponents in the South American qualifiers for very different reasons. Situated in La Paz, 11,932ft (3,637m) above sea level, the ground is one of the highest professional stadiums in the world and is regularly cited as offering an unfair advantage to the home side – even temporarily receiving a ban from hosting World Cup qualifiers for a short time in 2007.

An away match in Bolivia was one of the obstacles standing in the way of Luiz Felipe Scolari as he was drafted in to save Brazil's qualifying campaign in 2001. It seems incredible to think considering what the Seleção went on to achieve at the finals in South Korea and Japan, but the would-be champions were in serious threat of missing out on qualification until Scolari was hired. With only five matches left of the 18-game mini league,

Every game we played we had to add points to make sure we could go through, winning or losing we were always in trouble. But with that, we started to create a group.

Brazil were clinging on to the top-four spot they needed by virtue of goal difference. With tricky away trips to Bolivia and runaway leaders Argentina still to come, every point mattered if Scolari's rescue act was going to be successful.

But while their struggles weighed heavily on them, this qualifying emergency turned out to play a crucial role in creating the winning spirit that carried them all the way to lifting the trophy less than a year later.

'Every game we played we had to add points to make sure we could go through, winning or losing we were always in trouble,' Scolari recalls. 'But with that, we started to create a group. I started to trust the most experienced players, started friendships – not just as a manager – and so we formed a group between us where I had to take some decisions that helped the group to become stronger. So they trusted me a lot and I trusted them, there was reciprocal care, friendship and work, and that's how we formed an environment almost like a family.'

The 'Scolari family', as it became known in Brazil, was a cornerstone of the successful camp at the finals. Yet it was only a final-day victory against Venezuela that allowed them to book their plane tickets to the 2002 World Cup.

The role qualifying plays in the journey of some of the most famous World Cup runs is often overlooked, with the significance of overcoming adversity as a group before a finals long forgotten by the time they progress to the tournament's latter stages.

But if the stars align for a nation, however far away the finals are, the psychological impact can be huge if a certain significance is placed on particular matches or sequences. It was another technique Croatia manager Dalić took full advantage of when he was brought in ahead of the critical Ukraine qualifier in 2017. The tie followed the path taken by the great side that reached the 1998 semi-finals, who had to get past the Ukrainians in a play-off to qualify 20 years earlier.

'It was a very important motivation for our players, especially the older ones who remembered the World Cup in 1998 quite well,' Dalić explains. 'Many of them said several times they always dreamed of going back to Croatia and getting a huge welcome from the fans after producing a great result.

'They remembered that team [of 1998] and it gave them both the self-confidence that a small country such as a Croatia can do it, and the motivation to experience something like that. I always repeated to them and to the media that I truly believed they could do something similar in Russia and tried to get that into the players' heads.'

Synchronicity can have the opposite effect on teams, though. The expectation that history will repeat itself can pile on the pressure, only ramping up the prospect of letting a hopeful nation down. Falling short at club level can be bad enough, but making history for all the wrong reasons when there's a fanatical country that sees failure to qualify as a national shame is enough to make the blood of even the most seasoned player run cold. And it's up to the manager to shield his squad from that.

'I said to my parents, "If we don't qualify for the World Cup, I'll give up football". It's something I really felt. That night, I got night fevers and that was something that never happened to me,' says Jonás Gutiérrez, who was part of Diego Maradona's Argentina side that qualified for the 2010 World Cup by the skin of their teeth.

Maradona arrived mid-way through Argentina's faltering qualification campaign, but his charisma, status and eccentricity meant all eyes were on him alone by the time the final round arrived. He fiercely defended his team to the media – despite calling up 70 different players during qualification – and seamlessly remained the main talking point at all times.

When Martin Palermo threatened to steal the headlines from his boss by scoring a 92nd-minute winner in the penultimate match against Peru, Maradona unleashed a penguin-like belly slide along the touchline to keep the attention on him. It wasn't premeditated and neither, presumably, were his impassioned press conferences – most memorably after winning qualification when he grabbed his crotch and challenged Argentine journalists to 'suck it and carry on sucking it' – but he managed to divert all attention away from his players.

'It was the best and you had to experience that to understand it,' Gutiérrez continues. 'Maradona understood the person, he lived with pressure, so it was like a normal day for him. For most of the players, it was like we were relieved of that because all the pressure was on him. But he liked that and he knew how to deal with it, so for the players it was something important that he was the manager of the team.'

* * *

Not every manager can avoid the potential banana skins qualifying throws down and there have been some high-profile casualties down the years. Alongside Italy's Ventura and Mancini in the hall of shame sit some of world football's most notable managerial names: Louis van Gaal, Sir Alf Ramsey and Gerard Houllier. Other than the obvious, what binds the stories of each of this trio together is the seemingly fine margins that stopped them from being successful.

'The record of van Gaal as a manager speaks for itself. It was not that he was a bad manager, but sometimes the timing is wrong,' midfielder Bolo Zenden tells me about the Netherlands side that failed to qualify for the 2002 World Cup. 'Sometimes things occur that, as a manager, you don't have that much influence on, but those incidents decide whether a manager is said to be doing a good or bad job.'

For van Gaal, he took the Dutch job on the back of a successful decade managing Ajax and Barcelona, and thought he could take a talented Netherlands team one step further after consecutive semi-final defeats on penalties in the 1998 World Cup and Euro 2000. Yet they finished third in their qualification group, four points adrift of Portugal and Republic of Ireland.

Far from being an unmitigated disaster, Zenden's memories of van Gaal's first stint as national team manager are characterised by bad luck and circumstance. 'The game against Portugal at home, there was a fan in the stands who blew a referee's whistle, so we stopped and the Portuguese kept playing and scored a goal. We ended up losing the game,' says Zenden. 'We played a good game [in the return match] in Portugal, but then Frank de Boer conceded a penalty in the last minute and Luis Figo scored. But I don't want to make excuses because in the end we weren't good enough and we didn't play well enough.'

As many managers have found to their cost in the past, falling on the wrong side of too many close calls is enough to cause a team's qualification campaign to end in failure. And when every bad result builds more pressure, it's easy to see why narratives can form around just one or two key moments. Normally, though, those instances are symptoms of a broader problem. In the Netherlands' example, van Gaal's assessment was that the squad he inherited wasn't as motivated to win as they were when he worked with some of the players when they were younger – and it showed when it mattered most. It was something that stayed with him until he got a second bite at the cherry ahead of the 2014 World Cup, when he took a different approach to leading the Oranje through qualifying and on to the semi-finals.

Publicly, these stories rarely focus on root causes of problems and it's perception rather than fact that dictates how the manager at the heart of it all is remembered. Take England's most famous failure in 1973, when a Wembley loss to unheralded Poland meant the nation failed to qualify for the World Cup for the first time. The story of the calamity always focuses on Polish goalkeeper Jan Tomaszewski, who put in a superhuman display as England peppered his goal with 36 shots but only scored once as the Poles grabbed the point they needed to qualify at the expense of their hosts.

But look at the campaign as a whole and the Three Lions' failure had probably more to do with the end of the Ramsey era. Just seven years after being world champions, they only managed to win one match out of four in a qualifying group that also included Wales. That record was hardly the hallmark of a side that was simply unlucky to go out. 'England's tactics were wrong,' Wales defender John Roberts told the *Sports Argus* in 1973 about England's 2–0 defeat in Poland, prior to that night at Wembley. 'If you admit that, you must admit Alf Ramsey was wrong, because he has sole charge of selection. England played it the continental way, holding off and needing time and space – that played into Poland's hands.'

Ramsey's problems weren't confined to this qualifying campaign, though. England's performances had become stodgy, with the team failing to score more than once in 14 of Ramsey's last 22 games in charge, and he faced regular criticism for his timidity when it came to using substitutions.

Those issues were laid bare during that fateful World Cup qualifying campaign, as England only scored three goals throughout, with Ramsey introducing Kevin Hector from the bench against Poland at Wembley with just two minutes left on the clock. Despite that, if England had managed to score more than once from all the chances in the 1–1 draw, things might have been different.

'We were committed to going forwards and committed to scoring goals, but they never came unfortunately and the longer the game goes on, the frustration and desperation grows,' said Ramsey in his post-match interview with the BBC. 'Instead of playing it coolly and calmly in the hope the goals will come… I think we were pushing forwards much more at that particular time and we gave a goal away. We were maybe a little unfortunate because we were in the same situation many times during the match.' Ramsey left his post soon afterwards, but the path of history may have been different if England had found a way past Tomaszewski to qualify.

The reality is, zoning in on a solitary reason for a setback isn't always healthy for a national team, regardless of whether the manager stays on or not. While England slipped into a malaise after missing out on the 1974 World Cup that they never really shook off until the 1990s, other nations use their own low points as a springboard for a brighter future – even if it's not so obvious at the time.

Just as with England's defeat to Poland, France manager Gerard Houllier blamed one incident – or more specifically one person – for costing Les Bleus a place at the 1994 World Cup when they conceded a last-minute goal to Bulgaria in a qualifying showdown.

Houllier branded Ginola 'the murderer' of French hopes and said he'd 'sent an Exocet missile through the heart of French football and committed a crime against the team'.

Winger David Ginola was the target of Houllier's ire after the substitute tried to pick out Eric Cantona with a 90th-minute cross rather than hold the ball in the corner to defend the point they needed to qualify ahead of their opponents. Ginola's centre was overhit, gifting possession to the Bulgarians who quickly broke and scored. After the match, the normally mild-mannered Houllier branded Ginola 'the murderer' of French hopes and said he'd 'sent an Exocet missile through the heart of French football and committed a crime against the team.'

While Ginola's lack of game management was clearly an error, it's unfair to place all the blame on him. The defeat was France's third in a 10-match group – their second at the hands of Bulgaria – and they'd failed to win two of their three previous games, to relinquish top spot. If anything was to blame, it was a mental block.

'I didn't play the last game because I was suspended, but it's more of a mindset issue that we missed that World Cup because we were thinking we had already qualified when we had been five or six points ahead at the top of the group,' France midfielder Christian Karembeu recalls. 'After that it was a lesson for everybody that in football, you cannot underestimate any opponent. We lost many points against Israel and Bulgaria, and that last defeat was a shock.'

While France wouldn't travel to USA for the finals, four years later they were celebrating winning the World Cup for the first time. Houllier lost his job in the immediate aftermath of the Bulgaria defeat and his assistant Aimé Jacquet took over, and it was Jacquet's intuition that France's demise wasn't as simple as blaming Ginola's cross that led to that success.

'We learned from this and I think Mr Jacquet took and studied all these parameters to give us the stability, hope and know-how to achieve that goal,' Karembeu continues. 'He understood from 94 that individuals could make the difference, but you can make more of a difference as a collective group. He'd been through that experience at the time and there were many, many talented players – David Ginola, Eric Cantona, Jean-Pierre Papin and so on – but we didn't get through. He made some choices in the end to prevail as a collective.'

For France, their greatest-ever moment rose from the ashes of the nation's shame. Although as some other managers have found during their quest for glory, there's not always time to rectify their errors if they make bad decisions on their travels.

CHAPTER 4
IN THE LINE OF DUTY: DANGER

The power of the World Cup can be measured by what it does to a country's streets. Football can empty usually busy roads as locals gravitate towards television screens to watch their national heroes in a crunch match, or it can fill those same thoroughfares after a crucial victory, attracting a swell of celebration and noise. The sport's influence can be felt everywhere.

But while the promise of World Cup glory can see communities grind to a halt as it grabs attention in a way few other things can, its high profile can also attract the wrong kind of focus, such as the ability of the criminal underworld to make a statement while all eyes are on football's biggest prize, or the unstable situations it can place national teams in. It follows that being an international manager can come with its dangers.

As the figurehead of a nation's football hopes, it's not unusual for a coach to pay the price if things don't go to plan. But in some situations, getting the sack is the least of their worries. Down the years, managers have found themselves in tricky scrapes, or have become the target of dangerous plots simply for doing their jobs. Particularly when managing smaller nations, working in locations where security is an issue becomes commonplace and, when tensions come to a head, there can be frightening consequences.

Elite-level nations aren't immune from unsavoury incidents either, with some World Cup managers being the subject of kidnap plots and death threats. To paraphrase Liverpool legend Bill Shankly's famous quote, football may not be a matter of life and death – it can be a lot more serious than that.

* * *

Peter Butler knew something was amiss. As the then-Botswana head coach and his staff wandered through Bamako, the Yorkshireman's sixth sense clicked into overdrive. Butler's adopted nation was in the Malian capital for the second leg of a crunch 2018 World Cup qualifier, but the former West Ham midfielder had sensed tension since he'd arrived. And it was more than pre-match nerves.

Going into the match with a slender 2–1 advantage, Butler should have been fully focused on masterminding a famous victory for the Zebras. Instead, he was on edge. 'The security wasn't great when we got there and I wasn't really happy about it. I went to the [British] embassy and they couldn't do anything,' Butler recalls.

'We were staying at the Radisson Blu hotel in the city and although we got beaten 2–0, we went out for a few drinks afterwards. There was an eerie feeling and a strange environment. The next day when we checked out of the hotel and flew back, there were already Islamic jihadists in the hotel. And later that day they stormed the hotel and shot 20-odd people dead.'

Butler's brush with insurgents isn't the only time he's found himself in a precarious position since he traded a role as Halifax Town's caretaker manager in 2000 for coaching adventures further afield. As a club manager, he's been attacked on the pitch by angry officials in Indonesia, come face to face with would-be match fixers in Asia, and inadvertently become a pawn in military junta Tay Za's plans to gain global acceptance for his misdemeanours after being asked to organise a meeting with the British ambassador while working in Myanmar.

Those situations might not be something many coaches used to working on plush training grounds would consider as being reasonable to contend with, but for Butler it's the price he's willing to pay to 'row my own boat' as a manager.

He said up there is [convicted war criminal] Charles Taylor's training base. You've got to watch your Ps and Qs, watch what you say, be respectful and never look down on anybody whatever they're doing.

Since moving into international management – initially with Botswana and then Liberia – he sees his roles as humanitarian as much as sporting, even if he does hope to move up the ranks to get the chance to lead a major African nation to a World Cup in the future. To flourish, he needs to adapt to the environments.

'I was driving up to Ganta [a town in Liberia] and stopped at a checkpoint in a village,' Butler says. 'I said to the lad stationed there, "Where's this?" and he said up there is [convicted war criminal] Charles Taylor's training base. You've got to watch your Ps and Qs, watch what you say, be respectful and never look down on anybody, whatever they're doing. A smile goes a long way in Africa.'

Being streetwise and having a good set of manners will only go so far. While several coaches have found an unlikely sense of security in some of the most troubled nations on earth as they gain the adoration of the locals, the value placed on an international manager couldn't be greater – especially if they're a foreigner.

And sometimes being lulled into a false sense of security can be the most dangerous thing. That's what much-travelled boss

Stephen Constantine found when he decided to expand his knowledge of players at his disposal while Sudan manager. After deciding to stray away from capital city, Khartoum, his fearless nature landed him into a perilous situation.

'Under previous coaches, 95 per cent of the players selected were from Khartoum, but I wanted to go to see other teams and players, so I travelled four-and-a-half hours with a driver to travel outside of the capital,' he says.

'We were four hours into the trip when my boss, president Dr Kemal, called and said, "Stephenson, where are you?" and I just said, "I'm not sure, there's sand behind, sand in front and sand all around". He asked me to pass the phone to the driver and they started shouting at each other, then I got the phone back and he tells me to "turn the car around because you're not safe, you could be kidnapped or killed, we cannot guarantee your safety in this place".

'I said I was half an hour away and that I could see the city limits between the sand dunes. He puts the phone down and calls me back a few minutes later to say somebody is coming. About five minutes later, a massive pick-up truck appears with extremely big guns and I thought, "This is it, we're going to be snatched and killed". It turns out they were local security the president had sent to come and get me. They took me out of my car and put me in their truck to escort me to the stadium.'

Butler and Constantine's near misses at least suggest that a modicum of caution – and help from influential friends – can help the discerning manager pick his way through life working in more dangerous countries. But what happens when the authorities who are meant to be looking out for you are the ones placing a crosshair on your back?

That was the situation facing Tom Saintfiet when he became Zimbabwe manager in 2010. The Belgian's decision to accept a job in a country with a fractious political environment and questionable human rights record was possibly never likely to end well, although within only two weeks he found himself being smuggled out of the country by the cover of darkness.

'I was a few days into camp before a qualifier and the general secretary came to me to say I had to leave on a flight he'd arranged for me that evening at seven o'clock, otherwise the army and the police will arrest me for working without a work permit,' Saintfiet reveals. 'It was not my responsibility [to sort out a permit] and as a UEFA Pro Licence coach with experience in Europe and Africa, there should never be a problem. I stopped training immediately and went to the federation's office, where the lawyer from the federation was calling the police and immigration to try to solve the problem. I'd missed my flight, was sat in my training clothes and couldn't go to the hotel to pick up my things because the police were already there. In that moment, you're very scared because you don't know what's going to happen.'

Stranded in Harare, hundreds of miles from the border and with a net closing in around him, Saintfiet's only solace was regular contact with the German ambassador and his family. There was nothing left for him to do, but sit tight until darkness fell and put his trust in the staff he'd only met a fortnight earlier to help him evade prosecution.

'I had to get in a car with a driver I'd never met before and by night he drove me through Zimbabwe towards Botswana,' Saintfiet continues. 'Then at four o'clock in the morning when we're about to cross the border, a police agent stops us at the control post and looks in the window. I was wearing a baseball cap so as not to be recognised but he said, "Are you the coach?" I thought the game was up but then he turned to me and said, "Good coach, good coach," and waved me through. I guess he didn't know I had to be arrested and he allowed me to leave Zimbabwe. I left the country and couldn't return. What happened was completely unacceptable for any person or national team coach, knowing someone who came to help a country was chased away full of fear.'

Saintfiet suspected his sudden problem was linked to an ongoing match-fixing scandal in Zimbabwe at the time and that his desire to run the national team in his own way had made

What happened was completely unacceptable for any person or national team coach, knowing someone who came to help a country was chased away full of fear.

him persona non grata. This link was never directly proved, but the suspension of 98 Zimbabwean players and officials for their involvement in the Asiagate scandal that alleged match-fixing in a series of friendlies between 2007 and 2009 shows the environment Saintfiet had entered. In early 2012, it was reported by the Zimbabwean news network, NewsDay, that ZIFA chief executive Jonathan Mashingaidze was kidnapped and later freed as the lurid episode unravelled.

Such criminal misdemeanours might seem like the scourge of football's lesser-vaunted nations, but they've spilled out on the biggest stage, too. Rumours about the controversial 1978 World Cup have long surrounded Argentina's former dictator, Lieutenant General Jorge Rafael Videla, who is alleged to have rigged the competition in the home nation's favour.

But beyond doubt is the impact Argentina's political situation had on the 15 visiting sides for the tournament. Security was on red alert across Argentina as opposition to Videla's murderous dictatorship, which had seized control in a military coup two years earlier, attempted to use the tournament to shed light on the country's desperate situation. And it left France's manager, Michel Hidalgo, fearing for his life.

As Hidalgo and his wife, Monique, drove from their home in the south of France to Bordeaux train station, where the French boss would travel to Paris to join up with the rest of the party and fly to Buenos Aires for the tournament, his car was stopped by armed men. '[One of the attackers] pointed a gun at me and ordered me to go with him into a small wood 50 metres (160ft) away,' Hidalgo said in a TF1 news interview shortly after the incident. 'Meanwhile the other person took my place in the drivers' seat next to my wife. But I made a move once we had walked 15 or 20 metres (50 or 65ft) because I could feel the barrel of the gun in my back and I sensed I didn't have long to live. My reflex was to turn and grab the barrel of the revolver, which fell to the ground. I managed to grab it first, at which point he [the gunman] ran away.'

Hidalgo, gun in hand, headed straight to the nearest police station, where the firearm was found to be unloaded. An anonymous tip-off later that day claimed the attempted kidnap was carried out by opposition to Videla wanting to draw attention to France's supply of military equipment to Argentina.

In the immediate aftermath of the incident, Hidalgo initially decided 'there was no point in going' to the World Cup as sport paled into insignificance when held up against safety, but quickly reconsidered. 'Sport won out,' he said of his U-turn. 'I'll soon be back with the players [in Argentina, for the tournament] and we need to pursue our pacifistic actions that bring people together rather than driving them apart.'

But it wasn't just the French side that was heavily impacted by the situation in Argentina during the tournament. Whereas in previous competitions players had been afforded an element of freedom between matches, the nature of the trouble meant squads were securely isolated to avoid risking more high-profile incidents.

With the massacre at the 1972 Munich Olympics – which saw a Palestinian terrorist group kill 11 Israeli athletes – still fresh in the memory, organisers were acutely aware of how high the stakes were if security wasn't taken seriously. Holders West Germany were one of the sides closeted away in a camp dozens of miles from the nearest major city, with little in the way of entertainment, which created unrest among the group.

'He [West Germany manager, Helmut Schön] had the responsibility to make the stay safe for the team and we went out to a place 80km (50 miles) from Cordoba, which was very boring,' recalls midfielder Rainer Bonhof. 'There was nothing, there was just a military hotel with a small pitch on it and it made things not very likeable for the players. There was nothing to do. But at this time, the point was for Schön and the German federation to keep the team safe.

'He couldn't be open with us because of the political situation. There was no chance to create a calm or likeable situation in the camp. We were controlled by the military. We went to the opening match of the World Cup against Poland in Buenos Aires, but we went straight back home afterwards. Normally, we'd have the chance to enjoy Buenos Aires for a couple of hours, but we had to go straight back after the match. There was no chance for us to clear our minds because of the political situation in Argentina.'

The approach for the Dutch side, who lost the final to Argentina, was to focus on what was happening on the pitch and try to ignore everything else surrounding the tournament. As centre back Ernie Brandts recalls, the side was aware of the stories about Videla and the atrocities his troops were reportedly carrying out, but most pushed it to the back of their minds.

'The crew of Holland said to put everything on the pitch and try not to talk or think about it [what was happening in

Argentina],' he says. 'One player who went to see what was going on was Wim Rijsbergen. He went to see the mothers who were marching in Buenos Aires because their children had gone missing. So we knew something had happened, but we didn't know exactly what was going on.'

The incident Brandts is referring to was the gathering of mothers and grandmothers in Madres de Plaza de Mayo. The group congregated every Thursday to demand to know what happened to the thousands of young men and women who simply disappeared in Argentina at that time, after being suspected of opposing Videla's regime.

Of course, the football world wasn't supposed to be exposed to this side of Argentina and Rijsbergen's trip into the city probably wasn't advisable. Brandts admits to feeling protected from the full extent of the Videla's murderous ways. 'At the time, I heard that Videla was not a good man and people had been killed, but we didn't know [to what extent] and we couldn't see any of that,' he recalls. 'After the final we told them [the authorities] we wouldn't take our medals. There was a lot of frustration because we then heard a lot of things about people being tortured and how they were taking people to the stadium and saying, "Look everybody, all the people are happy".'

While Brandts says the Dutch management kept the players away from the details of what was happening across Argentina in 78, not all coaches have shared quite the same luxury. Colombia's manager, Francisco Maturana, and his team were subject to multiple death threats from drug cartels throughout their calamitous 1994 World Cup campaign in the USA. In fact, the pressure on Maturana got so severe, he was even forced to drop midfielder Gabriel Jaime Gómez for the game against USA after a series of faxes promised to blow up Gómez's Colombian home if he featured in the match.

It was reported by some Colombian television stations that Maturana considered resigning, but while he denied that notion, the severity of the situation was laid bare by the sight of a plexiglass screen behind the Colombian bench and security officers stationed nearby.

Upon Colombia's exit from the competition, Maturana holed up in the United States due to the continued threats and suggested the players did the same. Tragically, defender Andrés Escobar, who scored the unfortunate own goal that eliminated them against the US, chose to face the music back home – and was murdered only weeks later.

The threats of violence if Colombia failed on the pitch had sadly been real. 'The law of the boss is the law of the land,' said Maturana in an interview for ESPN documentary, *The Two Escobars*. 'When Escobar died, the earth shook and the wind cried "Escobar". As of that moment, you had to be on guard at all times. You couldn't trust anyone. Even a policeman could be good or evil.'

When the threat comes from within, it's even harder to hide from the potential repercussions. One of the most terrifying examples comes from Iraq's national side in the 1980s and 90s. Under Saddam Hussein's dictatorship, the Iraqi regime was notorious for its brutality, and that stretched into the national sport, too. One of Saddam's sons, Uday Saddam Hussein, was put in charge of the country's Olympic Committee and the national football team at the age of only 20, overseeing its successes and failures with an iron fist. Uday didn't officially take responsibility for the team until 1986 – the same year as Iraq's first and only appearance at the World Cup – but he was thought to be pivotal in hiring and firing a string of coaches before then.

Despite the World Cup qualification, managing the Lions of Mesopotamia wasn't a job many coaches stuck around to do for long. In the year running up to the 1986 tournament, it was as if Uday had fitted a revolving door on the manager's office, with seven managers coming and going between June 1985 and June 86.

While that volatility suggests a temperamental decision-maker at the helm, the reality of failing became much more severe as Uday assumed full responsibility. Managers were ordered to obey Uday's demands for team selection and threatened with violence, imprisonment – or worse – if they didn't get in line or deliver success.

That was relatively tame in comparison to what players who were deemed to be underperforming faced. They would be arrested and ushered to the Olympic building, where they'd be tortured for days on end in Uday's chamber. His lair was equipped with gruesome contraptions, such as a sarcophagus lined with nails, electric cables used to administer punishment by flogging or electrocution, and a vat of raw sewage to dunk players so their wounds became infected. Players were subjected to matches in the searing heat with a concrete football, 12-hour push-up sessions and being placed in solitary confinement. Some even suffered the ignominy of having their heads shaved before Uday urinated on them.

'[Uday] used to call the players before games and threaten them,' former Iraq manager Amu Baba said in an interview for *The Times*. 'Sometimes he telephoned the dressing room at half-time. He talked nonsense. I told him to go to hell. I said he knew nothing about football. How did I survive? Because the people loved me. Uday did not know the meaning of the word mercy… he did things even Hitler could not imagine doing.'

Baba, who claims to have been sacked 19 times by Uday, was told on multiple occasions he'd be killed or have his tongue cut out if he didn't follow his boss's orders and was once publicly beaten by Uday in front of 50,000 people at the Al Shaab

International Stadium. After a heavy 3–0 defeat to South Korea at the 1988 Olympics, Uday ordered their plane to taxi to the end of the runway, a mile away from Baghdad Airport's terminal. 'They did this to make us walk to the terminal, but the whole team just ran away as fast they could,' Baba told *The Times*. 'My son and I walked back to the terminal and when we got there, we were greeted by the secret police, who put guns to my head and stomach and dragged me away.'

There's no evidence to suggest the four Brazilian coaches who had a crack at the job in the run-up to the 1986 World Cup came face to face with Uday's violent wrath, yet

Baba, who claims to have been sacked 19 times by Uday, was told on multiple occasions he'd be killed or have his tongue cut out if he didn't follow orders.

the preparation was far from ideal. With just months to go before the tournament in Mexico kicked off, newly appointed coach Edu was given the sack and replaced by Ze Mario shortly after the squad returned from a successful training camp. Ze Mario was also gone after a month and finally Evaristo de Macedo took charge, although he never set foot in Iraq. 'We met in Europe and then went straight to Mexico because Iraq was at war at the time,' Evaristo explained in an interview with the BBC.

Evaristo's arrival preluded the high-profile dropping of star player, Falah Hassan, and lesser-known 20-year-old Jafar Abdul-Hussein, who had been selected by Edu to make his debut as a substitute against Denmark during a pre-tournament training camp.

Somewhat predictably, the decisions were taken from above the manager's head, with the political motivations emerging many years later. Abdul-Hussein's omission was rumoured to come on the back of pressure from Baathist government officials after his family was blacklisted for opposing the regime, while Hassan was deemed to be gaining too much influence due to his hero status and it was felt that would grow further if he appeared at the World Cup.

Despite the government interference and Iraq's relatively lowly status compared to their opponents, three single-goal defeats – to Paraguay, Belgium and hosts Mexico – meant the squad was invited to the Conference Palace in Baghdad for a television special dissecting what went wrong.

Uday hosted the event, blamed the team's failings on Evaristo and criticised outgoing Minister of Youth, Nouri Faisal Shaher, for the 'massacre' of Edu and his predecessor, Jorge Vieira, by sacking them in quick succession before the tournament. But of course, the decisions were instigated by Uday himself.

When Saddam's government was overthrown, the situation gradually got better. But with tensions still high when Bora Milutinović arrived to take the Iraq job in 2009, perhaps he had the right idea to keep his stay in Baghdad as brief as possible. 'I never stayed in Baghdad,' Milutinović tells me. 'I went to Baghdad only to sign the contract and nothing else. It wasn't scary, but I was unhappy there. When you come into a country like Iraq and you know everything about the country, you see how it is, how the people live and how scared they are to be alive. I was so unhappy in Baghdad, I only flew there.'

CHAPTER 5

LET'S GET THIS PARTY STARTED: HOSTS

It's long been said that a key ingredient for a good World Cup is for the host nation to perform well. As if there wasn't enough pressure from the natives already. There's little doubting that adage, though. The fervour created among the locals as a home nation moves towards the final can't be matched, with each victory stoking the excitement that little bit more.

For the team and manager caught in the eye of the storm, though, the mounting expectation can become unbearable. The partisan support has its benefits, of course, although while there are countless examples of teams enjoying home advantage and embarking on memorable runs, there are others who have frozen in key moments. Brazil's 7–1 hammering in the semi-final of the 2014 World Cup must surely rank as the tournament's ultimate capitulation.

That unenviable title is only challenged by another Seleção side, who came up short in front of their own fans when they lost against Uruguay in 1950. Known as the Maracanazo – The Agony of the Maracana – it was a source of national humiliation, until the 2014 defeat trumped that in the pain stakes.

The benefit of playing in a home tournament doesn't appear to be as pronounced as it once was. In the first 11 World Cups, the hosts won it five times. In the 10 tournaments since Argentina's 1978 success, only France in 1998 have reigned supreme on home soil, with four other nations falling at the semi-final stage.

Part of this is down to FIFA's insistence on taking the World Cup circus to new regions and cultures, ensuring that fewer of the elite nations get the privilege. This does create a new dynamic to contend with. Whereas all eyes were on the ultimate prize in previous decades, it's now up to coaches to set a realistic yardstick for their baying public as they get caught up in the excitement of a home tournament. With it, a host nation's focus has changed. For the emerging nations that are unlikely to get their hands on the trophy – even as hosts – innovative preparation techniques come into play as they try to inspire player development, both in time for the tournament and afterwards. With a yawning four-year gap between World Cups, the lack of qualifying matches can provide the perfect opportunity to prepare players for the biggest few weeks of their lives. But it's up to the manager to figure out how to take full advantage.

* * *

The pressure from the Brazilian public is huge for every World Cup. When you've won the title five times, nothing short of another successful campaign is tolerated. Regardless of the players, circumstances or opposition, if the Seleção don't bring home the trophy, it can only mean failure. So it doesn't take a genius to imagine the expectation piled upon Luiz Felipe Scolari's side ahead of the 2014 World Cup in Brazil – a competition played in world football's spiritual home. 'For a Brazilian, the World Cup represents the biggest universal tournament a player or a manager could imagine,' Scolari tells me in the soft tones that belie his Big Phil media persona. 'There is only one objective: to be champions. The Brazilian people don't accept second place.'

The then-65-year-old had an advantage as he prepared his charges for the 2014 tournament – he'd won it before. He had sampled the winning feeling and the adulation of the nation in the 2002 World Cup in Japan and South Korea. That experience would surely be the key to success again.

Only whatever Scolari had experienced in the Far East 12 years earlier wasn't on the same scale as what was waiting for him on home soil. The manner of Brazil's victory in

The demand and pressure to win the World Cup in Brazil was intense ... In 2002, we were a team that had a chance, but in 2014, Brazil were obliged to win the World Cup.

the Confederations Cup a year earlier – a 3–0 pasting of a previously untouchable Spain side – had fanned the flames of belief there was a bigger prize awaiting them. And this was taking its toll within Scolari's camp.

'The demand and pressure to win the World Cup in Brazil was intense and very different to the one in 2002,' he says. 'In 2002, we were a team that had a chance, but in 2014, Brazil were obliged to win the World Cup. So that pressure hanging over the manager and players can interfere with the quality [of our performance]. We had to minimise certain situations for our players and provide daily psychological support, so they would feel less pressure than normal. Because today everyone knows everything through the media, we needed to minimise certain situations, to protect the players as best we could. But you can't do that entirely.'

Wherever Brazil went, they were greeted with crowds of fans straining to see their heroes on their procession to glory. It's all people were talking about on social media, TV and in newspapers. Each match was a step closer.

Perhaps it's not a surprise their tournament ended in such calamity, as a shellshocked side suffered one of the worst defeats in World Cup history as they lost 7–1 to Germany in the semi-final amid legions of crying Brazilian fans.

Scolari admits his side were 'stunned and scared' by the potency of Germany's attack as they went 5–0 up within half an hour – scoring four goals in six blistering minutes – but says this was as much to do with Die Mannschaft's brilliance as Brazil crumbling under unbearable pressure.

'Germany played a perfect game and we made mistakes one can't make in a semi-final,' Scolari laments. 'If I had the chance to play the match again, I wouldn't change anything in terms of what we studied and the tactics we worked on [based on the process the team had in place]. We all know that game was one in 100 – one in 1,000 maybe – something absurd that happened, so if I could go back and change the team with the information we had gathered from Germany, we'd do the same thing again.'

Although as another manager who has taken a side into a home World Cup knows, witnessing the fans' emotions too intimately can have a negative impact on a manager's mindset. 'Of course, we as managers carry the expectations of the nation, but we can't internalise this pressure,' explains Philippe Troussier, who was Japan's manager in 2002. 'I feel this now when I'm watching a match at a restaurant or bar with the fans and that's fine when I'm drinking a beer, but you can't [afford to] understand how much expectation there is on a national coach when you play in the World Cup. I spent a lot of time after the World Cup in Japan watching matches on TV with the fans and saw how happy they can be if you win or upset if you lose, but this is pressure we can't allow to affect us. If you really think about the fact that people can die for a football match, maybe we wouldn't have the will to do the job.'

As Scolari pointed out, though, avoiding the furore of a home World Cup is practically impossible in the modern age. Controlling players' exposure to social media, television and streets lined with fans is a thankless task, as the alternative is to cut them off entirely from the outside world – something that wouldn't go down well with today's players.

Technology has played a big role in the explosion of global attention the World Cup now receives. Every four years, there is more coverage, more noise and more people critiquing the action, which brings an even greater focus on a squad's every movement. Back in 1966, removing England's players from the glare of the public eye was much easier. Alf Ramsey's team set up camp in Lilleshall, a small village in Shropshire that would go on to become home to the FA's Centre of Excellence in the 1980s. Extricating the squad from the growing delirium in London and pitching up nearly 150 miles (240km) away from Wembley – where England played all their matches – was a masterstroke as the team was immune to the frenzy their run in the tournament was causing.

'Generally, I never felt there was ever any great pressure on me,' says Geoff Hurst, England's hat-trick hero in the final. 'But you're in a little bubble and you're not really aware of the newspapers and what people were saying. There wasn't the coverage of that then, so you're not seeing it.'

Hurst is right. In 1966, football wasn't the front-page headline grabber it is today, but look at any pictures of the crowds in England around that time and it's clear the excitement started to build as a home victory inched closer. And that's where the decision to be based out in the sticks was so effective. Hurst remembers expectation being quite low on the England side before the tournament kicked off, and that opinion was frozen in time as the players lived away from the increasing level of excitement.

'Going into the World Cup, in terms of expectation, I don't think there was much from the supporters' point of view for a couple of reasons,' he continues. 'We didn't compete in World Cups before 1950, when the USA beat us, so we came into it as a new competition that people were only just becoming aware of, plus English clubs hadn't played much in Europe at that time. You need to put it into perspective – we'd hardly been interested in playing in European competitions, let alone in World Cups.

'Since that [1966] win, we've now generated the biggest TV audience, of more than 30 million. We've changed the way we look at international football, World Cup football and European Championship football – it's shifted dramatically over the years. There's a bigger expectation for us to do well now than there was at the time.'

But the idea of closeting players away to protect them from the public's gaze isn't universally popular with all managers. When it came to selecting a venue to base his squad during the 2006 World Cup, Germany manager Jürgen Klinsmann opted for the capital. Based in the five-star Schlosshotel Berlin, the team were only a few miles from the city's busy centre and regularly travelled to their two training grounds, which were several miles apart.

This wasn't a mere flight of fancy, it was part of Klinsmann's plan to bring the national team closer to the German people. He recognised the need for the public's perception of the side to change, and for the team to become a more modern outfit.

Connecting with the public during a home World Cup was central to that.

But the idea of staying among the people wasn't exclusive to the 2006 finals. 'I went to watch one of their matches in Frankfurt against Australia [in the 2005 Confederations Cup] and I was travelling alone on this assignment,' remembers decorated British journalist Patrick Barclay.

'I went to the game and came back, and there were loads of people in the lobby wearing tracksuits – the [German] team were staying in the same hotel I'd booked in. They weren't hidden away in a castle somewhere, they were slap bang in the middle of the city.

'It was a modest sort of hotel, the sort of hotel a newspaper can afford – three or so stars in the middle of town – and all the players were there. I remember I found a little sofa and on the next sofa were the Mertesacker family. The whole team was sitting around with their mums and dads and fans.

'It gave you the sense the team was part of a community. Whereas an England team would never stay in a city centre hotel, the Germans – they were the best in Europe and expected to be the best in the world – were staying in a three-star hotel, completely available to the public. I asked the journalists about this afterwards and they said it was like this because he [Klinsmann] believes you are like public property if you play for the Mannschaft.'

Klinsmann's side appeared to thrive on that feeling. Playing a more expansive style than the team that reached the 2002 final only four years earlier, they had an air of freshness and freedom – even if they did fall to eventual champions Italy in the semi-final. There was little sign of expectation affecting them.

* * *

The idea of a home World Cup being used as a watershed moment to beckon in a new era for a national team has become a more common strand in recent decades. With more emerging football nations earning automatic qualification for the finals as hosts, the likes of USA, South Korea, Japan, and South Africa have all held World Cups in the past 30 years.

By selecting non-elite nations, the onus on what those host countries can achieve has changed, since winning is unlikely. Instead, the pendulum of expectation has swung from home fans expecting victory to just a hope they aren't found totally out of their depth when the tournament begins. That brings no less pressure for managers, as well as providing a different challenge entirely. 'I had never been the manager of a host nation in a World Cup before and the emotion and feeling is completely different,' explains Carlos Alberto Parreira, who managed hosts South Africa in 2010. 'The population is involved, to be part of it for three-and-a-half years, to be part of the stadium construction, preparing the team, the players, until the final moment. It was a very, very positive experience.

'When I got there, someone asked me why [I accepted the job] and I said, "The only reason I came here was because I really wanted to be the manager of a host nation," and it was a really good experience.'

South Africa went into the tournament as the lowest-ranked side to ever host the finals. At 83rd, the Bofana Bofana were drawn in a group alongside perennial challengers France, two-times champions Uruguay and regular qualifiers Mexico. Suddenly the fear was they would be humiliated in front of a global audience.

To become the first hosts not to win a match at their home tournament – or worse, fall meekly to three defeats – would undermine the positive legacy the South African FA and FIFA hoped the tournament would leave. And since this was the first World Cup to be held in Africa, the continent wanted a strong showing.

'South Africa's group was a very hard one,' Parreira says. 'I remember to this day being at the draw and they put up the eight groups and due to technical results and past World Cups, France was not a top seed. Then Jerome [Valcke], who was FIFA's secretary general, joked that we will now draw a group for France to go in. And guess where France went in? South Africa's group.

'It wasn't a very well-balanced group and despite that we got four points, drawing with Mexico and winning against France. If we were in a different group, we'd have advanced to the round of 16. But I think the image that remained was a very good one, especially in the game against Mexico. It was the opening game, the whole world was watching and any disaster could have happened in terms of results, but we played a very decent game, could have won it, and ended up with a draw.'

To help with Parreira's task, the South African Premier Division ended more than two months earlier than normal to give the Brazilian more coaching time on the run up to the World Cup. This has become an increasingly common technique used by federations of lesser-ranked nations over the years, which aims to create a sporting advantage by getting more time on the training pitch. In fact, getting an uninterrupted four months ahead of the 2002 World Cup was a specific demand Guus Hiddink made to the Korean Football Association before taking charge. The K-League obliged and rescheduled. While that represented a victory off the pitch, Hiddink needed to find a way to do the same on it. In five previous World Cup finals appearances, South Korea had failed to win a single match and had gone 14 matches without a victory.

Hiddink's plan was to drill his players in the months leading up to the tournament, focusing on fitness and instilling more self-belief in the South Koreans to give them an edge on the opposition. Both of those factors were critical as the Reds shocked the world to become the first-ever Asian semi-finalists, so it's hard now to believe the Dutchman's methods were questioned when he first took charge in 2001.

Within months of arriving, Hiddink had earned the name Oh Dae Young – Mr Five-Nil – as South Korea suffered heavy defeats to France and Czech Republic, alongside other underwhelming results against strong opposition. He'd been at loggerheads with the national press for what he perceived to be preferential coverage of baseball rather than football and was in turn accused of being lazy and disrespectful because of a public relationship with his girlfriend – something frowned upon in Korean culture. There was little sign of what was to come.

'I had us playing tough European and African teams then and people wanted me to go home,' Hiddink said triumphantly after South Korea won their opening group match against Poland. 'But I stuck to my plans and look at us now. People had short-term views and didn't appreciate what I was doing.'

The former Real Madrid boss tried out 60 players in the 18 months leading up to the tournament, dropping several senior players to reawaken their hunger for the national team, then reintegrating them again later. Eventually it started to pay off on the eve of the tournament, thrashing Scotland 4–1, drawing with England, and going toe-to-toe with world champions France in a 3–2 loss.

Expectations suddenly ballooned from pessimism to belief they'd not only win a match, but progress into the knockout phase. One win turned into two, turned into three, then turned into a semi-final against Germany. But for all that Hiddink and the players achieved, midfielder Park Ji-Sung believes what made the vital difference was being hosts. 'If it happened abroad or in other countries, then we probably couldn't do this or perform like that,' says the former Manchester United star. 'The preparation for the whole one-and-a-half years, there were many training camps for the national team and it won't happen again. The whole country was just together for the goal of getting through the group stage of the World Cup. Then at the right time, a great manager came to Korea and everyone just followed what he said. It's not just only one thing that can make the success, it's everything together – the whole country makes that unbelievable thing.'

Allowing coaches more time to work with their players has a clear correlation with success in the modern game, especially when – like Hiddink – the majority of their players aren't playing in the elite leagues. And when it came to creative thinking to make up the gap, South Korea's 2002 co-hosts Japan went even further.

'I said to the JFA (Japan Football Association) that I needed to take care of three categories: the A group [the first team], the Olympics group for the 2000 Olympic Games in Sydney, plus the under-20s preparations for the World Youth Cup a year later,' explains Japan coach Troussier, who took the job in 1998.

'I explained my target was to bring through a new group of players. Because when a national coach creates his team, it's coming from a minimum of 60 or 80 players, not from [only] 20 or 30. It's coming from the players that are ready now, others that might be able to play in the next six months, and others that will be ready to play in three years… so that's why I wanted to identify immediately who were the right people to respond to me at the right moment in four years' time.'

It seems like an impossible job to manage three teams at once, but thanks to the JFA's flexibility and the luxury of having no qualifiers, Troussier managed it. He set a philosophy for every age group, graduating the top players from his under-20s squad to join the older group for the Olympics, before doing the same to create his senior World Cup side.

It ended with the Frenchman's Japan squad being among the youngest in the tournament, yet the group had developed a cohesion comparable to considerably more experienced sides. Troussier had taken advantage of a unique situation to create a group that some feel could have gone further than the last-16 of the tournament.

... my attitude was that of a teacher, I imposed how I wanted to play. I was like the conductor of the symphony.

'It's impossible to repeat what I did,' he affirms. 'The only way I did it was because 99 per cent of the players were local players and I automatically got camps with our own internal organisation between federations and leagues. We released the players differently. Now to be international coach of England, France or Germany, you have to follow the FIFA rules and you have players only five days before each match and it's completely different.

'Because my players weren't big names or big stars, my attitude was that of a teacher, I imposed how I wanted to play. I was like the conductor of the symphony. I had my musicians, each one is unique – this one plays violin, this one plays guitar, this one plays drums. And me as the conductor… I adjusted the timing of each one.'

But if Troussier's four-year hosting plan sounds like it stands out as the most ingenious, then Bora Milutinović may just pip that. The old hand had already managed Mexico in their home tournament in 1986 by the time he arrived as USA boss ahead of the 1994 World Cup, so had an idea of what was required to be successful. With no professional league in the States at the time, Milutinović created an intense four-year schedule of friendlies, playing 91 full internationals in that time so the players could get a flavour of what was going to happen when the tournament began.

'What was so important is that the players needed to feel what it meant to play at the highest level,' the Serb explains. 'We made a tour around the world. For example, we played Sweden in Russia, went to [South] Korea and South America, and played four games against Brazil, Argentina, Uruguay, Paraguay. It was simple – you can learn a lot about what you need to do and teach the players for many hours, but you can learn more when you play against teams like these. We learned what we needed to do to be better.'

Milutinović was working with a completely blank canvas and gave out central contracts to a group of college players to join him on the tour he created. Even this was alien to the vast majority of Americans, as most had never been on the books of a club previously. As defender Alexi Lalas describes, the players' experience was 'completely backwards'.

'Bora recognised he needed to blood us and this advantage, this strange silver lining of not having a lot of players playing around world, enabled us to function for all intents and purposes as a club,' Lalas tells me. 'It was spun to us as, "You've got this opportunity. There's the World Cup, then there's hosting the World Cup, then there's hosting the World Cup in a country like the United States, where you can do something that's going to be memorable and for your game". That sense of opportunity and of responsibility was a constant, day in and day out. "There's something coming, don't waste this opportunity, grab hold of it, be confident, be optimistic".

'It was this strange advantage that Bora had. We all know one of the biggest challenges and obstacles for national team coaches is the limited time you have together. So for the core of the team to be based day in and day out in residency in southern California and then to play basically seasons of games, that was a real advantage that Bora recognised and we used.'

Despite the central contracts, players came in and came out just as quickly as Milutinović ran the rule over dozens of hopefuls. He carefully honed and picked what he wanted within the camps, forming an environment of individuals who had the talent and mentality to succeed.

Milutinović may say it was 'simple' to identify the approach he did, but it remains the only World Cup preparation of its kind. And it created an environment where he'd managed to make a group of rookies feel entirely at ease with the idea of facing the world's best international teams in front of a cynical home support.

'When we stepped on the field to play at the World Cup, I had no reference in a club situation, the international game was just what I did and what I had done for two years, so that didn't faze me,' Lalas recalls. 'I know it's the same game and you're kicking a ball and it's the same laws. But in a strange way, none of us were fazed by the national game on a big stage like that because of the sheer amount of international games we had played in preparation for it.'

Time may have been on Milutinović's side as he plotted USA's moment in the sun, but it's not a luxury all coaches share when preparing a side for a World Cup.

CHAPTER 6

RACE AGAINST TIME: LATE APPOINTMENTS

Is it too much to ask for some continuity? We all know the life of a football manager can be precarious, but when the World Cup is every four years, the need for stability as a team tries to reach its peak is greater than ever. Yet dig into tournament history and a slew of managerial upheavals taking place right up to the big kick-off can be found. Caretaker bosses, last-minute appointments and general disruption can undermine a nation's biggest moment in the sun. In fact, some coaches even arrive at tournaments without having met all the players.

It sounds like a recipe for disaster – and sometimes it is – but there are also occasions when the short-term impact of a change is positive. Sacking an underperforming or unpopular manager is worth doing if he seems like a lost cause already, and when the replacement is a clear upgrade who can bring in some fresh ideas.

The installation of a head coach on the run up to a World Cup is more common in some continents than others. In Africa, for example, where jobs seem to change hands with startling regularity, the instability is exacerbated when the African Cup of Nations (AFCON) takes place in the same year as a World Cup.

All the good work of a successful qualifying campaign only months earlier can be undone in one fell swoop by a disastrous AFCON – and sometimes understandably. If a big nation fails spectacularly at one major tournament, what's the sense in doing exactly the same thing again a few months later?

Justifying the departure of an outgoing manager is one thing, but getting somebody in who can work wonders in a limited time is a different matter entirely. The challenges they face are the ultimate test of a coach's ability and quite often lead to some fascinating storylines.

* * *

There are only two days before Spain's opening match at the 2018 World Cup and Fernando Hierro is being hurriedly moved in front of the global press. As the former Real Madrid defender is ushered into the room for his hastily arranged unveiling, a cluster of photographers gather near his podium to snap a happy picture alongside Royal Spanish Football Federation (RFEF) president, Luis Rubiales.

It's all smiles, right up until the press officer has to address the elephant in the room: Julen Lopetegui. In particular, that Lopetegui is actually no longer in the room. Instead, he's on a plane from Russia back to Spain. Stripped of the chance to lead La Roja into a tournament he's prepared two years for, Lopetegui was ousted from his position after it transpired he'd agreed to join Real Madrid after the tournament without the RFEF's knowledge. Now it was left for Hierro to pick up the pieces.

'We've always said in the last hours that we wanted to touch the team and management we had as little as possible. It had to be somebody who knew the players, who knew this house,' Rubiales told the press.

Hierro's appointment was designed to be seamless. He was already out in Russia with the team as technical director, so was clued up on Lopetegui's methods and preparation. It was hoped a light touch would be enough to avoid widespread disruption to a side that was among the favourites to lift the trophy. Despite Lopetegui's departure, most of the staff remained, while 2010 World Cup winner Carlos Marchena was among three coaches flown in to assist Hierro in the dugout.

We can't change two years of hard work in the coming days... This is a marvellous group and what I've asked them to do is simply be themselves and follow their personality and world-class level.

'We can't change two years of hard work in the coming days,' Hierro explained at his first press conference. 'Many of the staff are still with us, we know how the next match has been prepared for and we're very close to it, so we have to be coherent and follow this direction. From now until the end of the World Cup, we don't have the ability to change much and we need to follow with the same work that has been done day by day that we have already been present for. This is a marvellous group and what I've asked them to do is simply be themselves and follow their personality and world-class level.'

The message was clear that Hierro would try not to meddle with what had gone before. After all, despite Lopetegui's perceived indiscretion, he hadn't lost a game in two years as Spain manager and his successor had only one season of managerial experience to fall back on, in charge of second-tier Oviedo.

A 3–3 draw with European champions Portugal in Spain's opening match had the hallmarks of a side that might be able to quickly move past what was happening off the pitch and added weight to claims they could still go far in the tournament.

Yet the laboured nature of the following performances was their downfall. A turgid 1–0 win against Iran was followed up by a 2–2 draw with already-eliminated Morocco, courtesy of a stoppage time Iago Aspas equaliser, before they failed to break down a resilient Russia side in the last-16 – eventually losing on penalties.

'The way he [Lopetegui] left illustrates the fallacy of the idea that managers or coaches don't matter in international football, where clearly they have a huge input, even among the top nations,' explains *The Independent*'s chief football writer, Miguel Delaney, who followed Spain's campaign. 'Hierro came in and it wasn't like he could just facilitate these good players in that way. Something very visibly became wrong with the team and how they were playing, but under Lopetegui they had a real sharpness about them and were cutting teams open.

'Under Hierro, they became almost a cliché of a modern Spanish team, which is a lot of passing and possession but no penetration or cutting edge. A cracking example of that is in the Russia game, which was one of the most frustrating performances I've ever seen because Spain seemed locked in this sort of stasis. It was almost this physical level of procrastination.

'I wouldn't blame Hierro for that, he was put in an impossible situation. But you couldn't get a clearer illustration of the importance of a coach at that level because Spain couldn't apply their tactics to the same degree and had nobody to change it.'

Delaney's assessment has credibility working in the other direction, too, with managerial appointments coinciding with upticks in form, however brief their tenure has been, although it seems there are a number of factors other than simply time in the role that can dictate if a job is a success or failure. Culture, expectation and circumstance are powerful drivers to what's set to come.

Hierro's stint as Spain caretaker does stand out as one of the most extreme examples of a manager being flung into a job almost overnight, but at least he was already familiar with the players he'd be working with. Incredibly, that's not always the case.

It's not unusual for a club manager to be hired and given only one training session before being expected to pick a team, but at least he'll have videos of matches from recent weeks he can watch to get to know his new players. At international level, games can be months apart and particularly in decades gone by, footage and statistics on the team could be scarce.

'The secret is to find the best 11 players as quickly as possible,' says Bora Milutinović, who accepted the Costa Rica job only 70 days before Italia 90 began. 'You need to share with them the mental side in those weeks [before the tournament]. They need to know what you're doing in training, how you train, and we must analyse and speak about every detail.'

To make the task even trickier when the Serb took over Costa Rica at short notice, the majority of the players were amateurs. Yet his method of communication worked, as he led the World Cup debutants to the knockout round courtesy of group-stage wins against Scotland and Sweden. They were an unknown quantity so carried an element of surprise, as well as being well-drilled and hard to break down. The relative lack of time on the training field soon became nothing more than a detail.

But while Milutinović seems to make it sound so simple and insists taking over a job so late in the day was nothing difficult – 'three years or 70 days, I don't care,' he claims – repeating the trick with Nigeria eight years later wasn't so easy. The coach was appointed as Super Eagles boss with five-and-a-half months to get to grips with his new charges. With little chance to get his players together before the tournament, though, he was left to perform another late, late show.

'He got the job months before the World Cup and that's a very short period for the players to know the coach, his tactics and everything. It takes time to adapt to his system,' remembers midfielder Mutiu Adepoju. 'When he was signed… the coach didn't know the majority of the players, so he was phoning the players because there weren't [as many] friendly matches as there are now.'

At first glance, it's hard to see why Adepoju seems so downbeat. Nigeria beat Spain 3–2 in a swashbuckling opening display, then got the better of Bulgaria in their second match to top their group. It was there they were dispatched 4–1 by Denmark, exposing the lack of understanding between players and coach.

A team packed with the gifts of Kanu, Jay-Jay Okocha and Finidi George had won gold at the 1996 Olympics and were fancied to fly the African flag into the latter stages in France. On paper, Milutinović had considerably more to work with than he had with Costa Rica. Although perhaps it highlights that in order to do a quick job well, taking over a side with low expectations and the ability to make big leaps forward by making basic tweaks has more of an effect. Hindsight suggests Nigeria needed more nuance to their preparation, taking into account what made them successful in the recent past.

'You'll see all the friendly matches prior to the World Cup we lost very badly and it was only in the main World Cup against Spain that we were able to do our magic,' ex-Real Madrid man Adepoju continues. 'Really it was very short and we didn't know the coach much and the coach didn't know many of the players to their full capacity. The tactics were entirely different [to what we were used to] and the system of play when we were preparing was 4-4-2. In the first game against Spain, you'll see in the first 15 or 20 minutes we were disjointed and all the players weren't getting things right.

'The team could have done more, but there wasn't enough time for him, or for the players to know the coach. When we lost the third group game against Paraguay, it exposed the weaknesses of the team and that's what Denmark capitalised on.'

* * *

To prove the managerial merry-go-round isn't exclusively a club phenomenon, the man who Milutinović replaced at Nigeria was Philippe Troussier. The Frenchman had led the African giants through qualification, but left following a contract dispute to take over Burkina Faso in January's AFCON – only to agree a deal to take South Africa to that summer's World Cup before the continental tournament had ended. Are you keeping up? In short, Troussier was also grappling with his own tight time frame to prepare South Africa for their World Cup bow, while Milutinović was suffering the same issues with Nigeria.

'I made my preparation and selection of the players without any camp – the first time I met my players was one month before the World Cup,' Troussier says. 'It was not an easy time and the preparation was under so much pressure. I did my best to share with the players a lot of information, technically and tactically. We had a lot of requirements and the job of a football coach is not that of a university teacher, it's a man who wants to inspire the players he wants to select, which meant doing it with no time was not easy or comfortable.'

Troussier used his short time in charge to visit possible training bases in France, introducing himself to key players around Europe and trying to identify others he could call up.

But as he tried to make the most of the limited time he'd got, he was also contending with the feeling he just wasn't wanted – or needed – due to the circumstances that led to him taking charge.

'I was in Johannesburg in January 1998 when I signed the contract, then I went off to play in AFCON with Burkina Faso,' Troussier explains. 'We got to the semi-final but South Africa reached the final under [previous manager] Jomo Sono, but he was going to be out of the World Cup process. Nobody could understand why South Africa were changing their coach after he got them to be runners up, so it wasn't a very comfortable position to be in at all.'

Festus Onigbinde must have had a similar feeling in 2002. Another former Nigeria manager who ended up getting the job quickly during post-AFCON fall-out, he had the advantage of having an in-depth knowledge of the Super Eagles' top stars when he took over only months before the World Cup. The catch was most of them were now in exile from the national team.

The veteran coach had no choice but to start almost from scratch. That meant a speedily arranged training camp in Europe, inviting a host of less experienced players to try out for the national side with the prize of a place at the World Cup up for grabs. It's not rare for a manager to arrive during a bad time, but the wreckage Onigbinde inherited was on a different level.

'There was the AFCON in early 2002 in Mali, and Nigeria didn't perform very well, so the team was disbanded. I was heading the technical department of the Nigerian FA at the time and was recalled to rebuild the team,' he tells me. 'The squad that disbanded in Mali said none of them would report for the national team again unless all of them were recalled, but I can't do my job that way. No player can dictate to me who to use, so I had to go round scouting for players.'

A group of 35 players assembled in London for Onigbinde's camp, minus a tranche of Nigeria's most-recognisable stars. One of the players previously on the periphery who got an invite was former Crewe Alexandra centre-half, Efe Sodje.

At 29, Sodje had made his Nigeria debut two years earlier, but had struggled to hold down a regular place until Onigbinde's call to form part of his new-look team. After impressing as a makeshift right-back in the camp's first friendly against Paraguay at QPR's Loftus Road, he came to epitomise what the coach was trying to achieve.

All the players want to do is play and that means nothing, the manager needs to come in and think about how he wants to play the game.

'It was all change. He [Onigbinde] changed everything and opened the camp and said to me, "If you want to come for trials, come",' Sodje says. 'Some of the main players had stepped down, but with the new ones it was just about getting on with it and pulling together in a short period of time.

'That's where Onigbinde came in and brought his old head to say how we should play and we had to do it all as a team. Football is all about teams because you can't have individual players, you need to have teamwork – he pulled us back together. It was more about how we gelled.

'It's difficult, but it all depends on the manager, everything relies on the manager. All the players want to do is play and that means nothing, the manager needs to come in and think about how he wants to play the game. If the manager comes in hard, he's going to lose the players because they're used to the old manager. If he comes in strict but friendly, that's the best way because you have to win the players over.'

Onigbinde appeared to be on to a winner. The new side moulded quickly and early friendly results encouraged the return of some of the more experienced players who'd originally rejected call ups. Front the outside, a combination of new and old appeared to be working, right up until the tournament itself. Even then, there was no shame in Nigeria being knocked out of the 'Group of Death' consisting of Argentina, England and Sweden.

But Onigbinde blamed 'suspicious performances' from a handful of the recalled players, which suggested his mistake was assuming those who had been involved in the AFCON months earlier had left their grievances behind so quickly. Sometimes only time can be a healer.

'We knew when the players came in that everything was moving on and there was no open confrontation between me and any of the players. But that is looking at people from the outside and you never know what they have in their minds,' he says.

'When building a team, the most difficult aspect is psychological fitness because that has to do with the minds of the individual players, how they feel, how comfortable they are and so forth. But when you're not with the team for a long time, it's difficult to make an accurate assessment of their minds.'

* * *

A late change of manager can prove to be the final piece of the jigsaw, though. In fact, it proved to be the perfect tonic to inspire a turn of fortunes for two of the World Cup's greatest-ever teams.

When football fans across the globe hear the names Mário Zagallo and Rinus Michels, they immediately think of Brazil's mesmerising 1970 team of Pelé and Jairzinho and the Netherlands' Total Football machine inspired by Johan Cruyff four years later.

What isn't so well known is that both got the top jobs in their respective nations with only a matter of weeks before their

World Cups started. It would be easy to say that they couldn't have had that much impact, particularly as their teams were stocked with great players, but this isn't true, especially in Michels' case, as the team he took over in March 1974 was a shadow of what they'd become that summer.

The Netherlands had been unconvincing in qualifying for their first World Cup in 36 years. And while Michels' predecessor, František Fadrhonc, had achieved great success to do that, he was struggling to bring together the talents of the two top Dutch clubs sides at the time – Ajax and Feyenoord – on the international stage.

'I talked to Johan [Cruyff] about it and he said – more or less – that "what happened was our instincts started to work. We used the Ajax style and put the best of Feyenoord in it and Michels managed all the pieces of the puzzle to put them in one complete piece",' says Jaap de Groot, Cruyff's close friend and ghostwriter of his autobiography, *My Turn*.

'Michels got the pieces and knew exactly how to put them in the right place. Johan used a very good example and said "nothing is invented by just one man. I don't think Thomas Edison invented light on his own, it must have been a whole team and everybody put a piece to it. Then there was one man who put the pieces all together to get it right".

'That's just what Michels did. He got all the pieces delivered by Cruyff and the other players, and his great contribution was getting everything in the right place at the right time with the right person.'

To label Michels' impact as a genuinely overnight success would be a slight embellishment. While his appointment did come relatively late in the day, the then-Barcelona manager was already the architect of the Total Football system that revolutionised the game during his time at Ajax years earlier.

Michels' innate knowledge of the system and close relationships with several of the Netherlands' leading lights – most notably Cruyff, his protégé and general on the pitch – made for a smooth transition to becoming national team manager.

There was the small matter of handling an internal dispute between the players and the Dutch Football Association, the KNVB, over pay before Michels could get started. There was even talk of the players striking before the new boss took a hard-line approach and promised to leave anybody still causing unrest off his final squad list.

With calm restored, Michels went about adding to the base Fadrhonc had been cultivating. His most notable move was to create a new-look central defensive partnership with midfielder Arie Haan and full-back Wim Rijsbergen. A bold move? Maybe. But one that represents the strength of mind the new coach showed.

'They [the players] loved Fadrhonc and he had a very good view of the game, but they needed a real captain of the ship after getting to a World Cup after so many years – they wanted it to be perfect,' de Groot continues. 'They had said they had Fadrhonc in the role and so many other coaches, but needed the name of Michels as the supervisor. They had it 95 per cent right, but needed Michels to make it 100 per cent right.'

Michels' fine tuning created one of the greatest teams never to win the World Cup as they wowed the world by sweeping aside the likes of Argentina and Brazil in a run to the final, where West Germany upset the odds to beat them.

Despite not getting their hands on the trophy, the 74 Dutch side remains celebrated as one of the best sides ever to grace the World Cup. Yet four years earlier, it was another team in the same bracket who were welcoming a new coach on the eve of the tournament.

Seventy-five days before the tournament in Mexico began, Zagallo was brought in to replace João Saldanha, a journalist who'd been given the job a year earlier, reportedly due to widespread criticism of the national team among the press pack. If that wasn't barmy enough, Saldanha's perfect six-out-of-six qualifying record wasn't enough to detract from his increasingly erratic behaviour. He was sacked following high-profile arguments with Brazil's military leader, Emílio Garrastazu Médici, and Brazil Football Confederation President, João Havelange. He also allegedly chased his predecessor with a loaded pistol after he criticised Saldanha, and – worst of all – he decided to drop Pelé, claiming the world's greatest player was going blind.

That cleared the way for Zagallo to pick up the reins, but not before Dino Sani and Otto Glória had turned down the chance to take the job. But despite the chaos that appeared to surround the side, Zagallo had the presence of mind to see a route to glory.

'I totally changed the team,' Zagallo told journalist Tim Vickery in an interview in 2005. 'I took over without a fixed idea, but I knew there would be a lot of changes because I didn't accept the idea of 4-2-4, which Saldanha had been using. There is no way we could have won the World Cup playing that system.'

Lack of preparation time appeared to be no barrier, though, as Zagallo quickly set to work on a pioneering tactical system to give the recalled Pelé, Jairzinho and Rivellino the freedom to create behind Tostão up front. The changes were simple, clear and effective, and seemed to surprise everybody how quickly they went from concept to football utopia.

'I'd won two World Cups with a 4-3-3,' Zagallo, who was part of Brazil's 1958 and 1962 winning sides, told FIFA.com in

2020. 'When I took over the Seleção, I had it in my head that that's what I was going to do. The changes I made were moving Piazza to play as a centre-back, bringing Clodoaldo into the team and managing to field all of those number 10s – Rivellino, Tostão, Pelé, Jairzinho and Gérson. They said it would be impossible, in such a short time, to make them all gel, but we won the World Cup.'

Zagallo and Michels' stories may make a mockery of the idea that time is needed to craft a winning side, although that must be tempered by pointing out how football – and coaches' use of tactics – have developed since the 1970s.

Yet there's still a beautiful simplicity to the way they masterminded those pioneering sides. Pick a system, get the players on board – and take on the world.

CHAPTER 7

BREAKING THE MOULD: FIRST TIMERS

Sometimes simply qualifying for a World Cup is enough for a manager to be immortalised. For the smaller countries, earning an invite to the globe's biggest football party is a dream come true. A vision they never thought they'd live in reality.

Since the first World Cup in 1930, 80 nations have taken up a spot in the finals, with teams from all four corners of the globe getting their chance to shine on the biggest stage. Among them have been some unlikely entries. Whether it's countries whose populations are dwarfed by the more-established elite, or those that don't have the same resources or history as their competitors, a steady flow of new names have rubbed shoulders with the best. From the likes of Iceland, Togo, and Trinidad and Tobago in the 21st century, to Zaire, Haiti and Kuwait even further back, World Cup history is peppered with different cultures and styles, not to mention some of the greatest underdog stories. And with the number of teams at the finals projected to reach an expanded 48 countries by 2026, there's going to be even more debutants over the coming decades.

Not all of the fairy tales have happy endings, though. The influx has meant the gulf in calibre between the top and bottom ends of the qualifiers are, at least theoretically, much greater, resulting in some pretty soul-destroying drubbings. A 10–1 shellacking, as El Salvador suffered against Hungary in 1982, tends to take the shine off that celebrated qualification.

Managers who were praised as messiahs upon qualification only months earlier can be transformed into hapless wannabes in an instant. It's a scenario that rubbishes the idea that going into a tournament is easier for teams who aren't expected to challenge for the trophy. Everyone has their own pressures and each manager has his own decisions that will leave a nation either brimming with pride or bristling with humiliation. The mountains they're climbing are just as great.

* * *

When Heimir Hallgrímsson was growing up in Iceland, everyone said that the Nordic nation was too small to ever reach a major tournament. That all changed in a scarcely believable few years, largely inspired by the dentist-turned-tactician.

When Hallgrímsson took over the Iceland national team as joint manager with Lars Lagerbäck in 2013, there was nothing to suggest any of that was to change. But by the time he stepped down, Iceland had been to a European Championship quarter-final – famously beating England in the last-16 – and had become the smallest nation ever to play at a World Cup finals.

Europe had fallen in love with Iceland's plucky character and the synchronised Viking Thunder Clap that followed the national team around France during the European Championships in 2016. This was an army of men who had shown themselves worthy of eating at the continent's top table and had a blatant disregard for their apparently lowly status.

They'd thwarted England and Portugal at the Euros and got the better of the Netherlands in getting there at all. But that counted for nothing when they kicked off their World Cup qualification campaign in Ukraine on 5 September, a little over two months after their famous run at the Euros had come to an end.

Hallgrímsson knew there were countless examples of smaller nations basking in their one tournament of glory and disappearing back to whence they came as quickly as they'd appeared – and he wasn't about to let that happen to Iceland.

'There was one big obstacle along the way and that was when you have

... when you have achieved something, it's really difficult to reach that again... Before the Euros, everybody had nothing to lose, but all of a sudden, we had it all to lose.

achieved something, it's really difficult to reach that again,' he tells me. 'Especially when we had achieved something like we did in the Euros, it was big and everybody was really happy. Before the Euros, everybody had nothing to lose, but all of a sudden, we had it all to lose.

'These guys now, from being almost nothing in Iceland, were national heroes, but were starting from zero points again... so it's really difficult to prepare psychologically to restart.

'The day after the party, the beer doesn't taste so good. So to go from bigger stages in Europe and the venues in France with full stadiums to that first game away in Ukraine with no spectators [Ukraine were serving a punishment to play behind closed doors following their fans' racist behaviour in a Euro 2016 qualifier] was a really big difference for these guys, who weren't used to doing all of this.'

Hallgrímsson's concerns were founded. Despite Alfred Finnbogason's sixth-minute opener against Ukraine, Iceland could only draw 1–1 in Kiev. A month later, they were 2–1 down at home to Finland and had to rely on an injury-time double from Finnbogason and Ragnar Sigurdsson to get the win. Victory against Turkey and defeat to Croatia left them with only seven points from four games, already lagging behind the automatic qualification place in third.

It was time for the coaching team to remind the players why they'd been so successful previously. They doubled down on the values that had served them so well, inspiring the team to five wins from the next six matches to carry them all the way to their maiden World Cup in Russia in 2018.

As much as Iceland's abilities on the pitch had served them well, it was what was between the players' ears that would make the impossible possible once again.

'It was about getting them [the players] to realise why we reached where we went in the Euros – it's never going to be given to us,' Hallgrímsson explains. 'We sat down and spoke about who we are, our identity and how we should always stick to that no matter what. If we did really well at the Euros, it was because of something and it wasn't because we are so good, so we really focused on our identity.

'A sentence we used a lot was "success is not a destination, it's a continuous journey in the right direction". So success for Iceland wasn't to get to the Euros or the quarter-finals, that was not the definition of success. We had to keep reminding them that while they did well, we had to keep doing the same things and have to improve what they're doing. That was the challenge.'

By extension, that also meant that qualifying for the World Cup did not mean they could all now just kick back. The idea that just because a smaller country has upset the odds to make it to a tournament that they can now sit back and relax when it comes around is misleading.

There's undoubtedly less external pressure on a nation not expected to go far, but that's no reason to be happy to make up the numbers, according to former New Zealand captain Ryan Nelsen, who led the All Whites to the 2010 finals.

'In 1982 when New Zealand last qualified, they celebrated getting there and that was the achievement,' recalls the ex-Blackburn and Tottenham defender. 'They got beaten and that's it, life went on. Just getting there was enough. That was the mentality we didn't want [in 2010]. Everybody else could say "well done, getting there for New Zealand is it", but no, we had a pretty decent team and a team that was pretty uncomfortable to play against.

'We knew that, so it was about shifting the mindset internally within our group to get this idea of just being happy to be there out of our heads now.'

With fewer than five million New Zealand citizens in 2010 – the equivalent population size of major cities such as Washington DC and Barcelona – on an island dominated by rugby and cricket, it's easy to see why there was a lot of back-slapping for reaching a World Cup. In 2010 the Kiwis had only 25 registered professional players to choose from and even fewer when they made their maiden tournament bow in 1982.

And while Nelsen is damning of the happy-go-lucky attitude shown in Spain during the summer of 1982, they were really up against it in a group including Brazil, Soviet Union and Scotland. They failed to lay a glove on their opponents as they shipped 12 goals in three matches to be sent packing. Twenty-eight years later, they were adamant their second bite of the cherry would be different. Ricki Herbert, a member of the 1982 side, was boss and he wanted to instil a positive ethos where they'd use the opportunity to make a statement, maybe even qualifying from a group that included reigning champions, Italy.

'We knew our limitations and were very self-aware, but we also had to bring in some kind of confidence that we can do something here,' says Nelsen. 'We had to infiltrate that all the way from the team to the coaching staff and the management. That was our biggest preparation task.'

Working in tandem, Herbert and Nelsen went about creating a belief. A combination of confidence and a system that played to their strengths was a recipe for giant-killing. The result? Three draws from New Zealand's three group games, which led them agonisingly close to the knockouts, and earning them the tag of The Unbeatables. And it was all made possible thanks to a deep-seated conviction created by coach and player.

'Coaches can stand up and say "we need to do this or that", but sometimes with players it's like fighting with thunder. It just kind of goes off and it's not real,' Nelsen picks up. 'As players, you can go in a bit deeper. The coach can tell me we really want to win and I say "yeah, I really want to win" and everybody is going to say that. But then you look in the mirror while you're brushing your teeth and you think "we've got no chance against Italy". All the thoughts and demons come into your mind. [The positive mindset] was a player-driven thing, helped by the coaches, because they wanted it and reinforced it whenever they could.

'Ricki [Herbert] had the formation he wanted to play which was really good for our team. There weren't any egos and everybody bought in pretty well, so whatever Ricki mentioned we just tried to doubly and triply reinforce because most of us were only going to have one shot at this.

'Did we want to be that team in 82 that says, "Well done guys, you fought admirably, have a pat on your back?" You want to be remembered for something different.'

Both Hallgrímsson and Nelsen's stories reference the idea of building on previous achievements with startling regularity. Having a previous focal point as a springboard is a crucial motivational tool when preparing for a tournament.

If a team's World Cup voyage is their first foray into unknown territory, though, the approach can take on a different form. Especially when qualification is such an unbelievable achievement in the first place.

'For me as a young lad growing up in Trinidad, getting to a World Cup was always a dream. So getting to a World Cup was surreal,' Stern John beams. 'We never thought it was realistic but then Leo [Beenhakker, the manager] came in and he made a massive difference.'

If we win a game, that's a bonus, but we're never going to qualify for the next round. We just wanted to go and enjoy ourselves and not get embarrassed...

Only once before had Trinidad and Tobago even come close, a 1989 play-off defeat to USA mired in controversy due to conspiracy theories that the game – unbeknown to the players – was rigged in the States' favour by CONCACAF bigwig, Jack Warner.

But Beenhakker made it all possible, moulding an ageing squad, predominantly scattered at less-heralded clubs around Britain, to reach the 2006 World Cup. The experienced coach married the hardened European nous he'd developed managing top sides, including Real Madrid, Ajax and the Dutch national team, with the best Caribbean traits to get the most out of Trinidad and Tobago's players.

The Soca Warriors had done the inconceivable and become the smallest nation ever to qualify for a World Cup (a record that lasted 12 years until Hallgrímsson's Iceland gazumped them) but there was a feeling they had reached the top of their Everest.

'Although we had some decent players, we were a small country and we weren't going to kid ourselves,' John says. 'If we win a game, that's a bonus, but we're never going to qualify for the next round. We just wanted to go and enjoy ourselves and not get embarrassed, we didn't want to be remembered for losing heavily – that's happened to countries before and we didn't want that.

'Leo [Beenhakker] knew exactly what we were coming up against and knew exactly what to speak to the lads about. He was always honest about everything with us, what he did and said, so it was good. The guys believed in him and the experience he was bringing to the table.'

A 0–0 draw with Sweden in the opening match, which John says was celebrated almost like they had won, was complemented by two spirited 2–0 defeats to England and Paraguay. It showed Trinidad and Tobago were competitive, but would Beenhakker have lost some credence if he'd expected more?

'Yes, 100 per cent,' John answers. 'We knew as professional players, we were there to enjoy the moment and make history as the smallest country to get to the World Cup. We can tell our kids and grandkids we'd been there, and he knew that too.

'Leo's motivational chat with us was that we're obviously underdogs and it's the first time we've been there [the World Cup], so we need to keep it as tight as possible. We don't need to go out and play open football and end up five- or six-nil down after 15 or 20 minutes.'

* * *

The fear of succumbing to a big scoreline while the world watches shouldn't be taken lightly. There have been 10 defeats of seven goals or worse in the tournament's history, with South

Korea's 1954 side accounting for two of them – suffering 9–0 and 7–0 losses to Hungary and Turkey respectively. Scant reward for the six-day trip the squad had been on to get to Switzerland for the competition.

If that jaunt didn't do much for the South Koreans' preparation, neither did the sparse pre-match team talk from manager Kim Yong-sik ahead of their ill-fated clash with Ferenc Puskás's Mighty Magyars. 'Everything was just foreign to us – the city, the crowds, everything,' defender Han Chang-wha told South Korean newspaper *JoongAng Ilbo* years later. 'We went to bed and the next day, we woke up and realised how big a game we had in front of us. Our coach [Yong-sik] didn't say much before the game. He was excited and probably as nervous as the rest of the team.'

In Yong-sik's defence, the 1950s wasn't an era known for managerial masterclasses. However, the same excuse can't be made in 1982 when El Salvador suffered a 10–1 defeat to a much less talented Hungarian side than in Puskás's day.

The tournament in Spain was the Salvadorans' second World Cup, although their first in 1970 hadn't gone too well either, as they lost all three matches with an aggregate score of 9–0. But after managing to navigate qualification for a second time, this time against the backdrop of a civil war, the Central Americans were cheered off as heroes.

The trouble is, manager Mauricio 'Pipo' Rodríguez may have got a bit ahead of himself. The 36-year-old decided the world was ready to be wowed by El Salvador's buccaneering style and after watching a video of opponents, Hungary, that players had pitched in to buy from a Spanish agent the night before the match, he unveiled his master plan.

'"They play just like Paris Saint-Germain," our manager told us while we watched it,' defender Mario Castillo told

FourFourTwo magazine. 'We had beaten them [PSG] in a friendly two weeks before. "We have to go and attack them as much as possible," he said. That was the biggest mistake of all time.'

Rodríguez's attacking plan soon backfired as the Salvadorans found themselves 3–0 down within 23 minutes, only for the young boss to introduce yet another forward midway through the first half to force the Hungarians back. This didn't work and despite the sub, Ramírez Zapata, scoring, El Salvador conceded seven more to lose 10–1.

As the goals flooded in, Rodríguez did ready number-two goalkeeper Eduardo Hernandez to come on, but changed his mind. 'I had wanted to protect [starting keeper] Mora from conceding more goals, then I realised that I risked two goalkeepers' confidence on the same day. I left Mora on the pitch,' the hapless coach said to *FourFourTwo*.

By the final whistle, Rodríguez's reputation was in tatters. Captain Norberto Huezo decreed that the manager 'doesn't decide anything' for the remaining two group games, and set the team up to play more conservatively in their 1–0 and 2–0 losses to Belgium and Argentina. Rodríguez returned home a pariah and never coached again.

Another nation used to being on the end of heavy defeats at World Cups is Saudi Arabia. In the five tournaments they've appeared in, they've lost five games by three goals or more, with the worst loss coming 8–0 at the hands of Germany in 2002. So when they were hit for five by hosts Russia in the opening game at the 2018 World Cup, manager Juan Antonio Pizzi relied heavily on his backroom staff to stop the rot getting worse.

'That [bouncing back after losing 5–0] was possibly the biggest challenge in my entire sporting career,' says psychologist Tim Harkness. 'When you lose a match like that, it opens up another world because that result has reverberations beyond just football.

'That result has reverberations into your life and into your moral identity, and that is the risk of the World Cup in that it becomes bigger and more important than it is, so has a negative effect on performance.'

Harkness and Pizzi worked on reasserting a sense of perspective within the group, trying to stop the players from becoming 'over-motivated' to correct the heavy defeat in the following matches and remain positive about what they do well. The Saudis only lost 1–0 to group favourites Uruguay in the next match and then beat Egypt in the final match to get their first World Cup win for 24 years.

'That was a really big deal for us when the Saudis played Egypt in the last match because we had to make absolutely sure there was no quitting there, given it was the end of a long and disappointing tournament, and they were playing a nation they all tremendously admired,' Harkness adds.

* * *

If the pressure of humiliation can weigh heavy on the shoulders of some of the smaller nations at a World Cup, it wasn't evident when Jamaica rocked up in France for their one and only finals appearance in 1998. Head coach Réne Simões had drilled the side to be more professional and was one of the first managers of a Caribbean team to take advantage of the so-called Granny Rule, to add a swathe of British-based players to the amateur 'taxi drivers and barmen' the Brazilian initially took over. Simões gave them a belief they belonged at football's top table.

'René [Simões] was a philosopher and he'd always keep you guessing and probe you with questions or [tell] stories of what could and would happen,' Deon Burton, one of the imported Jamaican caps, explains. 'The boys believed in it and we were listening to his every word. And it seemed to work. We were going to do it, 100 per cent. You need a strong person at the helm who can instil that and he definitely did that, especially with the players he had at his disposal. He set the marker down and if it wasn't for him, we wouldn't have been there.'

In fact, when Simões took the Jamaica job, he didn't want to be there. He'd already turned them down before political pressure from his own government convinced him to take a four-month contract in Kingston. Four years later, he led them out at a World Cup.

Simões overhauled the country's infrastructure, facilities, secured financial support for homegrown players to become professional, helped to arrange high-profile friendlies and went on several tours to Brazil to play the nation's top club sides. No wonder they rejected any notion of being underdogs.

'The players during the game do three things: they think, they decide and execute,' Simões tells me. 'So you have to make them have a strong mind. You don't get them with a strong mind by only putting them on the field, you have to work off the field to make them strong mentally. After that, you can change them and execute on the field. Off the field, we always had actors, singers, politicians and athletes from other sports coming direct to them to tell them their experiences.'

Simões's success story – that saw the Reggae Boyz miss out on a second-round spot behind superstars Argentina and eventual bronze medallists Croatia – has remarkable similarities to that of his countryman, Carlos Alberto Parreira. While Parreira is best known for leading Brazil to the 1994 title, he cut his teeth as Kuwait manager in the 1982 World Cup. The Asian outfit was exclusively made up of amateur players and because Parreira didn't have the luxury of calling up players with Kuwaiti heritage from around the globe, he had to make do with what he'd got. As Simões later did, Parreira decided the best port of call was to expand their horizons with global tours to ready themselves for big tournaments.

Money was not a problem, so we could take the team for 40 days in England, 30 days in Brazil and we took 35 players to play friendlies... We paid the Brazilian teams to play us.

'Money was not a problem, so we could take the team for 40 days in England, 30 days in Brazil and we took 35 players to play friendlies,' Parreira says of his preparation. 'We paid the Brazilian teams to play us. In those days, it was $10,000 to play matches with us. It was very interesting, the players really got inspiration and I kept one group through the years and kept improving. Every year, they were better.

'For a country with so many amateur players to win in Asia and qualify, to reach competitions where full professional players have reached...' he tails off. 'The team were prepared because I had them for two months without any problems from the clubs. Our president was the brother of the king and we had the power to have the players and stay with them where we needed.'

The group even practised at Bayern Munich's training ground prior to the World Cup, with the likes of striker Jasem Yaqoub and midfielder Saad Al-Houti honing their trade. They soaked up the experience so they weren't overawed on the big stage.

'We knew our World Cup was to reach [the finals]. If you can imagine from the whole of Asia, only two countries reached the World Cup, this is like winning for those countries in Asia,' the veteran coach continues proudly.

'Of course, we wanted to do well and go to the next round, but when you look at [group rivals] England and France, the difference is too big and there is a huge difference in history, culture, development, players. We drew with Czechoslovakia, we lost 1–0 to England and lost to France. But if you look back, it was interesting because we didn't embarrass ourselves.'

Parreira's pride is a fascinating insight into a coach's mindset. He's experienced the pressure of taking Brazil to two World Cups – winning one of them – but he bursts with just as much joy about his huge career achievement with Kuwait, although this barely registers with the wider world. Sometimes a first-round exit can still mean everything to people back home.

'It's a benefit of coming from a small country,' adds Iceland's Hallgrímsson. 'You can activate so many more people around you and the difference between people is less, so it's easier to get everyone around you.

'It's easier to empower and give ownership to the fans, the media and everyone who has responsibility for the national team because everyone benefits if we do well. Even the journalists, they travelled to Russia and France to follow the national team – it's nice for everybody in the country and unifies the Icelandic people.'

CHAPTER 8
THE PERFECT RECIPE: SELECTION

Good players make the best managers look great. It's a simple formula. With the best tools at his disposal, any coach stands a decent chance of having a certain level of success. But while some elite club bosses are branded chequebook managers for their propensity for splashing the cash in order to build the perfect team, it's not a luxury available in an international job. Instead, it's about making the most of what a nation has to offer and bonding it into a team that can make an assault on the World Cup.

Of course, taking over one of football's superpowers, or timing your appointment to coincide with the peak of a nation's most-gifted generation, is also a sure-fire way to make the team selection process a lot easier. Even then, getting the right blend of players to jet off together for an intense month-long tournament is easier said than done.

Just as picking the perfect starting XI isn't as simple as choosing the 11 best players and putting them on a pitch, the most successful World Cup squads aren't made up of the 23 most talented names within the national pool. Whether it's creating the right personnel balance, weighing up a wildcard pick or leaving behind one of the country's top stars, the decisions made before a manager announces his final squad can cast the die for the entire tournament.

Sometimes, it's not even the composition of the squad that makes the biggest impact, it's how a coach handles the delicate situation of breaking the news of who's in and who's out. Get it right and it'll go without mention, make a wrong call and it'll characterise an entire World Cup campaign.

The only consolation for today's managers is that they get the chance to fall on their own sword. In the World Cup's early years, squad selection was taken out of their hands. Committees of selectors, or a self-appointed individual from within the country's FA, would pick the squad, leaving the coach to make do with the players he was given. Back in 1930, Romania's King Carol II even stepped in to pick the Tricolori squad for that year's inaugural World Cup. While that might seem horrifying by today's standards – and possibly was even then for manager Costel Rădulescu – Carol II used his royal influence to secure the release of a large group of players who had initially been denied leave from the English oil company they worked for.

Not letting coaches make the selection also extended into the leading nations. Scotland's Andy Beattie cited meddling by his FA's officials as the reason he resigned during the 1954 World Cup, while England's first manager, Walter Winterbottom, would even have his starting XI chosen for him by a nine-man committee that would vote on selection.

As football developed, that archaic method soon died out. Winterbottom's replacement, Alf Ramsey, demanded full say over England's team – which gave him valuable control but also paved the way for his successors to be scrutinised for their choices for decades to come.

* * *

Cameroon's players were petrified of getting a knock at their door. The approaching footsteps in the dead of night, the shuffling outside of their room and the accompanying bang could only mean one thing. They were about to be removed. The men on the other side of the door would include Valery Nepomnyashchy. The Russian coach, flanked by a couple of cohorts, would be there ready to carry out the hit. Very few words were shared as the unfortunate player hurriedly packed his bag before being ushered out of the hotel. It was the end.

'Most of the players were afraid to meet Mr Nepomnyashchy, even out of training – it was so bad,' midfielder Emmanuel Maboang remembers of Cameroon's pre-Italia 90 training camp in Yugoslavia. 'You were afraid Mr Nepomnyashchy and his staff would come in your room at night to say, "OK, goodbye. Tomorrow there is a plane back to Cameroon, you can go back". That was the system [for selection] at the training camp in Yugoslavia, there was never a list of Cameroon players to say who was in and who was out.

Every night, the players – even Roger Milla, the best player in Cameroon – were afraid to go back to their room because Mr Nepomnyashchy didn't say anything, he just came to you in the night.

'Every night, the players – even Roger Milla, the best player in Cameroon – were afraid to go back to their room because Mr Nepomnyashchy didn't say anything, he just came to you in the night. He would just say "no comment" if you said anything to him.'

It sounds like the sort of harrowing story victims of a mafia attack might experience. Yet this was the way Cameroon's World Cup squad was whittled down, dropping like flies in the middle of the night, one by one.

A first ever quarter-final appearance for an African nation only weeks later suggests the system might have had merit, but the sinister approach adopted by the Indomitable Lions' mysterious coach doesn't seem like one that would generate the best atmosphere – not only among the departing players, but the ones left behind.

'We arrived at breakfast and you'd see that one or two players weren't there, tomorrow two more players [weren't there]. Players disappeared one by one,' Maboang continues.

'Every day I was counting "one, two, three… twenty-seven", "one, two, three… twenty-five" and you realised somebody had gone back last night. You couldn't speak a lot because tomorrow it could be you, while everyone else is asleep, who is sent back in the night. Then one morning at 9 a.m., he said "congratulations" and you saw you were in the 22.'

There's no good way to tell a player their World Cup dream is over. Monoglot Nepomnyashchy's inability to speak French or English closed off the lines of communication with the jilted stars being sent home from Cameroon's training base and while that may have felt brutal, it did stop his 'knock-and-drop' visits from becoming long, drawn-out affairs.

In another hotel room in La Manga eight years later, England manager Glenn Hoddle must have wished he was also incommunicado. He'd decided to leave Paul Gascoigne – England's Italia 90 star and one of the most talented players ever to pull on the Three Lions shirt – out of the 22-man squad for the 1998 World Cup.

Hoddle wanted to break the news to each player personally, explaining why he was leaving those out who didn't make it and what he was expecting from those who had. The night before, a list of one-on-one appointments were put up on the wall, but when Gazza got wind of the bad news before his allotted time, he stormed in to see Hoddle. Chaos ensued as the midfielder reportedly started hurling around the furniture as he launched into a tirade. Worse still, many of the other players were standing outside, waiting for their own appointments.

'We heard it, we heard him smashing up the room – I think there were a few tables thrown,' says fellow midfielder Rob Lee. 'As I went down the corridor to Glenn's room, there was a big backlog of players. I was probably behind Alan [Shearer] or Teddy [Sheringham] and there was a big backlog, there must have been four, five, six players and we knew something had kicked off – and obviously, we knew it was Gazza.'

Perhaps there was no good way to tell Gascoigne, by then 31 and likely to be too old for the next tournament, that he wouldn't get another crack on the biggest stage. Yet the ruckus soon made headlines and piled the pressure on Hoddle to prove he'd made the right call.

For Lee, though, who suffered the same fate as Gazza when previous England boss Terry Venables cut him from the Euro 96 squad, Hoddle's decision to time the meetings so the five dropped players could leave immediately on a private flight home saved some pain. Two years earlier, Lee had a 13-hour flight back from England's pre-Euros training camp in China after being told he hadn't made Venables' group. Other World Cup camps have their own nightmare scenarios, such as those not making it into France's 1998 squad being gathered together in a room and told as a group they'd be going home.

Despite the furore around Gazza having no place in Hoddle's England 22, there was sound reasoning behind the decision.

'It takes courage to leave him [Gazza] out and of course we know all about his drinking habits, but he was still a talented, talented player even then and it takes guts to leave somebody like that out,' Lee says. 'If Hoddle thought he's not right for the squad and has got problems, then he wasn't going to be a regular starter. Glenn had a way of playing and it surprised a lot of people, including me, because Gazza was still one of the best players on his day. But is Gazza somebody to have on the bench? Because as good as he would be, would he be happy on the bench?

'You've got to have a squad, certainly in a tournament, where people know they're not going to be playing and aren't going to rock the boat or be a pain if they're not playing. With Gazza, if we drew, the clamour to get him into the team maybe would have been too strong.

'It's very difficult. Sometimes you can't always have all the best players in a squad and you've got to have players who'd be happy to come and do a job and back the rest of the lads up, but if they are, they need to be good enough to do a job.'

* * *

It's scenarios like this, when the blessing of having too much talent, can perversely become a curse for some coaches. Strength in depth should be a good thing, but sometimes a squad overloaded with top stars can quickly create problems if players used to having key roles at their clubs find themselves sitting on the bench.

Especially in an intense tournament environment, the choice can be between giving certain players a starting berth or sending them home. But should managers decide to name the players in the squad anyway and take the risk of them becoming unsettled if they're not involved?

'Samir is an important player for Manchester City, but he has not performed that well with France,' France boss Didier Deschamps told TF1 after leaving Samir Nasri out of his 2014 World Cup squad. 'He is a starter at City, which is not the case with France, and he has made it clear that he is not happy when he is not [a starter] and I can tell you it can be felt in the squad. I built the best squad, I did not pick the 23 best French players.'

While Deschamps may have saved his camp from having a disruptive Nasri within its ranks, the diminutive playmaker's absence still hung like a shadow across French preparations in Brazil. Fuelled in part by Nasri's girlfriend, Anara Atanes, taking to Twitter to voice her dissatisfaction at Deschamps in a sweary post that led her to be taken to court, several senior French pundits and ex-players spoke out against the decision.

Deschamps simply brushed off any criticism. After all, he's no stranger to making controversial decisions involving several top French stars during his time as manager, with the likes of Karim Benzema and Aymeric Laporte consistently left out in the cold despite starring for some of Europe's leading club sides. Despite regularly finding the net for his club, Real Madrid, Benzema was exiled from the French side for six years due to his alleged involvement in a sex-tape scandal with team-mate Mathieu Valbuena, before earning a shock recall before Euro 2020. Laporte wasn't so lucky and eventually decided to switch nationality to play for Spain after successfully becoming a Spanish citizen in 2021.

Naturally, the French boss has the luxury of a huge pool of players to choose from, so some big names are always likely to miss out. And when asked why he chooses not to select certain players, Deschamps has pointed to the need to maintain a consistent seniority in the team, sticking with the players who are familiar with the rules and standards he expects of the side.

It's an approach other managers take, too. By identifying a core group that will always remain in place throughout a tournament cycle, an element of certainty can be established in what can otherwise become an unsettled squad that fluctuates due to form and injury.

'There are always decisions to make that will upset players who won't be part of the squad,' says Ottmar Hitzfeld, who took Switzerland to the 2010 and 2014 World Cups. 'I always had around 16 or 17 players who were the same in each squad though, so it was just a matter of adding a few players. You can't change national teams too much, you need a core group of players.

'If a player has a small crisis in club football, you have to keep in mind that his national team is a different team in a different environment and they can play well with you again. When players were out of form with their clubs, I kept faith in them.'

What I learned in my first camp was that I couldn't pick my best 23 players, that would never make the best team.

By retaining a similar squad during a campaign, then a consistent set of values and a hierarchy can form, even though players aren't together for long stretches of the season. There's still flexibility within that, but players can learn to understand their place within the national team – something that has caused unrest in the past if there are several individuals all vying for a limited number of positions in the line-up.

'What I learned in my first camp was that I couldn't pick my best 23 players, that would never make the best team,' explains Belgium manager Roberto Martínez. 'It was about selecting the best 23 individuals to make the best team for Belgium. When you say the best team, that means in every aspect of the role of playing for your national team, not just playing a game or two in the space of 10 days.

'It means possibly living together for 50 days in a major tournament. What that means is a player who is the main player for his club comes to the national team and if you can't give him the same role it's going to be very difficult for him to act as the team needs.

'That was the initial shock that I got when I went to the national team because I was expecting to always pick the best 23 players at each specific moment. I realised very quickly that wouldn't bring the stability, togetherness and the team discipline to face adversity.'

Even the slightest misjudgement can feel like putting an elephant opposite a mouse on a seesaw, with Germany's experience in 1998 a perfect demonstration of what can happen if that balance is askew. European champions from two years earlier, Germany would have expected to be one of the favourites going to France. Yet the sheer strength in depth of Berti Vogts' squad seemed to be their undoing.

'We had too many problems and too many players who expected to be in the first XI all the time,' Christian Ziege tells me. 'There wasn't a good mood through the team, which we had when we played in 1996… not everybody was going in the right direction. Everybody was saying, "I have to play, I need to play"… but the whole team wasn't up for it. The players weren't happy with not being involved in the tournament or a particular game, but we'd never blame just one person for that.'

Despite dispatching group opponents USA and Iran with relative ease, Germany relied on a pair of late two-goal salvos to avoid defeat to Yugoslavia in the first phase, and then to turn around a one-goal deficit late-on against Mexico in the last-16. There was no Houdini act as they were thumped 3–0 by Croatia in the quarter-finals, though.

On paper, a squad bristling with talent and experience of winning major titles, looked formidable. Dig a little deeper and Ziege's point begins to show: 12 of the players in the squad were 30 or over, with a further five aged 28. The youngest was Jens Jeremies at 24.

'We had so many leaders in that team, or at least too many players who thought they were leaders, who had to be in the first XI and had to play,' Ziege continues. 'Sometimes it's about taking a decision that says OK, this is a fantastic player and he has so many abilities, but in this position I think the other person is better than him. Then you have to think if it's intelligent to take two strong players in the same position. If you leave one out, he's not happy. So the mood was not good in the team.

'In 96, everyone knew what role he had and there were young players, there were leaders, there were fighters – not necessarily the best players in terms of quality, but in terms of mentality, sticking a team together. If you're cooking, you need a bit of salt, pepper, you need everything. If you just put salt in your food, it's salty and not tasty. You need the right balance.'

It seems almost too simplistic, but age is a great indicator when it comes to creating a balanced squad. Finding the sweet spot between being loyal to the senior players who have served so well in the past and blooding the next generation is the challenge. Across 16 years, Denmark coach Morten Olsen became familiar with the need to regularly breathe new life into his side as he led them to four major tournaments. But football isn't perfectly cyclical, with a conveyor belt of players appearing in the necessary positions just as the previous ones depart.

'Having a generation of younger and older players is important, but you also have to have players who are stable in their games, otherwise you have a problem,' says the former Ajax manager. 'Sometimes you have a situation where you have to choose between young players who are maybe not so stable, but are talented. Sometimes, this guy is stable, but he's not as good as two years ago.

'But you have to choose between these two kinds of players – the talented player who is not so stable, but maybe in some games can make the difference, or a more stable player who has won many games in a European Championship or a World Cup. Small countries that don't have the same possibilities as the five or six big countries in Europe will always have this to deal with.'

While the issue isn't so pressing for the bigger nations, the clamour from fans and the media for the next big thing to receive an international call-up can be even louder. There is sometimes a tendency to always be looking at what's coming next in international football, so it's a manager's responsibility to decide when the time is right to blood new talent.

Some coaches like to stick with the tried and tested faces, whereas others welcome the chance to throw a fresh name in, regardless of their age.

'If I'm in charge of a national team, I'll try to put young players in my squad as soon as I think "this is something special",' ex-England boss Sven-Göran Eriksson told *FourFourTwo* in 2019. 'If you think that a player might become very important for the country today or tomorrow, pick them. When you think they're ready – physically, tactically and mentally – put them in the team.'

During his five years with the Three Lions, Eriksson became known for experimenting with his squad, picking 82 players of all ages to join an England camp at one time or another. Two of his memorable debutants were Theo Walcott and Wayne Rooney, who both took their England bows at a time when they were barely out of school uniform.

While Rooney's talent and subsequent performances showed he was more than ready for the call up, Walcott's inclusion in England's 2006 World Cup was more puzzling. The pacey forward had only turned 17 less than two months earlier, had never played in the Premier League and Eriksson had never seen him play a competitive match. Seasoned strikers Jermain Defoe, and Darren Bent, who'd netted 22 goals for Charlton Athletic that season, were left out.

In his press conference announcing the squad, Eriksson told the media he was 'not crazy' for picking Walcott and reasoned the element of surprise could work in England's favour as opposition managers wouldn't know much about him. It was a ploy Sir Bobby Robson deployed in 1990 when drafting in Steve Bull from the lower leagues, although the Wolves hitman was a seasoned goal-getter by that time.

'If you don't have a clear [other option], why not take a young, talented one for the future?' Eriksson reasoned when asked about Walcott on Sky Sports' *Monday Night Football* in 2020. 'Because the player picked at number 23 will not win the World Cup for you, for sure.'

While Walcott didn't play a single minute of England's campaign, Eriksson's other gamble to take Rooney paid off. The team's undoubted star, the Manchester United frontman had broken his metatarsal in the run up to the tournament and faced a race against time to be fit – managing to start three of England's five matches.

Eriksson's quandary over Rooney's fitness isn't uncommon in the run up to a big tournament. When a key player is injured, making a call on whether he should take up a precious place in the squad can become the big focus as the announcement approaches, with the scrutiny lingering well into the tournament.

Eriksson told Sky Sports that 'if Rooney has a small chance to play, you have to pick him' and it was a move mirrored by Roberto Martínez with Belgium in 2018 when Vincent Kompany suffered a hamstring injury in a warm-up game against Portugal. If there's a chance he can play, he should be picked, was his attitude.

'We took an injured Vincent Kompany to the World Cup,' says Red Devils assistant manager Graeme Jones. 'He'd injured his hamstring on 6 June and he played 20 minutes against England on 28 June about 22 days later, then he starts the last-16 match against Japan and scores in the quarter-final against Brazil.

'With a lot of work in between with the physios, the sports scientists, the coaches on the training ground to get him to that level when it really mattered, could we have Vincent Kompany available? Yes, because he was imperative to what we were trying to do.

'Vincent Kompany was the best representation of the mindset that was required for winning tournaments. I've been lucky to work with some top players, but he had the best mentality of a player I've ever worked with.

'And he would echo the coaching staff and the manager's message because he believes in it, but not because he's a yes man. Anybody who knows Vincent knows he'll make his own mind up. But once he was convinced, he would echo our ways, our tactics, our thoughts and he was a strong leader and everybody respected him. Vinny was huge for that.'

* * *

Getting to grips with the players and characters making up a national team is much easier for coaches taking charge of their own country, or one packed with high-profile players. But for international managers who travel the globe taking on sides with smaller reputations, quickly familiarising themselves with the players at their disposal can be a challenge – especially when they don't get much time together.

By the time Bora Milutinović took charge of the USA ahead of the 1994 World Cup, he'd developed a clear idea of what he needed to do in order to be successful after leading Mexico to their first ever quarter-final in 1986, and Costa Rica to the Italia 90 knockout round. The Serb had a secret formula in his head of how to turn unfancied outfits into competitive tournament sides and devised a way to decide which players had the characteristics he needed to weave his magic.

'He would drive players crazy with what he did, but Bora was the ultimate man-manager in that he was constantly testing us, on the field and off the field,' says US star Alexi Lalas. 'He knew he had to assess who these players were, not just by kicking a ball, but who they were to get that best group of players. Whether it was making me cut my hair when I first got to camp, how a player tied his shoes, or plays soccer tennis – I mean, I literally saw a team-mate make the World Cup team by the way he played a soccer tennis game on one of the last days before cuts.'

> *He would drive players crazy with what he did, but Bora was the ultimate man-manager in that he was constantly testing us, on the field and off the field.*

Yes, that's right. A game set up like a volleyball match, apart from the fact that players would kick and head the ball instead, was the vital factor.

'We knew he took it [soccer tennis] seriously because he played it [himself],' Lalas continues. 'For him, the assessment of that soccer tennis was more about how that individual – or individuals when they're in tandem – approached the game. What are the things they're doing? How competitive are they? How did they take losing? How do they co-operate? How do you pick your partner? All of those different things.

'I'll be honest, I rolled my eyes at it quite a lot. And to be quite honest, I think he assessed me in different ways. But for other players, it really went into a formula that only he knew that was going to spit out who the players were that he wanted on that team.'

One of Lalas's primary tests surrounded his hair. The central defender became one of the cult heroes of USA 94 in part due to his flowing red locks and big personality. It was all part of a carefully created image Lalas had developed, but Milutinović wanted to see quite how important it was to his player shortly after taking over as manager.

> *Bora's assistant pulled me aside and said, "Bora wants you to cut your hair,"… I was irritated and pissed off and I started ranting and raving about "this is America" and individualism … But the fact is, I'd have done anything to be on that team.*

'I had really long hair and I remember we were in Phoenix, Arizona, and Bora's assistant pulled me aside and said, "Bora wants you to cut your hair",' Lalas recalls of the instruction. 'I was irritated and pissed off and I started ranting and raving about "this is America" and individualism and "this isn't right". But the fact is, I'd have done anything to be on that team.

'I remember walking down the street to the local barbershop and cutting my hair, and I came back. We had a team meeting that night and it was the first time Bora saw me [since]. He walked in, he just acknowledged me in the form of nodding his head and just carried on.

'That was a year and a half before the World Cup. He never said another thing about my hair or how I looked because at that moment, I had passed that test and there were plenty of others to come, but he wanted to see. For me, he knew hair was important. For somebody else, it might be something he tested them on to see how they reacted.

'From that moment on, I grew my hair out, I grew my goatee – if I had to sacrifice it at that moment, I was going to come back with a vengeance.'

Whatever the methods and considerations a manager must weigh up as he decides his final World Cup squad, the lesson of an old master of the game remains possibly the most important of them all. When England's World Cup-winning manager Alf Ramsey was selecting the players he wanted to take into battle with him, one criteria stood out above all else: trust.

'Alf had done a lot of the work [in the years leading up to the 1966 World Cup] and moved out the players who he thought were going to let him down, so he had the trust of the players,' Sir Geoff Hurst reminisces. 'Once he'd done that kind of work, with the pattern and the discipline, he put the team sheet up knowing those players, who are a hard-nosed group of players, fantastic characters and nice guys wouldn't let him down. All the hard work had been done in those three years leading up to it on how he wants to play, the players he picked, and so on.'

CHAPTER 9

PICKING A GENERAL: CAPTAINS AND LEADERS

A good manager knows he can't achieve his dreams without the help of others. So appointing the right leadership group to reaffirm messages is crucial if a national team is going to be successful at a major tournament. At the centre of that is the captain – the coach's representative among the players, a strong voice on the pitch, and a regular confidante to speak to about new ideas or concerns. Cultivating the right relationship with a skipper can make all the difference. Get it right and the back-up can be all-important in key moments; get it wrong and it could be a boss's downfall.

By nature, captains are usually one of the senior members of the team and hold a strong influence in the dressing room, so striking the right balance between allowing them responsibility to contribute and not allowing them too much power has caused many managerial headaches. There's no one-size-fits-all approach to perfecting a captain-manager relationship, though. It all comes down to different characters, having an understanding for each other's strengths and weaknesses, and managing expectations based on previous experiences.

But don't be mistaken in thinking that simply giving one player the armband is the end of it. History recalls several high-profile fall-outs – sometimes on the eve of World Cups – as existing captains were replaced, or other senior players had their noses put out of joint by being overlooked. Whether a manager's captain is the most experienced player, his biggest star or somebody he has a long-standing partnership with previously, that call needs to be the right one.

* * *

Mick McCarthy had been left out in the cold. The no-nonsense centre half was expected to be one of Jack Charlton's key allies as he took the reins as Republic of Ireland boss in 1986, yet he hadn't even made the first squad.

It was a decision that took a lot of people by surprise. The duo had created a strong relationship years before Charlton stepped into international management, when they lived close to each other in South Yorkshire, regularly meeting for a pint and a chat about football.

McCarthy, by then marshalling Manchester City's backline in the top flight, shared several football values with Charlton and had proved himself to be a strong character and leader. The perfect man to have around when starting a new job – or so you'd think. But the snub of Charlton's future captain wasn't all that it initially seemed.

'He [Charlton] said he didn't pick me because he knew me already and wanted to find out about everybody else,' says McCarthy. 'He appreciated the way Kevin Moran and I played together, and we were more of his ilk of centre-backs in that we kept the ball out of the net rather than building up from the back, which suited me and suited him.

'I had the utmost respect for him. I loved Big Jack and I know he had real respect for me because he [eventually] gave me the captain's job, and we remained lifelong friends.'

McCarthy's temporary hiatus from Charlton's Republic of Ireland revolution didn't stop him from making his voice heard when he finally got called up. While Frank Stapleton was the Irish captain for Charlton's first two years – having been retained in the role given to him by previous boss Eoin Hand – McCarthy's influence was felt within the squad, before he took the armband himself during the 1990 World Cup campaign.

He would be tough on me because he put me in the team and made me the captain to make sure what he wanted done on the pitch got done. So if I started p***ing about, I'd be getting it in the earhole.

'Mick acted as Jack's enforcer in those early years,' remembers Niall Quinn, who made his debut under Charlton in 1986. 'He had this really vociferous grip on the dressing room as a player himself and Jack knew he had a leader, not just an individual as a player.'

McCarthy went on to be Charlton's Captain Fantastic and became a trusted general in and around the Ireland camp. Needed a message reiterating on the pitch or a player pulled into shape? McCarthy was his man.

But while they'd built a special relationship that stood the test of time, with both manager and player staying in touch until Charlton's death in 2020, McCarthy didn't get any preferential treatment. Quite the opposite.

'He would be hard on me if I did something he didn't want me to do, like roll the ball into midfield or a square pass – I had a couple of up and downers with him about that,' McCarthy explains with a smirk. 'He would be tough on me because he put me in the team and made me the captain to make sure what he wanted done on the pitch got done. So if I started p***ing about, I'd be getting it in the earhole.

'We had a committee [of players] that dealt with bonuses and stuff, and I wasn't part of that. I was the captain of the team. It was more that we had a certain way of playing and he knew that whatever he told me to do, then I would make sure we were doing it on the pitch.'

McCarthy was the man to replace Charlton when he left the manager's hot seat in 1996, which may suggest a grooming of him as captain with an eye to him eventually taking over in the future. But McCarthy says there was none of that in his time as a player.

'He trusted me to make sure things were done,' McCarthy adds. 'All these good players we had, I wasn't some sort of second boss on the field, I would be encouraging our players to play that way and do what he was asking of us.'

For a manager, having a captain who can be relied upon to walk through walls for them is the perfect scenario. And when there's a trusted group of players all with similar beliefs that ethos becomes even stronger. It's a cliché to say a manager needs multiple captains, but it's true.

That sort of bond takes time to grow, but Bobby Robson reaped the rewards during his time as England boss. When first-choice captain Bryan Robson was forced to pull out of England's squad early on in their run to the 1990 semi-finals, there was a host of strong options to choose from as a replacement.

While Robson the player was a notable absence, the team was able to move on seamlessly, as was the collegiate way Robson the manager worked with the senior members of his squad and his coaching staff. And Sir Bobby was able to call upon Terry Butcher, a man he'd worked with as captain at club level.

'I was probably the longest-serving player under his stewardship, so I got to know him pretty well, but as with most managers, you don't become best friends – having been in management myself, you realise you can't get too close to players because that creates problems,' says Butcher.

'At Ipswich, I lived probably about a quarter of a mile from Bobby and we'd frequently meet walking the dogs. I had a labrador and he had a spaniel called Roger, named after Roger Osborne, who scored the winner for Ipswich in the 78 FA Cup final. It wasn't planned or anything, but we'd be two people walking the dog, having a chat.

'I never wanted it to go any further than that in terms of popping round for a cup of tea. That was never going to happen because Bobby was quite aloof

Because the players wanted to play for him and loved him, they tried really hard to make the new system work.

at times and then was very friendly when he had to be, as any manager is. He had to mix the camaraderie with being the boss and guvnor, and he managed that very well.'

Robson's management goes to show the value of having several captain-like leaders all over the team, so while goalkeeper Peter Shilton took the armband in the matches Butcher didn't play, the defender picked up the baton again without disruption when he did.

In both of Robson's World Cups in 1986 and 1990, some accounts from the time suggested the senior players had big says in tactical decision-making, too. But Butcher's memories as part of that group are nothing more than a healthy working relationship with key members of the team.

'I never got the impression he worked a lot with the senior players. He'd ask our opinion and speak to us individually to see how we felt, so he did take on board the advice, but he was very shrewd,' Butcher tells me. 'For us, making the change was pretty seamless and pretty comfortable. He instructed us what to do and we went on and did it for him. If you've got a good team and a good relationship with the players, you could change systems during the World Cup and during games, the players have got to have the confidence to manage that switch very well and know what they're doing.

'Because the players wanted to play for him and loved him, they tried really hard to make the new system work. It was pretty seamless and pretty good to be part of because if you had to change, you changed.'

If Butcher's understanding of Robson's wonts felt natural, the philosophical understanding between Rinus Michels and Johan Cruyff was another level entirely. It was almost telepathic. Their relationship went even further back than those that McCarthy and Butcher had with their managers. Michels and Cruyff's bond had grown outside of football, long before the mercurial forward had even made his Ajax debut.

'When Johan was 12, his father died,' Cruyff's ghostwriter Jaap de Groot explains. 'His father had a grocery store and, at that time, there was no [social] security, so they had a hard time making ends meet. There were some people who helped the family – the mother and her two sons – get through, and one of the people who did that was Michels [who knew the Cruyffs through Johan's involvement in Ajax's academy].

'For example, when Johan was a kid and he had to go to the dentist or whatever else, Michels said, "I live close to the dentist, I'll pick you up in the car and take you there". That situation of Michels caring about Johan – and there were three or four or five people who took care of him from Ajax at this critical time – he never forgot that.'

For that almost-paternal bond in Cruyff's formative years to have blossomed into manager-and-captain roles at the 1974 World Cup is an incredible escalation. But while the benefits of such a foundation is there for all to see in their joint success, it did mean Michels and Cruyff sometimes had private spats that perhaps wouldn't have developed in the same way if they weren't so familiar with each other. Despite that mutual reliance to deliver the Total Football ideology Michels and Cruyff are famous for, there's no doubting there was still a hierarchy to their relationship.

'I got to know Cruyff reasonably well and did a few interviews with him over the years – the first time was when he was playing for Barcelona and the manager was Michels,' BBC commentator Barry Davies reveals. 'We did the interview in the referee's room at Camp Nou and he came in smoking. He put the cigarette down on an ashtray and said, "If Michels comes in, that's yours, OK?" That was the first thing he ever said to me. It just shows there was a strength in Michels to create an element of fear, even in his greatest player.'

* * *

Not all international managers can benefit from having prior relationships with key players before taking over, though – especially if they're a foreign boss being drafted into work in a new country.

Coming into it cold can help when making certain big decisions, but it also can mean snap judgements are needed before fully understanding the foibles of the squad. That can make selecting a new captain tricky or, if there's a stand-out candidate who's held the armband for a long time, make winning their approval one of the first priorities.

When German coach Winfried Schäfer took over Cameroon ahead of the 2002 World Cup, he remembers one particularly big test early on in his tenure to win over captain Rigobert Song and the other senior players. It happened within minutes of his first team meeting.

'I spoke to them about discipline and said, "The players who won't fight for the team or for the country can go home because that's something that's very important to us",' Schäfer explains. 'My English was not very good at the time, but I talked mainly in English. I said, "When we have a problem with the family or your club or your coach, call me," and I gave them my number. Patrick Mboma, who was not the captain, but was a leader and a very good player asked "in which language?" because my English wasn't good and we had many players who spoke French and English. I went to him and looked him in the eyes and I said, "Patrick, what do you need, a coach or an English teacher?". Then I went to my room. After 50 minutes, there was a knock at my hotel room door and five players came in my room – Patrick Mboma, Samuel Eto'o, Rigobert Song, Marc-Vivien Foé, Raymond Kalla – and they said, "Coach, the language of football is international, we go with [support] you".'

That established power dynamic may have already existed in Cameroon, but wasn't the case when Sven-Göran Eriksson arrived as England manager. The Swede had been brought in during a period of flux for the national team, with the side struggling in their World Cup qualification group and without a permanent captain following Alan Shearer's international retirement a few months earlier.

'You need a captain who is respected by the whole team,' Eriksson told *FourFourTwo* in 2019. 'He doesn't need to shout or speak all day, but when he speaks, the others listen. Normally you can feel who it is. You see the player who the others respect; the one who can stand in the dressing room and say, "Hey come on, we're defending badly," or whatever the problem might be. If it's someone who knows the team and has been there for a while, even better, although that's not necessarily the most important thing.

'Picking David Beckham to be my England captain was a very easy choice, even if we later had many potential captains –

Rio Ferdinand, John Terry, Frank Lampard, Steven Gerrard and others – that I could have chosen. But everyone respected Beckham, not just the players, but also the people around the team and the general public.'

Although there was some criticism of Eriksson's decision – something the coach said he 'didn't understand and didn't listen to' – his gut feeling to name Beckham as captain paid off. The midfielder flourished with his new responsibility and became the team's talisman, regularly playing the starring role during Eriksson's reign. And as Eriksson's fellow countryman Lars Lagerbäck assesses, sometimes changing a captain can just feel like the right thing to do.

'It's a little bit about the dynamic of the group,' the former Sweden and Nigeria boss says. 'It's important for you to have good leadership from the team captain on the pitch, but also off the pitch. Sometimes we [during his time with Sweden] felt we needed to change the leadership of the squad a little bit because when some players go and some players come, they can change the dynamic inside the squad. That's the reason why we changed captains sometimes, the main reason anyway.'

But sometimes gut feelings can be wrong, even for the most experienced managers. After taking charge of the Netherlands for the second time in 2012, Louis van Gaal decided he needed to learn from the mistakes of his first stint as Oranje boss and build his side around younger, hungrier players.

That meant marginalising 29-year-old Robin van Persie, a man who had just top-scored in the Premier League the previous season and was in the process of securing a move to Manchester United. The pair had never crossed paths previously, creating a strained first meeting.

'It's quite remarkable because van Persie's first impression of van Gaal was "what a strange person, he's really awkward",' says journalist Robert Heukels, who wrote van Gaal's 2020 biography. 'In the first dialogue between the two, van Gaal said, "You're not going to play here [the national team] anymore," so van Persie said, "OK". Then van Gaal asked, "So you're staying?" and van Persie said, "Yes, I'm staying, I'll be a substitute, no problem". In the beginning, van Gaal picked Klaas-Jan Huntelaar as his first-choice number nine and van Persie was his number three or four because van Gaal didn't believe he had the motivation anymore.'

A combination of van Persie's attitude to being told he was no longer an automatic choice and his impressive start to life at Old Trafford soon changed van Gaal's mind. But instead of simply reinstating the striker to the starting line-up, he had an even more pressing question to ask him.

'Van Gaal always gives people a second chance, so the next game he said, "You are my centre-forward and I have another question, do you want to be my captain?"' continues Heukels. 'For van Persie, it was "what's happening here? First I'm out, now I'm captain". But they just had a conversation between the two of them, they found they both had the same humour and are both a little bit strange in conversation.

'They clicked and van Persie became the real star of the Dutch team. He went on to become Netherlands' all-time top scorer and van Gaal spoke about everything with van Persie before he announced it to the Dutch squad.'

Adversity may have been the catalyst for van Gaal and van Persie's relationship to blossom, but the closeness they achieved as a result is what many managers need. They shared thoughts on tactics and formations, discussed ideas and went on trips together as they attempted to plot Netherlands' path to glory. Van Persie became an extension of van Gaal's inner circle and was the conduit between the coach and the players. It's a model that's been successful for plenty of managers, and the added responsibility given to a captain means that messages can be seeded with more subtlety from a different voice.

Sometimes it's clear a player is management material, so he relishes the chance to be part of the preparation and add their own ideas when asked. For that approach to be successful, though, the manager needs to have complete confidence in his captain to communicate his message in the right way, and be prepared to listen if they disagree.

'You get some managers on different sides of the spectrum,' explains former New Zealand captain Ryan Nelsen. 'With some, every single pass and everything needs to be perfect, then they take away some of the freedom and expression of the players. With others, they are very open and personable and let players talk, so it's a collaborative thing. Then you get the ones who are in between, and it's those managers who don't end up being successful because there's no clear message.'

Nelsen says the All Whites' boss for the 2010 World Cup, Ricki Herbert, was happy to let his captain take the lead when the time was right. On the run up to their match against world champions Italy, the centre-back even stopped a video session and asked the coaching staff to leave so the players could discuss the opposition themselves.

It's a bold move that could have backfired if Herbert took umbrage with the interruption. Yet his ability to relinquish control and recognise Nelsen's experience when approaching a big game relieved some of the formality – and pressure – in the build-up to the match.

'He [Herbert] would say, "What do you think, this is how we play, you guys have got to do it on the field," so it was very open,' says Nelsen. 'It's a really hard thing to do as a manager, especially at the top, to sit there and listen, but the difference in the New Zealand team is that you've got 20-odd guys on the same page and when anybody spoke it was for a greater reason, there were no individual egos. In the Premier League, if the manager asks what we should do, you'd get 20 different answers because it suits them better. That's where Ricki was good... and it worked.

'We took a lot of that [approach] from speaking to ex-New Zealand players, the All Blacks, some of the good cricketers. It's generally a New Zealand-type thing because it's our culture and mentality. The All Blacks do that quite often and the players have a leadership coaching team inside the team, there are coaches all the way down.'

* * *

A nation's culture may have a lot to do with how effective certain manager–captain relationships are. For smaller countries, in particular, a captain's role is far greater than on-pitch duties and they can become a figurehead for the team itself. Managers may come and go, but the captain remains.

This can be for a wide range of reasons, such as the strength of leadership a certain player demonstrates, or if there's a single elite-level superstar among the ranks. The captain becomes the protector of their team-mates and the representative of their nation.

Some players are born leaders and appear destined to be the national team boss when their time as a player comes to an end, whereas others have their sights set on even higher plains.

Even as a player, Paraguay's José Luis Chilavert's status meant he was considered by many as a future president of the South American nation. The larger-than-life goalkeeper became a cult hero all over the world for his goalscoring exploits as much as his shot-stopping abilities, and was renowned for his forceful nature – a characteristic many managers fell foul of.

When I spoke to him – only days before he officially announced his intention to stand as a candidate in Paraguay's 2023 elections – Chilavert was philosophical about some of the stories from his playing days but spoke about his openness with La Albirroja's managers. According to several newspaper and television stories at the time, Chilavert used his influence to stop Brazilian coach Paulo César Carpegiani from selecting Julio César Romero for the 1998 World Cup by threatening to pull out of the squad if Romero was picked. And four years later, Chilavert reportedly led a player revolt against Italian boss Cesare Maldini by speaking in native Guarani to ignore Maldini's instructions at half time in a crunch group match against Slovenia – managing to overturn a 1–0 deficit and win 3–1 with only 10 men.

Contrary to quotes attributed to him at the time, Chilavert now denies either of these incidents played out in that way, blaming the 'lies' of the 'very mediocre and quite awful' Paraguayan press as the origin of these falsehoods. Yet he does admit having a big hand in the decisive turnaround against Slovenia that saw Paraguay progress to the second round in 2002.

'Slovenia were winning, so we [the players] spoke with Maldini and we decided to take a risk,' Chilavert recalls. 'He brought on [Nelson] Cuevas who scored two goals and we managed to win 3–1. It was important to make that change and to stop the *catenaccio* [Maldini's favoured defensive tactic] and to put more pressure on going forwards.

'I collaborated in having Cuevas brought on the field because I was shouting to Maldini to get him on. He adjusted to that and took that on board, he made that tactical change – he was good and had such an open mind because we were able to win the match.

'It's very important to have a good relationship [between manager and captain]. Maldini was a very open-minded person and he listened to our advice. That's good because we're the ones who know our skills and our strong points, so that in return was a big help for him. With that change, we managed to defeat Slovenia and make history in the World Cup of 2002.'

Wherever the balance of power sat between Chilavert and Maldini, the story shows quite how influential a captain can be in getting the best outcome. Franz Beckenbauer's increasing role during the 1974 tournament in steering a misfiring West Germany side towards World Cup glory further illustrates that, at times, the skipper can know best.

* * *

Creating a role for a senior player who feels the captain's armband is theirs by right can backfire if another candidate arrives on the scene, though. If a captain has been in post for a while or another player believes they are the rightful successor when he stands down, it can cause ructions in the camp if the manager decides to make a change.

The fall-out Argentina boss Carlos Bilardo faced by naming Diego Maradona as captain ahead of the 1986 World Cup could have derailed their entire campaign. Bilardo's backing of El Diez was already contentious enough among large sections of the Argentinian press and fans, so throw into the mix that Maradona would be replacing 1978 World Cup-winning captain Daniel Passarella created a perfect storm of controversy.

Passarella, by then 33 but still an important figure in the team, initially threatened to quit the team if Maradona took his role, but soon changed his mind when it became clear Bilardo wasn't budging. But that didn't stop splits in the camp threatening to ruin preparations.

After Maradona and some team-mates arrived 15 minutes late for a meeting, Passarella launched into a vicious diatribe, suggesting his new captain and the players he was with were delayed because they were taking drugs.

We wouldn't have won the World Cup without Maradona because he was the engine of the team. He was conveying happiness and would motivate the team, he'd help us concentrate and was permanently enthusiastic.

'Ok, I'll admit to taking drugs, but not this time,' came Maradona's retort. 'You're landing others in the sh*t, kids who were with me and didn't do anything. Have you got that, grass?'

Another run in between Maradona and Jorge Valdano – another long-serving member of the squad – revealed more bad blood between the new and old guard. But Bilardo showed no sign of diffusing the situation and picked Passarella in his squad anyway, although a bout of enterocolitis intervened, forcing the former captain to withdraw himself.

For all the controversy that surrounded Maradona being named as captain, defender Néstor Clausen believes Bilardo's decision to give him the armband was pivotal to the team's success. The new skipper was more than simply Argentina's best player, he was also chief entertainer and cheerleader rolled into one raw bundle of talent – and he needed to have the freedom to lead the team.

'We wouldn't have won the World Cup without Maradona because he was the engine of the team,' says Clausen. 'He was conveying happiness and would motivate the team, he'd help us concentrate and was permanently enthusiastic.

'I cannot imagine Maradona not being our captain because, for us, Maradona was already a leader. Passarella was a leader as well, but Maradona was a leader not only for us but a world leader because he was number one worldwide. No one could have imagined that he was not captain of the team.'

Call it manager's instinct or simply seeing the blindingly obvious, but Bilardo was unwavering in his decision. He just knew Maradona had to be his man.

'People said, "Maradona failed in the national team [before the 1986 World Cup], why do you trust him?" But I trusted him because he was going to be the best player at the World Cup,' Bilardo explained in a 2005 interview for FIFA.com. 'It was my time to coach and I trusted Maradona. I believed that with him, if he was really fit, we could tip the balance in games.

'I was not only impressed with his talent, but I was also convinced of his leadership qualities. I believed strongly in Diego from the start and he never disappointed me. Just imagine – four days before we were due to leave for the World Cup in Mexico, people were sniping at me because of Maradona.

'As it happened, Diego played a brilliant tournament, led us to the title, dominated the World Cup like no-one else either before or after that, and ended up becoming a world star.'

CHAPTER 10

A HOME FROM HOME:
THE RIGHT VIBE

It's every player's dream to be selected to represent their country at the World Cup. Running out on the pitch, soaking up the adulation of your nation's fans and showing the world your talent.

Nobody ever thinks about what it's like outside the glorious matchdays a major tournament has to offer. Weeks on end away from home, sometimes with limited contact with loved ones and plenty of time to burn between matches. Sometimes wiling away the days between one game and the next is where championships can be won or lost. Are players in an environment where they are primed to perform at their best, or is homesickness and boredom setting in?

When you've got a squad teeming with superstars living in a hotel for a month-long tournament – not to mention the pre-tournament preparation – issues can fester in the background, undermining what's being done on the pitch. It's not always possible to let the players roam freely around the places the camp is based in, while managers are always trying to find the balance between allowing their players some freedom – then perhaps having to deal with their mischief – and stifling them.

Some coaches don't see this as their domain, as their job is to only look after football-related matters and are relatively hands-off, while others diligently schedule activities, ignite hilarity, or even set strict diets for players to follow.

The importance of these approaches can't be underestimated. A successful camp may get little more than a cursory mention as the players return home, but be prepared to hear the grumbles of discontent if things haven't been right. In the past there have even been suggestions some players have become ambivalent about being knocked out of a tournament: professionally they want to progress, but personally they can't wait to get home.

There are no hard-and-fast rules for creating the perfect vibe during a World Cup training camp, but atmosphere is definitely a key factor when it comes to bonding a successful side.

* * *

A puddle of urine starts to form around Alex Ferguson's feet. The Scotland manager is stood in near-complete darkness in the bathroom of his suite at the Tartan Army's 1986 World Cup base in Mexico, but quickly works out what's going on. Ferguson's toilet seat has clingfilm stretched across the top of it, deflecting anything that tries to enter straight back on to the floor.

'He was raging,' chuckles former Scotland boss Craig Brown, who was part of the coaching team in 86, as he thinks about the prank, which was sprung by Ferguson's own players. Earlier that day, they'd gained access to the gaffer's room, unscrewed all the light fittings and set the trap.

'I think it was Charlie [Nicholas] who masterminded the clingfilm,' Brown continues. 'He [Ferguson] was next door to me and came through and said, "I can't get the lights on, is there a fuse in here?" I came through to next door and he was trying the lights and even the lamps in the bedroom. He went to the toilet while I was there and when he came back, he was raging because they'd clingfilmed the toilet.'

A HOME FROM HOME: THE RIGHT VIBE

The Manchester United legend's no-nonsense reputation might suggest what happened next. But, somewhat surprisingly, Ferguson didn't unleash his famous 'hairdryer treatment' on the players. Instead, it went to show the jovial spirit that existed in the Scottish camp, with Ferguson laughing it off as one of many japes to expect in a relaxed environment. He wanted the players to feel at ease, enjoy their time in Mexico and feel ready to focus when the serious stuff arrived on matchday.

Fergie's wet feet weren't the only victims during Scotland's stay. The kitman once went into his bedroom to find 32 bags of equipment in there, while the kit room had been turned into his bedroom. But Brown says it wasn't just the players pulling the pranks.

'I took training quite a lot and at the end of the session, I would always pick two teams: Old Firm players against the rest, or the Anglos who played in England against the rest, or the good-looking team against the rest, those who had lost their driving licence and those who still had it,' the future Scotland manager recalls. 'I remember coming back from the 1990 World Cup and this lady came to my car and she said, "Why was my husband in the ugly team?" and I said, "I need your surname". She said "MacLeod," to which I replied, "Murdo MacLeod? Ugly team – dyed hair and false teeth".'

'We tried to have good humour and one of the ways to do that is to have fun games. We had a lot of head tennis and the staff would referee the game and we'd try to get a reaction. We wanted that banter going.'

Things may not have gone as Ferguson, Brown and Co had hoped on the pitch during the tournament as they went out in the first round, but there was little doubt a strong team spirit had been garnered. It seems such an obvious asset to have when you're away from home for a major tournament.

Northern Ireland's 1982 World Cup hero Gerry Armstrong spoke to me about how a strong camaraderie was one of the key ingredients manager Billy Bingham created during the golden era of his leadership. There was a sense of personal – as much as professional – desire to be named in the squad.

'Nobody wanted to miss a call-up for the national team because all your mates were there and it was fun,' says Armstrong. 'It was great representing your country and you're always proud,

Nobody wanted to miss a call-up for the national team because all your mates were there and it was fun.

but to see all your mates and have so much fun with them – as they say in Northern Ireland, the *craic* was brilliant.'

Stories of such wholesome enjoyment when going away with the national team weren't lost on one international manager in waiting. As Gareth Southgate emerged as a player in the 1990s, he was used to hearing tales from players in the other home nations about their international experiences and it stuck with him. By the time he took over as England manager in 2016, he'd inherited a side stilted by the expectation of pulling on a Three Lions shirt and often split by club divisions. He knew that had to change if they were ever going to be successful.

'One of the first things Southgate did was to talk to Irish or Scottish or Welsh players he played with and noticed how they'd look forward to going to international camp, whereas the English players used to dread it,' says the *Independent's* chief football writer Miguel Delaney.

'The first thing he tried to do was create a similar atmosphere and that was through the implementation of a whole manner of rules and stuff he did. Like in 2017, when he got them all to an army boot camp to create a group cohesion. He followed that sort of New Zealand rugby thing of "no d***heads" to ensure there was a good atmosphere. That was key to Southgate that international football was not a chore for players in that way and it's something they wanted to be involved in.'

By the time England jetted off to Russia for the 2018 World Cup, there was a completely different feeling around the squad. Admittedly, reduced expectation compared to previous teams meant there was less pressure on Southgate's 2018 vintage, but it's hard to envisage the pictures of players splashing about on inflatable unicorns emerging from past tournaments.

The former defender also introduced wellness questionnaires to encourage players to be more open, invited the usually critical British press into camp to play darts and pool with players to break down barriers and introduced *kabaddi* – a quickfire Indian team sport similar to tag – to promote team spirit.

'Those small things that are fun so that they can go and mess around really is part of the switch off, without feeling too conditioned and organised,' Southgate said in an interview with the BBC's *Football Focus* after the tournament. 'I don't think anybody likes organised fun, we've all been in those sort of situations – and you can imagine, 23 footballers, not really what they're up for, so we've got to be a bit creative.'

But while Southgate's style was to make the World Cup atmosphere feel natural, it was carefully orchestrated. Even his handling of the press, which has a knock-on effect on external perceptions and the pressures that come back on the team, was expertly handled.

'It's quite a basic thing and it's mentioned a lot, but things like darts with the media does have a multiple effect in itself,' Delaney says. 'If you make it fun and break down the boundaries, so the media aren't seen as opposition… on a subconscious, psychological level, you're probably less inclined to immediately criticise someone or go for the strongest possible criticism when something bad happens because it tempers your approach. It creates a more positive atmosphere around the national team.'

While positive results and a run to the semi-finals undoubtedly helped, the noises coming out of England's 2018 camp were poles apart from previous tournaments. Following a disastrous 2010 campaign when England limped through the group stage before being dumped out 4–1 by a rampant Germany in the last-16, several players came out to voice their dissatisfaction at manager Fabio Capello's authoritarian rule.

A lot was made of the players complaining they weren't allowed to do certain things, which I just thought was an excuse for poor performance.

The Italian was accused of being a 'control freak' by some players, pointing out that draconian rules (such as banning ketchup and butter from team meals), boredom caused by restrictions on activities, and mixed messages, left players in a bad frame of mind.

Defender Jamie Carragher has an alternative view, though, and points out that sometimes complaints over camp conditions can be a ploy of players covering up for their own failings.

'A lot was made of the players complaining they weren't allowed to do certain things, which I just thought was an excuse for poor performance,' he argues. 'I enjoyed the World Cup in South Africa and the base. We didn't have to travel to the training pitch and the facilities we had on the base were fantastic. I was a bit bemused when I heard all the criticisms and complaints when I got back from that World Cup. I just thought they were excuses.'

If pinning all of England's struggles on the reduction of some luxuries does seem a little extreme, what did Carragher make of the ruckus about Capello's ketchup ban?

'You're a professional athlete and if you can't have ketchup…' he answers, momentarily tailing off. 'Whether you've had ketchup or not doesn't make too much difference to your performance. Is it that much of a big deal to moan that you can't have ketchup with your evening meal? I mean, come on. People who complain about things like that, it just makes them sound immature.'

Regardless of whether some of the specifics of the criticisms from England's 2010 camp were warranted, there's definitely something to be said about showing players trust and allowing them some freedom to keep themselves entertained during a tournament.

Some coaches are more comfortable than others when it comes to loosening the leash, although the difference in profile between certain teams can also impact how much flexibility a manager has.

A prime example of those contrasting styles were Denmark and France as they holed up less than a mile apart in the Western Cape of South Africa in 2010.

'They [France] had a good hotel and we had a fantastic hotel with beautiful surroundings, but our players were more free and they could go down to the city, no problem,' says Danish boss Morten Olsen.

'France had a great team, but they didn't succeed because it was a prison where they were. That was different [for Denmark] and we always believed in the players, we're one big family. There's always a good atmosphere and we tried to be professional, and everything around the training facilities and hotel is there, but sometimes we went for a day on safari or something. We took the time for the players to rest and not think about football all the time.'

It could be argued that the sight of some of France's stars walking around was likely to get more attention than the Danish players, but providing some form of escapism seems to be a common theme with many successful World Cup camps.

An increasingly digital age when fans can snap pictures or videos with their smartphones and upload them instantly to social media inevitably encourages more caution among managers, as what can start as an innocent trip can quickly become a media storm.

When squads are so closely guarded, allowing players the chance to let off steam can provide extra motivation. While there have been stories of players being indifferent about tournament progression because of their boredom living on training bases for weeks on end, coaches can use the prospect of some freedom as an incentive for good performances. Just as Vicente del Bosque did with Spain as they marched to glory in South Africa.

> *I saw a rash of players come back absolutely f***ing legless and every one of them was on time for the bus the next morning.*

'When they got Portugal in the first knockout, he [del Bosque] said, "If you put them away, you're out all night",' says journalist Graham Hunter, who had access to La Roja's World Cup 2010 squad. 'He said, "It's been hard work… and we won't fly back immediately so you can go out all night".

'Being a Scot, growing up with Jimmy Johnstone stealing a rowing boat and Willie Johnston being sent home in 78, to let players out like that? But nothing went wrong. I saw a rash of players come back absolutely f***ing legless and every one of them was on time for the bus the next morning, and that's all del Bosque had asked them to do.'

With a quarter-final against Paraguay only a few days away, it seems like a monumental risk for del Bosque to have taken with his World Cup favourites. Yet when Hunter quizzed the veteran manager about that, the Spaniard's response showed what can be allowed if a healthy respect has been created within the squad.

'I asked him [del Bosque], "Wasn't that a big risk? What if somebody had been arrested?"' Hunter continues. 'He said, "One, I wouldn't change my mind, it'd be a rarity if one of these guys misbehaved or got into trouble and, two, I'd take whoever was involved aside and have a chat with him and I'd ask him to be more careful. But I'd treat them like adults – I gave them a reward for their hard work to incentivise them and I know what they'll do with it. If something went wrong, I'd do it again next time if I thought it was appropriate".

'That's the level of elasticity in his relationship with them. He definitely didn't think there was no chance of anything going wrong, it wasn't complete naivety. It was a guy who knew his squad well enough to know there weren't any idiots, there wasn't anybody who'd get drunk, fall asleep in the nightclub and miss the plane or whatever – and he was right.'

It all comes down to that 't' word again: trust. Although perhaps the key to maintaining control is to never truly let it go in the first place.

Whether it's leaning on coaching staff or creating a hierarchy of leaders within senior players in the squad, the groundwork a manager puts in place to build faith with certain individuals can pay dividends to keep the ship in order. It can become management by proxy.

'Jack [Charlton] had this way of making us almost into his family,' recalls Republic of Ireland forward Niall Quinn. 'He was warm and such fun, but also so serious and he had lots of messages pinned to the wall. Andy Townsend told me one of them said, "You're to be a dictator, but the trick is not let anyone know you're a dictator," which is a brilliant summing up of it. He [Charlton] was a dictator and he was who he was, he did it his way, he didn't suffer fools along the way, but everyone loved him. That got us into a position with a bond that all of us bought into.'

That feeling of being part of a family unit stretched even further in Hungary's hallowed Golden Team that went to the 1954 World Cup as favourites. Head coach Gusztáv Sebes formed a network of contacts among the players' relatives to keep a beady eye on what they were doing and to make sure nothing upset the kilter of his squad ahead of the tournament.

'For the sake of the coming event, our trainer [Sebes] sought the cooperation of all the wives and mothers and asked them to make sure their husbands or sons led a quiet, untroubled life and went to bed early,' Ferenc Puskás wrote in his eponymous autobiography. 'Once one of our players went home later than expected. His wife had sat worrying and waiting up for quite a while, but in the end she went to bed. Her husband, who had a bad conscience, took off his shoes and crept into the bedroom anxious not to disturb his sleeping wife. His luck was out.

'"Is that you, Jancsi?" she asked in an angry voice. "Of course, it's me," he answered, but instead of letting well alone, added, "Did you expect it to be someone else?" The next day, we all knew about the family quarrel and poor Jancsi was in hot water with our coach for disturbing the even tenor of his training. We always looked upon our team as a large family and treated each other accordingly.'

* * *

The topic of families has long been a bone of contention when it comes to creating the perfect balance in a World Cup training camp. While some managers are dead against the idea of allowing wives, children and parents to have more than a fleeting presence in players' tournament experience, others believe they provide a healthy dose of normality.

The truth is, there seems to be no clear answer to how much family time is enough, but as Belgium boss Roberto Martínez points out, modern beliefs appear to suggest going cold turkey isn't conducive to a happy atmosphere.

'It's not normal for a player not to see their family for 50 days,' Martínez tells me. 'These players are playing big games [for their clubs] and they prepare by training, by being on the training ground and getting the best support they can. But then they go home, they sleep in their own comfortable environment, they see their families and then they go and perform on a pitch with huge audiences.

It's not normal for a player not to see their family for 50 days.

'Now when you go to a World Cup, all of a sudden you have to do something you've never done before, which is having to play games, without seeing your family. It's how you cope with being a father, a husband, a brother and a son without seeing the people you love and something you've never done.'

Martínez's attention to detail led him to study the different ways countries prepared for the 2010 and 2014 World Cups and discovered European nations in particular created 'almost too alien' conditions to isolate them from regular family contact. Conversely, he says the South and Central Americans were a lot more relaxed in that regard.

'It made total sense to bring the families into Russia,' Martínez says of Belgium's approach to the 2018 World Cup. 'That was the biggest part of the normality we achieved. The players could concentrate on playing for the national team at a World Cup that's more intense than club level, but you shouldn't pay the price of not seeing your loved ones, who you see when you play for your club.

'We brought the families into the base camp and they [the players] were able to have good quality family time and we were able to keep not [just] the footballer – because he doesn't need a lot when he's engaged in the World Cup – but the human being *and* the footballer satisfied in that experience.'

One of the first squads to be publicly recognised for including families as part of their World Cup preparation was the Netherlands' 1974 side. Images of the Dutch players going out on boats and enjoying some free time with their wives form part of FIFA's official tournament film, *Heading for Glory*.

The idea of allowing players the chance to relax and spend time with loved ones fits like a glove with Dutch culture and the style that Rinus Michels' swashbuckling side had as they swept all that stood before them in their run to the final. But most of all, it was an indication of a team free to make their own decisions both on and off the pitch, which was built into a lot of the players from a young age.

'Johan [Cruyff] always had a vision when he was a manager,' says his ghostwriter Jaap de Groot. 'He always told his trainers and coaches to "do your work and do it good, but also let everybody have fun. When we work and when we train and when we're busy with the group, we're serious, but also remember we must have fun as well".

'That is also from the Ajax school and its free spirit. At that time, they showed a magnificent level of discipline when they were on the pitch and they knew exactly what to do. I think Michels even talked it over with Johan and asked, "What do you think, shall we get the wives along?" and he said, "OK, good idea, get them in". This team was able to get their focus back one hour before the game, no problem.'

The idea that families can be a distraction doesn't come from nowhere, though. One of the most high-profile instances was when England's 2006 World Cup crusade was overshadowed by the party of wives and girlfriends (or 'WAGs' as the British press called them) based in nearby Baden-Baden.

Pictures and stories about the group regularly appeared in the national tabloids, which told tales of debauchery with gusto. At times it was hard to tell whether it was the players or their partners who were of greater interest to the press.

It was all part of manager Sven-Göran Eriksson's masterplan to lead a talented team to a first international win in 40 years, but when they lost a quarter-final penalty shoot-out to Portugal, the microscope examined why – and it was the WAGs who got a lot of stick. But while Eriksson's decision to keep families close is regularly cited as an example of why it's a bad idea, Carragher disagrees.

People make a big deal of this with the WAGs in 2006, but I think a lot of it was nonsense to be honest.

'We trained in the morning and saw our families in the afternoon,' says the former Liverpool defender. 'People make a big deal of this with the WAGs in 2006, but I think a lot of it was nonsense to be honest.

'A lot of it was baggage you didn't need in the press every day and it's maybe not a good look when you see certain things going on with families and wives, but I don't think it affected the results on the pitch in any way, shape or form.

'When we were winning big games with Liverpool, we'd train in the morning and come home to our families in the afternoon, it was just the same at the World Cup. I don't think anybody's focus was not on football, and it's what you do at club level.'

For a manager, leaving an avenue open to allow for additional criticism is unlikely to be a favourable option and the negative press that Eriksson attracted for 2006 might have impacted successor Fabio Capello's decision to limit family time to one afternoon a week.

Interestingly, Carragher appears to go on to draw a correlation between how a manager chooses to handle the controversial family issue and the type of camp they're likely to put on for their players.

'Sven wasn't the sort of manager who would get involved too much with the players, but he wasn't the type of manager who'd set all kinds of rules and regulations – he almost sort of let the players do what they want and get on with it,' he adds. 'I think that's why he was so respected and liked by the players, he treated them like adults. Sometimes that can come back to haunt you because there will sometimes be a player who crosses that line and brings the team or manager or the squad into disrepute. But that's the way he managed and I think that's why he was respected.'

Earn that respect and a lot of other key blocks start to fall into place. Fail to do that and disaster could be waiting around the next corner...

CHAPTER 11

A SHOT IN THE BALLS:
BIG CONTROVERSIES

Not everything can run smoothly and for every World Cup success story, there's normally a tale of woe. But while early exits and bad results can leave a nasty taste for some of the world's biggest nations, the damage of a truly catastrophic exit or headline-grabbing incident can leave an indelible mark.

Mention certain tournaments, countries or people and thoughts immediately turn to the high-profile moments that have become as much a part of the tournament's history as events on the pitch. Just try saying Republic of Ireland and Mick McCarthy to even the most casual football fan and memories of Roy Keane come flooding back.

For a manager caught in the centre of the ensuing media storm, the scrutiny couldn't be higher. As well as dealing with internal issues, the press and fans judge how he deals with the situation and the players involved. A bad performance on the pitch? That'll be the hangover from the incident everybody's talking about.

Not every flashpoint results in negativity, though. One of the best examples of a coach using the circus surrounding his team to inspire his charges to success was Enzo Bearzot, who went from being the unpopular manager of an Italy side dealing with the aftermath of a match-fixing scandal to a World Cup champion. The siege mentality is alive and well.

Over the years, the World Cup has seen more than its fair share of controversial moments and blow outs. Whether it's the high-stakes pressure hanging over the teams, bad timing or simply the amount of time teams spend closeted away together in training camps, the tournaments have been magnets for big dramas.

But what can a manager do to salvage those situations – and is sending players home really the only way to diffuse a situation?

* * *

France's players were refusing to get off the bus and it was causing chaos. Les Bleus stars had arrived at their Western Cape training ground in South Africa and had briefly greeted a group of fans who had come to watch them, before stubbornly getting back to their seats. The squad was revolting against manager Raymond Domenech in support of striker Nicolas Anelka, who had been sent home following an altercation with the manager at half time of their game against Mexico days earlier. And now they were on strike.

While the majority of the players were sat in their seats, captain Patrice Evra was out on the training pitch, remonstrating with Domenech as the latter quickly lost control of the situation. National team director Jean-Louis Valentin quit on the spot and fitness coach Robert Duverne angrily launched his whistle into the surrounding trees.

And the head coach? He took the bizarre decision to read a statement the players had prepared to the watching press. The same statement that openly criticised Domenech's own actions.

'We regret the incident which occurred at half time of the match between France and Mexico, we regret even more the leak of an event which should have remained within the group and which is quite common in a high-level team,' Domenech read on the players' behalf.

'At the request of the squad, the player in question [Anelka] attempted to enter a dialogue but his approach was ignored. For its part, the French Football Federation has at no time tried to protect the squad. It has made a decision [to send Anelka home] without consulting all the players, on the basis of the facts reported by the press.'

Anelka did not react in the most suitable fashion... What was important was that it made the front page of a newspaper and that exposes the internal life of the squad.

To fully understand how such a messy incident occurred, it's important to go back to half time of France's second match in their faltering 2010 World Cup campaign. After drawing 0–0 in their opener against Uruguay, the 2006 finalists were struggling to make inroads against Mexico, with Domenech picking out Anelka for special criticism during the break.

Anelka, a strong character, reportedly launched a verbal volley back at Domenech – one that later proved to have been exaggerated by the French press. The striker didn't re-emerge for the second half, although the issue was never properly addressed. Domenech made no effort to clear the air with Anelka and instead appeared to be waiting for the player to apologise to him. Senior players even attempted to arrange a reconciliation between the two but, as the story goes, Domenech didn't go to meet Anelka at the pre-agreed time. Eventually, Anelka was sent home, leaving his manager to explain away a situation that seemed completely avoidable.

'People cannot imagine the pressure,' Domenech said when asked about the incident at the time. 'We are in a dressing room, the coach says something to a player who is already under pressure, he can react and with strong words.

'Anelka did not react in the most suitable fashion, but if it was just a guy sitting in his corner and muttering, that would not have mattered had it stayed there. What was important was that it made the front page of a newspaper and that exposes the internal life of the squad. I sorted out the problem internally [by sending Anelka home], and as far as I was concerned it was done and dusted.'

Soon, too, was France's World Cup campaign. They'd gone on to lose to Mexico following the dressing-room row and rounded off their tournament with a 2–1 defeat to hosts South Africa.

Based on the sequence of events later reported, Domenech's managing of the situation seems far from ideal in a World Cup environment, leaving a problem to fester and cause a greater rift. Disagreements and players going home early aren't unusual at the World Cup. But when the blue touch paper is lit beneath a squad, it's a manager's responsibility to extinguish the flames before they rage out of control.

Often, dressing room fall-outs can be quickly repaired after everyone has calmed down, but sometimes it's impossible to simply brush an incident under the carpet. Then it becomes a case of damage limitation.

'Big events happen at World Cups,' says Mick McCarthy, who was caught up in a media storm when a dispute with captain Roy Keane blew up ahead of Republic of Ireland's 2002 campaign. 'I look back on those stories: there was England and Bobby Moore [when the England captain was falsely accused of stealing jewellery in Mexico in 1970] and the Hand of God with Maradona.

'The story that came out of our camp was equally as big as those. In fact, in Ireland, it was a damn sight bigger. So then you've got to deal with it and so we did. We dealt with it pretty well I thought, but it was running through the ether of everything we did.'

McCarthy and Keane famously clashed at Ireland's pre-World Cup base in Saipan, where the squad was staying ahead of moving to their tournament base in Japan. The intention had been for the players to unwind for a few days and do some light training before the real hard work began when they moved to Isimo, but the story goes that Keane expected a more intense preparation.

To add to the frustration, the facilities they'd been promised in Saipan didn't come to fruition. 'It was unforgivable really because considering the climate, the one thing they could have grown was grass,' McCarthy quips. Instead of keeping a lid on his frustration as McCarthy instructed the players, Keane vented to the press.

That was the catalyst for a huge argument in front of the entire team, with Keane effectively booking himself an early flight home when he reportedly questioned McCarthy's Irish heritage, branded him a 'f***ing w***er' and told him to 'stick your World Cup up your arse'. But while all the media focus was on Keane, McCarthy worked wonders not to let the incident divide the whole camp.

'From the outside, our camp appeared to fall apart, but we worked hard behind the scenes to make sure we got good performances and we could put the distraction of the Roy Keane stuff behind us by the time the football started,' recalls forward Niall Quinn. 'Everybody, fair play to them, came to the table with their A-game, we were as fit as we could be and as assertive as we could be with the type of football we were going to play and not let the occasion or distractions of the Roy Keane incident get to us.

'It was very important that we stored all that stuff for when we got home and put it all to bed then. The plan was to forget about it, put it in a box and we'll open it when we arrive back in Dublin – and let's see if we can stay here as long as we can before we go back and do that.'

That approach seemed to work and there was little evidence of a hangover as the remaining players put on a series of rousing displays to reach the last-16, only missing out on a quarter-final spot following a penalty shoot-out defeat to Spain. But while the players appeared to rally round McCarthy's leadership, he remembers feeling some apprehension the first time he faced the Irish crowd after the Keane row.

'It was amazing how the squad did come together and galvanised after the event,' McCarthy adds. 'I remember going out on the field before we played our first game against Cameroon and our fans were all behind us and going mad singing and shouting for the lads. The lads went over and enjoyed it, but I remember feeling not quite sure. It was like feeling lonely in a crowd, not knowing what the reaction would be.'

More often than not, a manager is left with little choice but to remove a player if their authority has been called into question. A small pocket of dissent can soon become a revolt that threatens the coach's leadership. But as McCarthy found, the decision to weed out an individual is much harder when you're sending home one of the team's biggest stars.

Attempting to smooth things over by offering a second chance may appeal to all parties, but it rarely works out if egos are involved. Srečko Katanec discovered that the hard way in 2002 when the then-Slovenia manager tried to repair the

▲ Victory! **Alf Ramsey** celebrates England's World Cup success in 1966 with captain **Bobby Moore** and **Nobby Stiles**

▼ History under a cloud? Italy's **Vittorio Pozzo** is the only manager to retain the World Cup with victory in 1938. But were his fascist leanings a bit too close to the bone?

▶ **František Fadrhonc** (right) stepped aside on the eve of the 1974 World Cup to allow **Rinus Michels** (left) to take over as Netherlands boss

▼ West Germany captain **Franz Beckenbauer** and manager **Helmut Schön** enjoyed a very close relationship, with some stories suggesting the former played a dominant hand in winning the 1974 World Cup

► Under-fire Italy manager **Enzo Bearzot** knew patience was the key to getting the most from star man Paolo Rossi in 1982

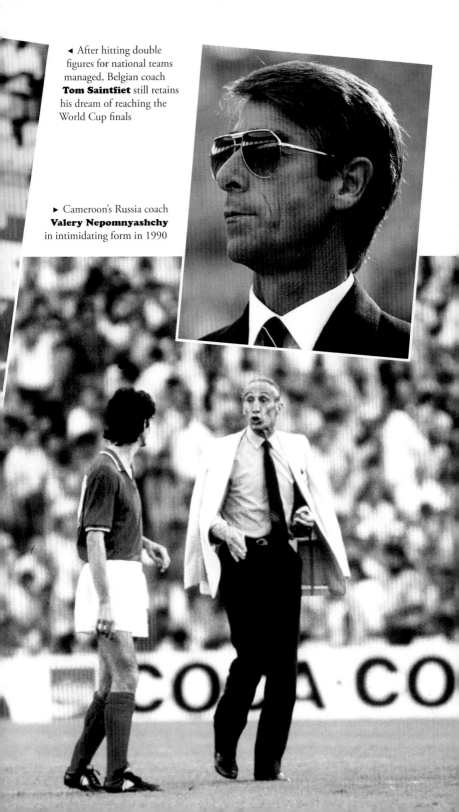

◄ After hitting double figures for national teams managed, Belgian coach **Tom Saintfiet** still retains his dream of reaching the World Cup finals

► Cameroon's Russia coach **Valery Nepomnyashchy** in intimidating form in 1990

► England manager **Gareth Southgate** comforts **Ashley Young** as the Three Lions lose the 2018 semi-final to Croatia

▼ Belgium's **Roberto Martinez** and **Graeme Jones** celebrate a game-changing tactical switch to progress in 2018

◄ Mr Cool **Joachim Löw** makes it look easy as he oversees his former champions from the dugout. But should he have bowed out after Germany's 2014 victory?

▼ I've got an idea! Netherland boss **Louis van Gaal** congratulates goalkeeper **Tim Krul** in 2014 after introducing the penalty expert moments before a shoot-out with Costa Rica

◄ Veteran German coach **Otto Pfister** nearly missed out on his World Cup bow in 2006 after siding with Togo's players in a pre-tournament bonuses dispute

▲ **Guus Hiddink**
(far right) joins in the
celebrations as **Park
Ji-Sung** (left) fires hosts
South Korea into the 2002
knockouts

▼ **Carlos Bilardo** and
Diego Maradona embrace
as Argentina celebrate a
1986 World Cup success
that hadn't seemed likely
before the tournament

▲ West Germany rejoice as England's **Chris Waddle** looks crestfallen in the background following the 1990 semi-final penalty shoot-out

▲ **Vicente del Bosque** is mobbed by Spain's victorious players in 2010

▶ From wannabe physio to World Cup winner, **Carlos Alberto Parreira** proved nothing is impossible

◀ **Luiz Felipe Scolari** despairs as Brazil lose 'one in 1,000' semi-final with Germany in 2014

▼ Secret weapon **Roger Milla** proved his worth for Cameroon at Italia 90

▼ Captain and manager bond on show as New Zealand's **Ryan Nelsen** and **Ricki Herbert** depart South Africa 2010 as The Unbeatables

▲ **Didier Deschamps** gets his hands on the World Cup trophy as France captain in 1998 (top) and again as manager in 2018 (below)

damage after star man Zlatko Zahovič caused a scene at being substituted in their opening match of the tournament.

The playmaker initially lashed out at Katanec with stinging criticism before revoking his comments, which meant he could stay 'for the good of the team', only to repeat the claims again two days later. There was no third chance and Zahovič was eventually sent packing.

Sometimes, when a tough decision has to be made, it's best just to make it quickly and move on, just as Croatia's Zlatko Dalić did to great effect in 2018 when Nikola Kalinić refused to come as a second-half substitute in their match against Nigeria. The coach's move was swift and decisive, and showed the rest of the players who was boss.

'It was the hardest coaching decision in my career because I valued Nikola's quality and I believed he could contribute to the team during the tournament,' Dalić reasons. 'However, I had to make that decision because he was not ready at that moment to contribute to the team. I didn't want to speak too much about that then and I won't speak too much about it now – details are something that should stay in the dressing room.'

Showing a player the door isn't necessarily the perfect remedy for every incident, even if it seems the most immediate way to stop an issue from distracting the rest of the squad. In the heat of a World Cup, it's crucial for a manager to accurately read the room before turfing a player out.

When pressure was being applied by FA bigwigs for Alf Ramsey to take action against Nobby Stiles for his robust challenge on Jacques Simon in England's group clash with France in 1966, a lesser manager may have buckled. The diminutive midfielder was a key link in England's first XI and a highly respected member in the dressing room, so the impact of giving him an internal ban to uphold the nation's reputation for fair play didn't compare to the upheaval it would cause within the squad. Ramsey backed his man instead.

It was the perfect decision. Not only did England avoid losing a key player, but Ramsey brought the side even closer together under his leadership – turning a potentially negative situation into a positive.

'You've got to look at Alf's actions and they refresh us all on what he was like,' says 1966 hero Geoff Hurst. 'The FA committee members wanted to remove Nobby after that tackle. Alf asked him, "Did you mean it?" and he said "No". Then there was more pressure on him [Ramsey] but Alf said – and this is great support – "if Nobby Stiles doesn't play, I'm resigning as manager". There's no greater support than that, which was, of course, unbelievable.'

* * *

If sending a player home during a tournament can cause turmoil, losing a member of the squad due to actions outside of the team bubble can be even more unsettling. Whereas dropping an individual is a proactive measure to nip internal issues in the bud, the impact of an external scandal can attract even greater scrutiny.

While a manager's decisions about his own squad may be front-page news in his own country, the story usually stays relatively local. But if an individual has brought disgrace on himself in some way, it can become a global phenomenon – especially if it's the world's best player.

'When Julio Grondona told me Maradona was expelled from the World Cup and he couldn't even talk to any of us, I wanted to shoot myself in the balls,' Argentina's 1994 World Cup boss Alfio Basile told TyC Sports more than two decades after his star player was banned following a positive drug test.

The shock reverberated around the globe as Maradona, who had played a key role in La Albiceleste's perfect start to the tournament, was banned by FIFA for taking the banned substance ephedrine.

This was a man who had thrilled the world as Argentina won the World Cup in 1986 and had carried the nation to the final four years later, despite nursing an injury. El Diez was considered by many to be the best footballer to ever walk the earth, but had struggled with well-documented drug addiction, so naturally the speculation around the incident reached fever pitch.

Maradona's demise was the hottest topic at the tournament and while his brilliance would inevitably be missed by Argentina, it also created overwhelming attention on the team-mates he'd left behind. For Basile, his TyC interview shows how he, too, thought the ban was a turning point in Argentina's campaign. 'He [Maradona] was our absolute best player during that tournament and that wasn't all,' the veteran manager said. 'On that day [Claudio] Caniggia suffered a muscle tear that also affected us. We were doomed after that.'

The promise of convincing wins against Greece and Nigeria soon evaporated as Argentina lost their final group match to Bulgaria, before a husk of the team that started the tournament were dumped out by Romania in the last-16.

Maradona's untimely departure had obliterated the team's focus and confidence to such an extent that Basile was fighting a lost battle to separate the incident from what was happening on the pitch. Yet Basile defended his man, instead choosing to call out FIFA for what he perceived as unfair targeting of Maradona. So instead of putting an end to the saga, the manager caused it to drag on.

'When you're out there, it's sad but you've got to get on with it because there are bigger issues, like playing for your country and playing at the World Cup,' says Willie Donachie, who was part of the Scotland side that saw Willie Johnston banned for a similar offence in 1978.

But that's easier said than done. The press want a reaction and there's a tricky tightrope for a manager to tread when deciding which route to follow. While Basile backed Maradona, when Johnston tested positive test for the stimulant Fencamfamin, which he inadvertently consumed when taking over-the-counter hay-fever tablets, he wasn't so well supported.

Manager Ally MacLeod, who was himself coming under increasing pressure after Scotland lost their opening match at the tournament to Peru, had taken Johnston's positive test badly. It was another body blow to his ailing dreams of World Cup glory.

The day after the match, MacLeod had a run-in with journalist Trevor McDonald at an official function when the ITN reporter started quizzing Johnston about the positive test – the Scottish boss causing an unnecessarily big scene in front of a room packed with people. The next day, Johnston was isolated from the team camp and informed by the Scottish FA that he'd never play for the national team again, despite his protestations that the breach was accidental. MacLeod then reportedly went to the extreme of confiscating every pill the players had and disposing of them.

If the mood had been bad before, now it was terminal. 'Everyone felt for Willie because he's a nice man and for that to happen to anybody is a disaster and a shame,' Donachie says. 'The timing of it was really bad because the pressure was building on Ally all the time. He seemed to be ageing by the day and it was a shame – Ally was always strong, but it was a very difficult time for him.'

MacLeod's emotional reaction meant he now had crosshairs on his back. He didn't attend the SFA press conference announcing Johnston's punishment, so when he next faced the media ahead of the match against Iran, the furore had reached fever pitch. He faced questions about a swirl of rumours accusing other players in the squad of taking banned medication and stories from before the tournament that he'd threatened to quit over a row over player bonuses. He strongly denied both.

MacLeod may have been blindsided by some of the issues he faced while in Argentina, but it's difficult to argue his own actions didn't play a significant hand in putting pressure on his team. Ever the optimist, the Scotsman had declared himself a winner upon his appointment a year before the finals and bravely predicted Scotland would return from the World Cup as champions. His words created fervour among the Tartan Army, building a sense of jubilation throughout the country before they'd even left, and it wasn't popular among the players. 'Nobody liked it, but it was just the way Ally was,' Donachie explains. 'When we left to go to Argentina, we had to go to Hampden Park, where there were 30,000 people in the ground to wave us off – and again, none of the players liked that [either]. Then we got on the bus to go to Prestwick Airport, which is an hour's drive, and all the way there were people on the street waving flags. It was crazy.

'In 1966, Alf Ramsey had said England can win the World Cup [before the tournament] and it was a very bold statement in those days because people didn't ever say things like that. It just wasn't the British way to be brash and super-confident, you're always cautious about that sort of thing because it can come back to bite you. I think Ally looked at that [Ramsey's statement] and thought that by saying we could win, he was trying to be positive – that's the sort of person he was.'

The storms facing MacLeod and Basile – and their different approaches to dealing with it – shows how difficult it is to recover when bombshells of that size hit. It's not impossible, though. Italy's unlikely World Cup champions of 1982 and their manager Enzo Bearzot were the subject of vicious criticism from their home press before they'd even made it to Spain for the tournament. Add two dreadful performances to the fractious atmosphere caused by the match-fixing scandal hanging over the team and Bearzot's unpopularity left the Italian coach saying he had 'Brutus at my back', ready to stick in the knife. But it was his response to that that arguably inspired the greatest turn of fortune in World Cup history.

'They went to 82 and the press hated them,' explains Italian football historian John Foot. 'And Bearzot was a kind of taciturn man from the north, famously not talkative and not very charismatic, very quiet. A players' kind of manager. A lot of Bearzot's selections for 82 were very controversial and a lot of the press were on his back, but he turns that around by really creating a group that's "us against the world, us against the press, we hate the press, we hate everybody".'

All press were banned from the Italian camp and, like an opening batsman on the first day of a test cricket match, they put the shutters up. Nothing was getting in and nothing was getting out. Initially that only poked the hornets' nest externally, but the spirit it created inside the group was incomparable.

'The relationship with [Dino] Zoff was so important. He was like Bearzot, from the same area, very quiet and he was the captain, the old guy, the goalie,' Foot continues. 'So Bearzot put Zoff up in the press conference and he gave one-word answers, the press couldn't get anything out of him and it was brilliant. That sort of "f**k off" to the press was great and it was what they needed because they [the press] were really going for them [the team] – and they won the World Cup against that [backdrop].'

* * *

The media can be a valuable tool in a manager's armoury if used with care and consideration. While Bearzot wanted to shut them out – and others arguably should have done the same – there are other occasions when going public is the best remedy for issues threatening a World Cup campaign.

Arguments over performance-related bonus payments have threatened to derail several tournament preparations over the decades, with the manager sometimes becoming the main conduit between the players and their federation. With a foot in both camps, the man hired to make sure there's success on the pitch can become a line of communication between the two warring factions. Depending on the circumstances, the coach can have a huge influence on which way the negotiations tip.

Managers, such as Rinus Michels, have threatened not to call up players striking to secure bonuses in order to remove the issue from the camp, but when the problem is about unpaid cash that has been promised to the players following qualification, it changes the complexion of the problem. When that happens in the smaller countries, where the players aren't highly paid, it's often the manager who can force the hand of the national FA if he plays his cards right.

'There was a question about the players as the federation didn't pay the bonus for qualification,' recalls Togo's manager, Otto Pfister, about the minnows' build up to the 2006 World Cup. 'Less than two weeks before our opening game against South Korea, we had a friendly game in Vaduz against Liechtenstein. I was told that the next morning we'd have a small training session and then the players would strike.

'I called the captain [Jean-Paul Abalo] and said, "It's not long until our opening game, we can't strike," and he tells me, "We're striking because the federation isn't paying the bonus". I was straight on the phone to the president and I told him, "My friend, you have to pay the players". He told me it wasn't possible and I said direct that I couldn't work like this and I'd give up.'

The German coach's unwavering support for the players and threat to join the strike action set off a domino effect that soon came to the attention of FIFA. If Togo's FA couldn't pay the players what they owed, FIFA would stump up an advance so the bonuses were paid, averting the possibility of a team refusing to fulfil its fixtures.

What would have happened if Pfister hadn't been so forceful is unclear, but his access to the world press to talk in support of his players was a powerful tool. His willingness to side against his employer, despite coming under intense pressure, was arguably even greater.

'I was on the side of the players, it's clear,' Pfister says. 'The President came into the training camp with the Minister of Youth and Sport, and he said, "You're the manager, you're in charge of the discipline of the team". I said, "My friend, you are the president of the federation, if you don't pay the players, what am I to do?"

'That was a big problem for me and with a situation like this, if you're not mentally strong, the outcome can be very uncertain. But at the end of the day, we handled the problem.'

Sadly, these stories are far from uncommon in African nations. In fact, a fight for bonuses on the eve of a tournament has blighted two of Cameroon's World Cup campaigns, in 1990 and 2002. On both occasions, stand-offs ensued – although the managers' roles in them were at different ends of the spectrum.

The Indomitable Lions' Italia 90 story may be part of World Cup folklore, but it all started with a long night of drama before the tournament's curtain-raiser against reigning champions Argentina, a match the Cameroonians won 1–0 – a feat that's all the more amazing considering what went before it.

'We didn't sleep before the game because we were fighting about money,' Emmanuel Maboang tells me. 'I was one of the youngest players and I was the last to receive the money, and they gave me only half. I cried all night about receiving my money and the other players supported me. They asked our ministry about why they gave me half the money, but eventually I received my money in cash.'

> *We didn't sleep before the game because we were fighting about money.*

Player payments were just one of the issues facing Cameroon as they turned up in Italy, as they arrived with a lack of equipment, including boots, when they first reached their training base. On this occasion, though, the players couldn't count on the support of their manager in the negotiations. Maboang says Russian coach Valery Nepomnyashchy refused to get involved and said his only focus was what happened on the pitch. Considering his players were still going back and forth hours before their opening game, that stance seems churlish.

'Mr Nepomnyashchy never spoke about the money or administration,' Maboang continues. 'He was training, stop. He wanted the players fit and he said he never wanted a player to speak about the money they received, he had no communication with the players about money or the authorities.

'He just wanted his players fit for training and if you weren't, he said that if you don't want this, want this, want this, you're not in the team. Even [Roger] Milla was afraid. Even the strongest players and the ones with the biggest reputations didn't have any way to speak with Mr Nepomnyashchy. If you speak, stop.'

It was this experience that created the environment for what came 12 years later. Another issue over unpaid bonuses hung over a talented Cameroon side before they travelled to Japan and South Korea for the 2002 World Cup. The African Cup of Nations champions refused to fly to the Far East until a resolution was found. Instead, they holed up in a hotel in Paris, missing their scheduled flight to Tokyo and leaving an unsuspecting Winfried Schäfer trying to pick up the pieces.

'The players told me: "Coach, we don't go". I thought it was a joke – I didn't know before what was happening,' Cameroon's boss says. 'It was clear it was a catastrophe.'

Little did Schäfer know, the strike had been planned months earlier. Adding to past incidents around bonuses, the 2002 team decided they had to make a stand before going out to the tournament – sacrificing their preparation to help future generations in the same situation.

A senior member of the team told me the players trained in secret while in Paris and always planned to participate in the tournament, but couldn't let on to anyone – not even Schäfer – for fear of weakening their bargaining position. The German offered to help in a similar way that his countryman Pfister would do with Togo four years later, but he was powerless to make a difference.

'I talked to the players and said please go, this is your World Cup, you have been fighting four years for this World Cup. Maybe three players wouldn't go, so nobody goes,' explains Schäfer. 'We had a friendly match in Osaka against England and I asked them to go and play, and then if the minister doesn't pay their money, I would go into the press conference and tell all the journalists about it and I'd stop my work and go home.

The players said, "if we play he [the minister of sport] won't pay the money and we want to set an example for the future".'

When eventually the ministry backed down, Cameroon had lost almost a week in Paris. But before they touched down in Japan, they faced further upheaval when their chartered flight was forced to make an emergency landing in Bangkok after failing to gain permission to fly over Cambodian, Vietnamese and Filipino airspace. They were travelling for 48 hours and had no time to acclimatise to the conditions or the new time zone.

It meant a promising side that had won gold at the Sydney Olympics two years earlier and triumphed at the AFCON just months before wouldn't ever get up to full speed. Despite taking the lead against Republic of Ireland in their opening match, they were pegged back to a draw, before a sluggish victory against Saudi Arabia and defeat to 10-man Germany sent them home.

And Schäfer knows where the blame lies. 'The Minister of Sport didn't pay the team their money,' he says. 'He killed our team and we had a very good team, believe me.'

When things start to unravel, even the best coaches can be helpless to stop issues from taking centre stage.

CHAPTER 12
DON'T MENTION THE WAR: RIVALRIES

Sometimes a match is about more than simply a game. Whether it's a chance to settle an old score from a previous tournament, prove the doubters wrong or get one over on a hated rival, there are certain fixtures that have greater significance than others.

When it comes to pitching two nations against each other in the face of decades of global political and social issues, the World Cup has an unfortunate habit of pairing up some of the bitterest enemies.

Sport is meant to be a great way of bringing people together, but sometimes a football match, which at a World Cup has so much riding on it, only serves to add fuel to the flames. Particularly during qualifying, regional foes can regularly find themselves vying for only one World Cup berth. The Corinthian spirit is nowhere to be found.

It was that situation that sparked the 'Football War' between El Salvador and Honduras in 1969, when the Central American duo went head-to-head in a three-legged qualifier to reach the 1970 finals in Mexico. Rioting marred the matches, as historic tensions came to the fore. Thousands of Salvadoran immigrants were forced to flee Honduras, prompting the Salvadoran government to dissolve diplomatic ties and declare war on their neighbours. A four-day conflict followed, punctuated by air attacks and ground assaults, before a truce was called.

Thankfully it's rare for such an extreme reaction to take place but it goes to show the strength of feeling a match can evoke. And the pressure to succeed only grows when the match is played out in front of the world at a major tournament. Some of the greatest rivalries don't have to be down to politics or geography, though. Storylines can emerge in the most unusual places, when past sporting grievances or humiliations are dredged up again.

For a manager, it can be a case of finding a way to come out on top, whatever it takes.

* * *

'If I was to do it all over again, I'd make it more political,' admits Steve Sampson. 'I'd use history as motivation for my players that they [Iran] held American citizens captive for the longest period of time and are literally one of the greatest enemies ever faced by the United States.'

These aren't the words you expect to hear uttered by a former international manager, especially one who is looking relaxed in the middle of his spacious office in California Polytechnic State University where he now works. Despite his cosy surroundings, Sampson is matter of fact about where he believes his US team fell short when they lost 2–1 against Iran in the ultimate World Cup grudge match in 1998: he thinks he was far too diplomatic.

'I wanted to make it all about the football and de-politicise the whole event because, for me, our football was on display,' he recalls. 'Whereas for the Iranians it was their politics on display.'

When Iran and the USA were drawn together in Group F, the world collectively winced at the prospect of the two nations coming head-to-head on the football pitch. The duo had spent most of the previous two decades at loggerheads. They'd had no formal diplomatic relations since 1980, the USA had placed Iran under a trade embargo and, as Sampson referenced, the 1979–81 Iran hostage crisis saw 52 Americans held for more than 14 months in Tehran. There was no wonder US Soccer Federation President Alan Rothenberg had branded the tie 'the mother of all games'.

When the draw came out, we said that we're getting three points against Iran, boom, put that in the bag. If we don't do that, there will be big problems. Obviously, we didn't.

'I was coming at it as an American kid who grew up in the suburbs and looked at Russia as the evil empire and the big enemy – in the same way, it was like that playing in the World Cup against Iran,' USA defender Alexi Lalas remembers. 'What they represented at that time to a 20-something who had been growing up in the 70s in the United States… was about to play out on the field.

'From a practical perspective, this was three points. When the draw came out, we said that we're getting three points against Iran, boom, put that in the bag. If we don't do that, there will be big problems. Obviously, we didn't. They used the relationship and the history and the propaganda, if you will, to motivate themselves and we didn't match it with our performance.'

The public talk beforehand had been about smoothing relations, despite the Iranians refusing to approach the Americans for the pre-match handshake and rumours mounting of a terrorist group planning a protest in the stands during the game. Roses were exchanged before kick-off and it seemed football was the main focus.

But unbeknown to Sampson, Lalas and the rest of the US side at the time, the political rhetoric in the Iranian dressing room aimed to prise open old wounds to inspire the team to victory. It made the Stars and Stripes' more liberal approach look feeble in comparison.

'I later found out that at half time of that game when we were losing, a top politician from the Iranian government came down to the locker room and collected all the passports of the Iranians and said, "You lose this, you'll never return home",' says Sampson. 'I only know this because I met with [Iran] coach [Jalal] Talebi after the World Cup, so it's true.'

While Talebi may not have been the instigator and claimed, 'I'm not a political man, I'm a sportsman,' ahead of the match, the California-based Iranian will have been well-versed in how to put his Persian Stars in with a chance of beating their western foe.

'I achieved what I wanted to do, which was to make it a football event, not a political event, but the Iranians did exactly what they wanted to do,' Sampson concedes. 'They made it a political event, so much so that after they beat us, every single one of the players was awarded a new home in Iran, paid for by the Iranian government. That would never have happened in the United States.

'The fact they came into this World Cup not really caring about getting into the second round, all they cared about was beating the United States, they didn't care about their first match against Yugoslavia, all they cared about was their match against us.'

Whether all the pre-game posturing was an extravagant game of rope-a-dope to lure the US into a false sense of security is up for debate, but there was no hiding the political significance when two other rivals faced off in 1974.

The match between West and East Germany had been the hottest topic on both sides of the Berlin Wall when the nations were drawn against each other during West Germany's home tournament. Early group fixtures against Chile and Australia became mere footnotes to the main event, with the possible implications of defeat for either side discussed in the higher echelons of both governments.

West Germany's manager, Helmut Schön, became the centre of the story. Born in Dresden in the east of the divided country, Schön had defected from the Soviet regime in 1950 before becoming a critical part of predecessor Sepp Herberger's coaching staff – taking over from his mentor in 1964.

The issue of Schön's heritage had never been discussed as much as it was in the run up to the East Germany match and a strong feeling developed in the squad that victory would be as much for their manager as themselves. Captain Franz Beckenbauer proudly declared before the match, 'We're playing this for Schön.'

'The point of his [Schön's] history was that he was very important and a very good player for Dresden, which was on the opposite side of Germany that later became the DDR,' says midfielder Rainer Bonhof, using the acronym East Germany was known by.

'That was the key to him because he always knew if somebody was struggling themselves. He had escaped from the other part [East Germany] and that made him as a character, and he was very liked by the players.'

Be that as it may, West Germany were a side struggling to find their groove. They'd won their opening two matches in unconvincing style to book their place in the second phase before the East Germany match, whereas their rivals still needed a point to progress.

Anything short of victory would still be seen as a disaster, especially in front of their own fans. And so it proved as Jürgen Sparwasser's 77th-minute strike was enough to hand East Germany the win in the 'fight between brothers'.

'I remember sitting in the press conference when they [West Germany] lost to East Germany, which of course was a disaster, and everybody was after Schön among the German journalists,' recalls BBC commentator Barry Davies. 'There was certainly a strange feeling about playing the East and I think the West German spectators assumed they'd win that match. Schön hadn't quite found the balance that he wanted.'

There was certainly a strange feeling about playing the East and I think the West German spectators assumed they'd win that match.

Schön took the defeat hard and retreated into himself, spending the night soul-searching and chose not to emerge from his room the next morning to have breakfast with his players. There are even rumours he considered quitting there and then.

'Schön left straight after the match when we lost. He was knackered because we lost – not just against the DDR, but because it means we didn't win our group and the DDR went on ahead of us,' Bonhof remembers.

'It was very important to him that we didn't lose against the DDR, where he was born, and that made him so afraid. It became a very long night after the match and he spoke with Beckenbauer, he spoke with [Günter] Netzer and he spoke with [Wolfgang] Overath, and they convinced him to change a couple of positions and bring in some other players for the second stage.'

This is where Schön's story becomes unclear. History tells us West Germany ended up in an easier second round group and the changes made as a result of the devastating defeat to their neighbours triggered a run culminating with them winning the World Cup. Had the defeat come against an opponent with less national significance, there may not have been the same reaction.

But as the legend goes, it wasn't Schön calling the winning shots. The crestfallen coach allegedly suffered something close to a nervous breakdown in the aftermath of the East Germany defeat and captain Beckenbauer picked up the slack – selecting the team, suggesting a new tactical approach and attending press conferences with his manager.

It's not a version of events Davies subscribes to, though. 'It's generally thought that Beckenbauer took over, but I always thought that was nonsense,' the broadcaster says. 'I think Schön was canny enough to use Beckenbauer as his captain to get across what he wanted.

'While I don't believe they should have won the final, I saw their next match against Sweden, which was probably their best performance of the championship. I think Beckenbauer and Schön were very close, but I still think ultimately Schön was the boss.'

The Germans – West, East or unified – are no strangers to a rivalry. The Netherlands, England and France have historically placed a special onus on matches with their German counterparts. While much of that ire initially stemmed from the two World Wars, that ill-feeling has gradually subsided and been replaced by memories of painful losses instead, a currency Germany dishes out with regularity.

When revenge is on a team's mind, it then becomes a manager's decision to either bury bad memories and focus on the here and now, or try to use those grievances to inspire a different result. Which option to choose seems to depend on the circumstances of the previous defeat: was it the team's performance that cost them victory, or have they got a real reason to be aggrieved?

France's semi-final disappointment in Spain 82 is certainly in the latter category after West Germany's Harald Schumacher's hideous neck-high tackle not only left victim Patrick Battiston in hospital, but the goalkeeper facing no consequences. Throw in that Les Bleus gave away a two-goal lead and lost on penalties, and it's understandable the 1982 game was on French minds when they came up against each other in the 86 semi-final as well.

'It's a moment the players have been waiting four years for,' France boss Henri Michel said before the game. 'Seville in 82 will be on their minds and they are very excited at having the chance to take revenge.'

No doubting what Michel's pre-match team talk was about, then. But it didn't work, with France succumbing 2–0 to the West Germans this time.

* * *

If a match's significance is so obviously strong, perhaps there is no need for any managerial tub-thumping at all. With the Netherlands in the 1970s and 80s, every Dutch player knew what it meant to play against West Germany, with political feelings still strong following World War II, and the sense of injustice at their great 74 side being deprived of the World Cup still raw.

'Of course, Netherlands against Germany is always a special game because while nowadays relations are OK, in those days, we didn't like the Germans,' explains 1978 finalist Ernie

Brandts, who was part of the team that faced West Germany in the second round of the tournament.

'It was quite natural that you didn't have to motivate the players when you were playing Germany and you could see it in training. Everybody was motivated and there was a lot of concentration and everyone was training hard.'

It took 14 years to get over that [1974 loss]. Ever since the Netherlands had to play against German teams, there was a tension.

A draw with West Germany in 78 helped the Netherlands progress to the final but that still wasn't enough to expel the ghosts of the past. Leading Dutch journalist Jaap de Groot says the bad feeling lingered until redemption was achieved.

'Losing in the way they did to Germany [in 1974] while feeling they were the best team created a national trauma that was only resolved when we beat the Germans in the 1988 European Championship,' he says. 'It took 14 years to get over that [1974 loss]. Ever since the Netherlands had to play against German teams, there was a tension. Then there was Johan Cruyff's farewell game [when Bayern Munich beat Ajax 8–0 in a testimonial]. There was a lot of tension and a lot of people related it to the war, so it wasn't nice – German football was not number one on everyone's list. But after 1988, the trauma was healed and now it's over, it's history. But the wound was open, bleeding for 14 long years.'

But bad memories don't fade so easily and the significance of particular match-ups can still linger decades on. England may have won their World Cup Final with West Germany in 1966, but it didn't stop the bitter rivalry ramping up every time the two countries came face to face on the pitch.

Memories of two world wars were stirred up every time the pair came up against each other, with the tabloid press happy to dredge up memories of tanks, soldiers and trenches. Winning was a source of national pride and created a sense that the match was about more than simply sport.

Terry Butcher, England's captain for the Italia 90 semi-final against West Germany, said that the team tried to ignore the rhetoric around the match but, inevitably, they were aware of the extra needle felt in the stands. However, manager Bobby Robson unwittingly found a way to broach the subject.

'Gary Lineker said to the lads, and had written on the flipchart before the game, "I bet he [Robson] mentions the war," and put odds on there,' Butcher recalls. 'So when Bobby lifted the page – and he had already mentioned the war as a joke and a very flippant remark – it was quite funny for the players. It was the elephant in the room, "don't mention the war" like Basil Fawlty, but we all knew as British people you think about it and remember what happened, but I think we were [by now] a completely different generation in a completely different world.

'It was one of those things that was there and he got it out of the way, and let's concentrate on the football. It was quite a funny thing, but everybody had it in the back of their minds – although it [the match] wasn't about that.'

Butcher and England had found themselves in a similar situation four years earlier when they squared up with another country England shared a chequered past with. Argentina and England already had history from their 1966 quarter-final when Sir Alf Ramsey famously branded the South Americans 'animals', but the 10-week Falklands War in 1982 added a lot more spice.

England's 1982 side had already been subjected to chants of 'Malvinas, Malvinas' by Spanish fans in that year's World Cup, so it was another political issue the side was well aware of before their quarter-final meeting with Argentina in 1986. Once more, Butcher says, the squad tried to ignore what was going on and focus on the match itself. But by the time they'd left the field, international relations had worsened further thanks to Diego Maradona's Hand of God goal, when he punched the ball past Peter Shilton to give La Albiceleste the lead.

Without the benefit of the copious TV replays there are today, it wasn't until after the match that Maradona's actions became clear to England's players.

We'd have gone absolutely ballistic because that would really have been an affront to the way we played the game.

'After the game, I was in the drug-testing room and I signalled over to him [Maradona] and tapped my head and tapped my hand, and he tapped his head,' Butcher explains. 'It wasn't until much later that I knew how cleverly he'd done it. If everybody had seen it and it had been really clear cut, I would dread to think what would have happened. We'd have gone absolutely ballistic because that would really have been an affront to the way we played the game.'

Back home, the nation knew they had been cheated, which fanned the flames of dislike even more. And that ill-feeling continued to fester into the next generation. If Maradona was a key protagonist in the England–Argentina rivalry in the 1980s and early 90s, then David Beckham picked up the mantle in 1998 after he was sent off for a petulant kick at Diego Simeone in their last-16 tie.

Along with the feeling Simeone made more of Beckham's kick than was necessary, La Albiceleste further irked the Three Lions by taunting their beaten opponents as they got on their coach to leave the Stade Geoffroy-Guichard after the match. So when the two nations were drawn together again in the group stage four years later, the match was bound to carry a little extra bite.

'Having been involved in 1998 and watched the Argentinians celebrating on their coach, five yards from ours, I could have no more incentive to be jumped up for this,' said Teddy Sheringham in the pre-match press conference. 'I want revenge. I can't remember anything like that at any other game I've been involved in. I put it down in the little notebook in the back of my head and I hope it comes back to hurt them.'

With Beckham's transformation from national pariah to talismanic captain in the four years in between tournaments, the motivation for the squad to get redemption was clear. Manager Sven-Göran Eriksson tried to preach control and pointed out in the same conference Sheringham spoke at that the best way to get the result they all wanted was by not letting it become too personal.

'I know a little bit of the story and I saw some documentary film which was very interesting,' said the Swede, who took over two-and-a-half years after that night in St Etienne. 'If you take that into the match in a sporting way and have a great desire to win, then that is positive, but if you only look for revenge and you're feeling hate, then it's very dangerous.'

He added: 'I don't think we have to win at all costs, but it would be nice to win this match. It's a very important game and we have to get a result if we want to be playing in the World Cup after 12 June.'

Eriksson's words seemed to have had the desired effect as England delivered a controlled performance to beat Argentina 1–0, courtesy of Beckham's penalty. Running over to the corner flag in celebration, kissing the badge on his shirt, his outpouring of emotion showed how much was bubbling under the cool facade.

While it worked out for England on that occasion, the masters at triumphing in a grudge match are Germany, who always manage to find a way to come out on top whenever a tie contains an extra edge.

Whether it's France or the Netherlands wanting revenge for past defeats, or matches against England stoked by history, Germany have risen above the noise more often than not. But as 1990 World Cup winner Pierre Littbarski explains, part of that is due to the intensity that's maintained in every match German sides have played in down the years – regardless of the opponent.

We have a different motivation. It's a challenge for us to prove again and again that we are the best every time, that is what's driving us and pushing us to our limit.

'It's a question of pride,' Littbarski says. 'The Germans have a tendency to not want to lose, even against their best friends, so they develop a rivalry against other players, especially the top-class players, because they get the motivation to beat the likes of Maradona or Gullit.

'We have a different motivation. It's a challenge for us to prove again and again that we are the best every time, that is what's driving us and pushing us to our limit. That's inside the team and the training matches were like a battle every time.

'We like to prove every time we are the best, even if we compete with our team-mates, we want to show them we are the best. But it's not influencing our mental stability – we're not getting nervous because it's about believing in your own power and our own qualities. That maybe makes the difference.'

If everyone is viewed as an adversary in the heat of competition, then it stands to reason that the stimulation of a big game has much less chance of becoming overwhelming. But it's also possible that while other teams earmark their matches against Germany, these rivalries aren't as big on the other side of the coin. After all, if they're the ones more regularly coming out on top, there's nothing to fuel that ill-feeling.

So do Germany's managers ever try to play up to a rivalry to motivate the players against certain opponents? 'We don't have that much in the national team,' Littbarski answers. 'We use it a lot in the Bundesliga, but we don't use that in the national team. Especially in 86 and 90, we had enough personalities in the team, so there was no need to motivate again, so it's not really a technique we use.'

Stay cool, stay calm and the success will follow. It's a motto that's served many managers well in the past.

CHAPTER 13
MIRACLE WORKERS: UNDERDOGS

There are few competitions that throw up quite so many David versus Goliath contests as the World Cup. As the elite nations gather for a four-yearly party they've almost exclusively dominated, the expectation that the less well-established countries are just there to provide something akin to a warm-up before the latter stages begin has haunted many a superstar.

As a result, unexpected names have been able to forge paths to the final stages by leaving bigger sides in their wake. From shock victories to arriving at a golden generation's peak for one unforgettable summer, the underdogs' journeys form just as much a part of a World Cup's story as the globe's biggest names lifting the trophy.

An unfancied side's passage to those uncharted heights often requires more ingenuity, greater managerial nous and a healthier dose of opportunism than the sides laden with stars demonstrate. Yet those runs also, usually, end in heartbreak.

For every South Korea, Bulgaria or Turkey that has reached a World Cup semi-final, Croatia are the only nation from outside the traditional superpowers to reach a final since 1962. And even then, it's hard to consider a team boasting the talents of Luka Modrić and Ivan Rakitić as true underdogs in the same way as the amateurs of Cameroon, who became Africa's first quarter-finalists in 1990.

Sometimes it can be the most obscure details that transform the fortunes of an also-ran into a World Cup fairy tale.

* * *

There's always been a story that Cameroon's Italia 90 run was inspired by a chauffeur. That instead of Russian coach Valery Nepomnyashchy calling the shots as Roger Milla and Co broke new ground to become Africa's first World Cup quarter-finalists, it was his driver-cum-translator putting his own spin on instructions instead.

It's a tale that hasn't gone away in more than three decades since the Indomitable Lions' famous run. So much so, the idea that a man with no football experience was changing Nepomnyashchy's instructions into a winning formula has become part of tournament folklore.

But midfielder Emmanuel Maboang says the myth holds no water. 'Many people said the translator wasn't giving the true information – for me, it's lies. It's lies, lies, lies,' Maboang says as he crushes the rumour.

'I know some players want to make names for themselves, but there was no way [that could be true]. Nepomnyashchy was the coach. You could see that because when the translator didn't get it right, he said, "I didn't speak like this and didn't tell you to send the players here," and if someone wanted a change he said "no" and told him what the tactics were.

'Nepomnyashchy knew French a little bit, so he knew if the translator told you anything wrong – even if it was one missing word, he said "no, no, no". If we were working tactically and one defender was in the wrong place he'd say "no, tell him it's like this" and "if you play like this, you go home".'

Instead, Maboang points to Nepomnyashchy's fierce discipline, tactical acumen and unforgiving fitness sessions as the pillars of the Indomitable Lions' run. The Russian didn't care for building relationships with his players and was deliberately aloof, locking himself away in his hotel room, apart from training sessions and group meals.

In an era when the softer side of management wasn't considered as important as today, Nepomnyashchy's authoritarian regime worked. After shocking holders Argentina in the opening game of the tournament with a display of desire and physicality that unsettled La Albiceleste's players – 'they were afraid,' says Maboang – they topped their group and reached the quarter-finals with a win against Colombia. If it wasn't for a late Gary Lineker penalty in that last-eight tie with England, Cameroon could have made it to the semi-finals. No African side has ever gone further.

Despite that, Nepomnyashchy was never really lauded for the part he played because of his unapproachable manner. Yet it was partly that dour persona that made the difference. 'In Africa, we joke sometimes that Mr Nepomnyashchy doesn't smile, but in Africa sometimes we need people like this,' says Maboang, who was one of several amateur players in the 1990 squad.

'Even the coaches from Africa need to keep a distance from the players… they will go outside everywhere and do what they want. And the manager would come to your room and not speak because he was afraid of most of the players.

'This is not just a Cameroon or African organisation thing, most players need some authority sometimes. Nepomnyashchy in the World Cup camp, no one spoke to him, even the assistant was frightened to say anything. There are lots of stories such as if you were on the bench and he said, "Emmanuel, you need to warm up quickly," you run like a cat. There was no talking, he made his play and bang. But we needed this sometimes.'

Whether it was deliberate or not, Nepomnyashchy's treatment of his players was perfect motivation for them. They were primed for action and formed a togetherness by surviving a gruelling pre-tournament training camp of long fitness sessions and scant contact with the outside world.

Managing to take the temperature of a group to work out how to inspire the best possible performance from it is hard enough, but

We got so confident and because we were hosts, the fans were behind us in the stadium and gave us amazing support.

forming an environment to make that a reality and maintain it through an entire tournament takes something special. The resulting moment can be like stepping into the twilight zone, especially for an underdog performing miracles.

'We played against Portugal, Italy and Spain and probably a few months earlier we'd never have thought we were going to beat them, but during that time it started to fall in place,' reminisces Park Ji-Sung about South Korea's string of high-profile victims as they reached the semi-finals of their home World Cup in 2002.

'We got so confident and because we were hosts, the fans were behind us in the stadium and gave us amazing support. The circumstances probably made us a better team than we were. After the match, when we beat Portugal [in the group stage], the players knew we could play any team in this World Cup.'

The backbone to South Korea's success was a culture shift triggered in the squad by head coach Guus Hiddink shortly after taking over the national side. He identified a softness within the psyche of his players and moved to instil a nastier streak to give the Taegeuk Warriors the belief to compete with the best.

It was an issue a homegrown manager might not have recognised, yet Hiddink's experience of working in European club football and with the Dutch national team at the previous World Cup stood him in good stead to notice it.

'In Korea, we had a culture that if someone is even one year older, we have to respect them more and he [Hiddink] tried to break that down,' continues Park. 'So when they're on the pitch, they're the same – it's not that someone is older and someone is younger.

'In my country's culture, we add something on someone's name because he is older, but Hiddink didn't want that, and to make it quicker to call the name when they are on the pitch. That kind of thing makes it more equal and everyone has more motivation on the pitch to show he is capable of playing, rather than thinking, "He's older than me" [so must be deferred to]. This kind of thing made us more compatible as a team.

'He also communicated to the players that he wanted to see more anger and he wanted us to show that on the pitch. He always said Korean players are generally too calm and they have to react to something to have anger… these things make players more honest and then they can communicate directly with the coaching staff.'

There's no doubting the stars aligned for South Korea in 2002, with a partisan home crowd and one or two fortunate breaks as they got past Portugal, Italy and Spain to book a semi-final with Germany. But Hiddink stoked that fire.

Instead of bending to the more illustrious opponents South Korea faced, Hiddink tried to bottle the positivity around the nation by preaching about enjoying the moment and sticking to what had served them well so far in the tournament. It's simple psychology, but the message was that the team belonged in such exulted company and kept feeding the dreams of the nation's fans to continue pushing them on. In fact, Hiddink almost made it sound as though it was a contest of good versus evil.

'The Korean team is capable now of putting their opponents under pressure in a co-ordinated way,' said Hiddink prior to the Italy tie. 'They cover well. Two are always putting the player on the ball under pressure. That approach has broken down many teams recently.

'It's curious that you might find one of the biggest footballing teams playing one of the smallest, and the smallest attacks while the biggest defends. But if that's the case we have to cope with it.

'The Italians are different to the Portuguese who want, like the Koreans, always to attack. They get their results through another style. Italy don't care about playing good games, they care about the result.'

Riding the crest of a wave and taking opportunities when they arise was also the key to the run South Korea's northern neighbours embarked on in 1966. After being swatted aside 3–0 by the Soviet Union, North Korea got a late equaliser to draw with Chile before famously beating Italy to qualify for the quarter-finals.

The North Koreans received ferocious backing from the crowd in Middlesbrough, where they played all of their group matches, and benefited from the puzzling tactics of Italy manager Edmondo Fabbri to beat the Azzurri 1–0. Despite the general consensus that the North Koreans' biggest asset was pace, Fabbri named two slow defenders, Franco Janich and Aristide Guarneri, in his side, along with a half-fit Giacomo Bulgarelli. The stage was set for an upset.

'I think them [North Korea] losing the first game 3–0 helped because they looked down and out, and nobody wanted them to be murdered by the other teams in the group,' recalls commentator Barry Davies, who was stationed in the north east for the tournament. 'But nobody anticipated what happened against Italy and it was mostly the Italians' fault. The coach of that team was covered in tomatoes when they went back to Italy, along with the rest of the team. One of the players [Bulgarelli] was injured and it was the days before substitutes, so he played out on the wing and really couldn't contribute. That result wasn't meant to happen and it's quite extraordinary that it did.'

The North Koreans looked as though they'd make it even further in the tournament after racing into a 3–0 lead against Portugal in the quarter-final, but their own tactical misgivings meant they succumbed to a Eusebio masterclass to lose 5–3.

The idea that some of the World Cup's most romantic storylines boil down to timing may seem sanitised, but the ability of a manager to bring his players to a peak at the right time is a coveted skill. It's not an easy feat to work out how to fit them all in the same team without knocking them off course as the pressure of a tournament mounts.

That was one of the main factors Tomas Brolin thinks helped Sweden reach the semi-finals in 1994. Four years earlier, the Swedes were knocked out in the first round without earning a single point, but they had blossomed in the meantime and arrived in the USA without any major injuries.

'Tommy [Svensson] was a good trainer because he saw everyone's mentality,' explains Brolin. 'He knew we were all at big [club] teams in Europe and you can't change a player when they come with a natural game, so he had a look, put us together and found the framework we should play in.

'He trusted that we were good players and saw what we could do on the pitch, so we had a lot of self-belief going on the pitch and he let us do that. Maybe it's not always like that, it depends on what sort of players you have and how they are mentally. But in Sweden at that time, and with the players Tommy Svensson had, I think that was the best thing he could do and we got results after that.'

Only a late Martin Dahlin equaliser stopped Sweden losing their opening match to Cameroon, though. And it was Svensson's smart switch to move Brolin back into midfield to free up space for Kennet Andersson in the front line that unleashed their full potential to reach the last four.

'If you look at the teams at the World Cup in 94, it was Sweden who scored most goals in the whole tournament – that's quite amazing and surprising that little Sweden did that,' Brolin adds. 'I think it would have been different [if Svensson didn't move Brolin into midfield], but you can never know that and both Kennet and I were in really good shape, and Martin was in good shape. Sometimes it's risky to have three goalscorers in the team from the start, but Tommy knew I could play as a midfielder as well.'

Understanding each player's strengths in order to retain tactical flexibility and catch the opposition off guard has proved a priceless tool for countless coaches. Particularly in past World Cups, when tactical analysis and in-depth scouting reports weren't as available as they are today, it was possible for a manager to have an ace up his sleeve for when he needed it.

For an international boss to build up that background knowledge was difficult in a time when there was no technology to help. It took decades of work, which could all come to fruition at just the right moment, just as it did for Romania's

Anghel Iordănescu when they faced Argentina in the last-16 of the 94 World Cup.

'He [Iordănescu] knew us very well and knew which position to play us to get the maximum,' explains Ilie Dumitrescu, who was at the heart of Iordănescu's plan, which spawned a 3–2 win over the South Americans. 'For example, I was a left-winger most of the time, but in the match against Argentina, I played like a number nine because [Florin] Răducioiu had two yellow cards and was suspended.

We always said that football is 10 categories and we like to be the best in six out of 10 of those, rather than being semi-good in 10 out of 10.

'Sometimes at Steaua Bucharest [where Iordănescu had coached Dumitrescu before taking the national team job] he would use me like a number nine. If it was another manager, he wouldn't play me like a number nine in that match, he would put another player in that position and we wouldn't have a very good reaction – it was a big surprise for Argentina to face me playing as a number nine.'

Dumitrescu scored twice in the first 20 minutes before teeing up Gheorghe Hagi to slot home the decisive third to knock out a side that had played in three of the past four World Cup finals. Mission accomplished.

While Romania had a plan for Argentina, the secret to causing a World Cup shock can sometimes be simpler: do nothing. Just as Hiddink did with South Korea in 2002, the message of not needing to change an underdog's approach for a big match is bold and confident – and reaffirms the abilities of a team. Instead of dwelling on what a smaller nation doesn't have at their disposal when coming up against a bigger foe, perhaps there is merit in focusing on strengths rather than weaknesses.

'We always said that football is 10 categories and we like to be the best in six out of 10 of those, rather than being semi-good in 10 out of 10,' explains Heimir Hallgrímsson, Iceland's manager. 'So let's focus on what we're good at, let's not bother about some other areas that other countries will be better than us in. Let's not focus on that and try to work and spend our time to be the best in six areas out of 10.

'Of course, we need good football players, but this is part of the reason we did so well – we believed in the qualities we had and played according to them.'

* * *

Unlocking the motivation that inspires a team to overperform at a tournament can be the catalyst for a great run if a manager can retain that feeling for an entire campaign. Senegal's 1–0 win against world and European champions France to kick off the 2002 World Cup is a perfect example – it spurred the outsiders on a run to the quarter-finals. But without such a notable victory in their opening match, it's conceivable none of it would ever have happened.

Billed as 'France B', the Africans were managed by a Frenchman, Bruno Metsu, and 21 of the 23 players in their squad played in Ligue 1, creating an inferiority complex that could have weighed heavy on their shoulders.

'Above all, I try to make the players feel as confident as possible,' Metsu said in an interview with *World Soccer*. 'I talk very little to them about their opponents, a little bit at the beginning of the week of the match, then nothing other than to point out their weaknesses.

'There are coaches who emphasise the opponents to such an extent that the players come onto the pitch feeling frightened. I use videos a lot, before the opening match against France,

I showed the players all Les Bleus' weaknesses. I never spoke of the qualities possessed by Thierry Henry, David Trezeguet or Emmanuel Petit… the players knew them already.'

Metsu used the France B tag to fire up his team. Talking up his players as being worthy of having a place in France's all-conquering squad of superstars, and adding to their unity by backing Khalilou Fadiga after he allegedly stole a necklace from a South Korean jewellery shop as part of an ill-advised prank, were all part of the overall plan.

With less than a week before the France game, Metsu allowed Fadiga to remain in the team and challenged his side to banish the stories by putting on a good display for everybody to talk about instead. By the time the tournament started, the spirit within the squad was bubbling over.

The Lions of Teranga were ready to roar and went toe-to-toe with their more-fancied opponents, winning 1–0 courtesy of Papa Bouba Diop's close-range finish. Even though France boss Roger Lemerre credited Senegal's tactic of packing the midfield in order to get the upper hand, Metsu says the magic ingredient was more holistic.

'We worked as hard as any team in the world in training… but you don't have to be a great manager to send out a team in a 4-4-2, a 4-3-3 or whatever because anyone can do that,' Metsu told Senegalese radio in 2012. 'By contrast, channelling everyone's energy and strength in the same direction, that is something else. Motivating players, giving them confidence, making them mentally strong… football is not just about tactics and some people tend to forget that.

'I am a big believer in human values, if you don't love your players you don't get results. It's all about the little something extra that a manager can bring, the boost you give the players and they give you.'

Sometimes the source of that rise is clear and a manager doesn't need to do much in order to ignite a team's flame. For a national team, their country's own history can be a powerful motivator and provide extra significance for the players.

'[Miroslav] Blažević used our national pride long before the World Cup,' says Igor Štimac, who was part of Croatia's run to the 1998 semi-finals. 'He was well aware of our concentration, quality and tactical knowledge, so he made his point by talking about our nation's suffering and patriotism.'

Croatia was still a young nation in 1998, having fought for independence from Yugoslavia in 1991 and playing their first competitive match (since the reformation of the country) in 1994, so their World Cup performance was a powerful patriotic symbol.

Blažević was born in Bosnia, but due to the disparate nature of life in Yugoslavia at the time, he understood the experiences many of the Croatians had suffered. He recognised 'players who were ready to do big things for their country' and knew only a light touch would be needed to keep the Vatreni on track.

'We were all like brothers,' continues Štimac. 'Most of us had been playing for many years together in the two biggest Croatian clubs, Hajduk Split and Dinamo Zagreb, so creating togetherness, especially with the war going on, wasn't a big task. We were well aware of the results' importance for our countrymen fighting back home for freedom.

'You know how they say that the best coach is the one not doing anything wrong? That was him, letting us do our thing and shine, not complicating the simple game football is.'

Blažević arguably had an influence on Croatia's World Cup campaign 20 years later as they went one better to reach the 2018 final. The prospect of emulating the previous generation was a big motivating factor as Zlatko Dalić's side became the smallest nation since Uruguay in the inaugural World Cup in 1930 to play in the final.

The memories of some of their national heroes gave the class of 2018 the belief a country their size could reach the latter stages. As in 98, there was an amazing camaraderie among the team and a combined desire to achieve something special together that carried them through three periods of extra time – and two penalty shoot-outs – en route to the final. With a path through the tournament like that, there's little doubting how big a role team spirit played.

'There are two facts that say a lot about this team,' Dalić tells me. 'Firstly, in the 60 days that we were together, there were zero fights or any kind of verbal disagreements between any players or staff members. For 50 men to be together for so long and get along all the time, that doesn't happen often.

'Secondly, we didn't have one game where we didn't have all the players available. That shows we were very well-prepared conditioning-wise, but also that our players were focused, that our medical staff was great and that everybody was willing to sacrifice his body for the benefit of the team. That was huge for our success.

'We had quality in the team, but so did a number of other teams. What was key for us was this unbelievable togetherness, unity, brotherhood and belief that we could overcome any obstacle. That's why I will forever be proud that I was the head coach of such a special team.'

Momentum and belief alone aren't enough to carry a team all the way in a World Cup, though. Whether managers trot out clichés about feeling no pressure because nobody had expected them to get so far in a tournament or not, it's difficult for players not to feel the sense of occasion as the big games rack up – regardless if they play for an unfancied nation or not.

In some ways, when a coach is dealing with players who aren't familiar with being at the sharp end of major competitions, the focus on people-management becomes greater. While the biggest names who play for high-profile clubs are familiar with handling the pressure themselves, the lesser lights may need more attention.

Ahead of a must-not-lose final group match with European champions the Netherlands in 1990, Republic of Ireland boss Jack Charlton unveiled a blueprint for dealing with an inexperienced player as he threw Niall Quinn into the starting line-up for his first tournament start.

'Am I playing, Jack?' and he replied, 'Have I not told you? I must be losing it.'

'We had a light session in the morning and had a sleep in the afternoon in the hotel, but David O'Leary went for a walk because he couldn't sleep,' remembers Quinn. 'He came back and said there was a rumour among the press lads that I was going to play tonight. I said, "Don't be stupid, Jack would have told me if I was going to play".

'The bus drive to the ground with all the fans took about 45 minutes and nobody said a word [to me], so as far as I was concerned that was it. We got to the stadium and Jack told us to go out on the pitch for a walk maybe an hour and half before the game.

'I went out and had a 15-minute walk and the team still hadn't been announced. Jack was out there walking on the pitch talking to somebody and he called me over, put his arm around me and started walking with me.

'He said, "I don't want you chasing around like a headless chicken, I want you to hold your position, go to the far post, not coming to feet and I want you to hold the ball up and come back and defend when we need you to defend, but I want to make sure you're always on the far post". I said to him, "Am I playing, Jack?" and he replied, "Have I not told you? I must be losing it". We had a bit of a laugh and I went into that game without a nerve in the world.

'It was brilliant from him. You can keep all your psychology that's come into the game, to me that was just magnificent because I went into that game thinking, "This is brilliant, the manager loves me, I had right good *craic* with him". Whereas if he'd said "you're playing Quinn, you'd better do this and do that" in front of the lads it would have been tense. But to do it out in the open air of the pitch and have a big laugh about it meant I played like it was a Sunday morning game in the park.'

I think it's very important psychologically to limit the expectations and make it clear that players should do only what they can.

Making players feel comfortable and confident ahead of a big match is clearly an advantage for any team – Quinn's equaliser in the Netherlands match sent Ireland through – but overconfidence can even blight an underdog.

A healthy dose of realism may not be the bravado-building team talk of World Cup shock folklore, but it does have its merits.

'I think it's very important psychologically to limit the expectations and make it clear that players should do only what they can,' reasons Ottmar Hitzfeld, looking back at Switzerland's 1–0 win against Spain in 2010.

La Roja had been nothing short of awesome in the two years since they won Euro 2008 and arrived in South Africa as big favourites to take their first World Cup crown. They'd passed sides off the park with their lightning-quick, 'tiki-taka' style and at times appeared peerless as their classy juggernaut crushed all before them.

So it was no surprise the Swiss side weren't expected to pull up many trees in their opening match of the tournament. Although it probably wasn't what the players expected to hear from their manager, too.

'You always have to try to see your own strengths without paying too much attention to which is the better team,' the former Bayern Munich boss explains. 'Of course, Spain played the best football in the world, they were incredibly strong. We couldn't compete with them football-wise, but we had to be patient, sit back and be very organised.

'Even a team that has the ball most of the time will lose it at times and they will find themselves in a situation in which they aren't too organised and you have a chance to hit them on the break.'

Gelson Fernandes's second-half strike combined with a resolute defensive performance – not to mention some profligate Spanish finishing – earned Switzerland a win that stunned the world. Although when the group's final reckoning came, it was the victors who went out, while Spain recovered to win the group and later the entire competition.

The giant-killer not following up a famous result with more wins is common. So often teams come off the high of a notable result and get too far ahead of themselves, or struggle with the added expectation. It's the manager's responsibility to handle that.

This was the case for Algeria after their famous 2–1 victory over West Germany in 1982. The North African side were bursting with belief after the win, but succumbed to a 2–0 defeat against Austria in their second group game – a result that left them vulnerable to becoming the victims of the 'Disgrace of Gijon' as their two previous group rivals played out the outcome both needed to qualify.

'After the game against West Germany, the players got ahead of themselves and this is where experience makes the difference,' Rabah Madjer, one of the goalscorers in the famous upset explains. 'We were better than Austria's team, but in the end, the thing that made the difference was experience because it was Algeria's first World Cup, so the way we approached the game was [suddenly] new to us.

'The coaches [Rachid Mekhloufi and Mahieddine Khalef] were very cautious before the Austria game and in their pep talks they were saying it wasn't going to be an easy game, that we had to play in the same way we had against West Germany. We played well, but in the end, the factor that gave Austria the win was maybe their tactical plan and experience.'

Madjer says the confidence that came from the 'unthinkable' win against West Germany did have a more positive long-term effect on the nation as Algeria reached three of the next four African Cup of Nations semi-finals, and the next World Cup in 1986. And the former Porto striker points to the role joint-managers Mekhloufi and Khalef had on the North African nation's development by inspiring the victory that announced Algeria to the football world.

'The two coaches were the main factor in Algeria's success at the 82 World Cup,' Madjer adds. 'They're the ones who shaped us as footballers and gave us motivational speeches to help us overcome the fear we had before the game against West Germany. The coaches made us understand that we had amazing players in the Algerian national team.

'They're a big part of Algerian football and the chemistry between them was a big factor in the success of the team, whether it's in their way of thinking or their football strategies, they were complementary.

'The team's progress was a lot better because of the confidence they took from this particular game. The win against Germany changed Algeria's perception of football and helped to put us on the map.'

If one win is enough to inspire a new generation of heroes, it's clear the power belief can have on a team. Without believing the impossible is realistic, pulling off a shock is a non-starter.

'The fascinating thing is you don't have any other team sport where a third division team beats a first division team, but in football it can happen,' says experienced coach Lars Lagerbäck. 'That mindset is the best to have in general, especially when you're going to the finals with a smaller nation.'

CHAPTER 14

NOW OR NEVER:
GOLDEN GENERATIONS

A blessing or a curse? The term golden generation has been bandied around several of the world's greatest teams in the past, but very rarely does a side carrying the tag ever truly live up to the hype that's created around them.

Whether the tag creates an overconfidence within the side or the weight of expectation is too heavy for players' shoulders, it seems more common for these teams to fall short rather than end up with a trophy in their hands. In some ways, that failure only seems to further add to the image of their greatness, somehow preserving them, and protecting them from the glare of actually winning a major tournament.

Take Hungary's 'Golden Team' of the 1950s, which seemed destined to win the 1954 World Cup. A team blessed with the gifts Ferenc Puskás and Sándor Kocsis contrived to lose to West Germany in the final, despite crushing all before them for years either side.

They're joined by the likes of the Netherlands' losing finalists in the 74 and 78 tournaments, Brazil's great flair side of 1982 and England's team of global superstars of the noughties. The latter's inclusion goes to show how the term has become more prevalent in recent years, perhaps undeservedly. And with Portugal and Belgium also having sides adorned by the 'golden' tag, perhaps the modern media's use of the term plays a part in blurring the lines between a strong crop of players and the true immortals of yesteryear.

It also raises the question whether each golden generation should reasonably be expected to win major trophies, even though some do go on to hoover them up. With so few pieces of international silverware available to compete for, perhaps a team having a memorable run or challenging at the sharp end of major tournaments is enough vindication of their status.

In some cases, it can mean even less than that. While the mainstream global press may only remember the biggest and best teams, smaller nations champion their own golden generations, too – groups of players who far exceed previous expectations and carry the hope of the nation on their shoulders to achieve something significant.

One thing's for sure, once a team is anointed as a golden generation, a manager will be forever connected to their success or failure. Can they handle the pressure?

* * *

Roberto Martínez was unsure how to embrace the attention. Everybody was talking about Belgium, the quality of their squad and falling over themselves to point out the arsenal the new manager had at his disposal. The prospect of working with such a talented bunch was what had enticed the former Wigan and Everton manager into international management in the first place.

But now he was at the helm, Martínez felt uneasy about playing up to the idea of this being the nation's golden generation. With two years to go before a World Cup campaign when he took charge in 2016, many around the globe expected the Red Devils to be contenders, which left the Spaniard feeling cautious.

'The golden generation tag needs to be something that is a positive way of describing our group,' Martínez explains. 'Clearly, in 2016, this was a special generation and a team with huge potential but they weren't the golden generation because that was in 1986 in Mexico when Belgium finished fourth

The golden generation tag needs to be something that is a positive way of describing our group.

in the World Cup. It was quite worrying that that [achievement] brought an expectation that was quite powerful and I thought in the beginning could be a little bit negative.

'I publicly tried to say a few times this group of players was the best I'd worked with, but not the golden generation of Belgian football because that was 86. I didn't want that to be an extra pressure on the players, even though these players are used to having to win and play in the best competitions in Europe and around the world – it was too much when you have the whole country behind you.'

Martínez's hunch wasn't without basis. Belgium's current crop of players had been talked about for years, but never really excelled at a major tournament. Predecessor Marc Wilmots had led them to the quarter-finals of the 2014 World Cup, where they lost to eventual finalists Argentina, and then to the last eight of Euro 2016, where they were stunned by defeat to Wales.

When they first moved to Belgium, Martínez and his assistant Graeme Jones quickly went about changing that culture. The duo arrived just as the Belgium FA's new national football centre was opening in Tubize, which automatically breathed new life into international training camps. Alongside this, they tried to break down traditional cultural differences by agreeing all sessions would be carried out in English – a neutral dialect every player spoke – rather than choosing either Flemish or French, the two dominant languages spoken in Belgium.

Upon their arrival, Martínez and Jones also recognised what they considered to be a Belgian characteristic that meant people weren't as comfortable with confrontation and wouldn't fight their corner in quite the same way as other nationalities would. That inner steel had to be developed before any talk of a golden generation could be used.

'It was very clear for everyone to see the group of players in that dressing room was going to be the best group of players Belgium had ever had in their history,' Martínez says about the squad he met when he arrived in 2016. 'So it wasn't a question of talent or a question of developing our team from a technical or tactical point of view. It was more about bringing the purpose of that talent for the reason of winning games. It's not about trying to play the game to see how we can do, it's the opposite – it's what do we need to do in order to win?

'I think that was just trying to change the mindset… I felt we had to start working on the winning mentality. The purpose of playing football is to use individual talent to perform well as a team and, as a consequence, to win. My first impression was that that would be the task, not trying to highlight the talent we had, or instil confidence.'

It seems incredible to think a team brimming with quite so much talent would need that. But compare the pre-Martínez Belgium to the 2018 World Cup semi-finalists that battled from two goals down against Japan in the last-16, beat Brazil in the quarter-finals and pushed France all the way in the semis and it's clear what's changed.

And so, too, has Martínez's opinion of the golden generation moniker. 'After the 2018 World Cup, that golden generation tag became very positive because it was true,' he adds. 'This group are the golden generation of Belgian football and these players are used to having that sort of stimulation in the game, but that's something you can control because it's true.

'And you can work with that by the way you talk about it. [Previously] you almost leave that elephant in the room because you don't want to talk about it if you're not going to be able to handle it and it's going to affect you. Now we've got a dressing room with six players with 100 caps and now you can approach it very front-faced and manage those expectations.'

Even if Belgium are now better equipped at dealing with pressure, it doesn't mean they have any god-given right to sweep their way to glory. Even if they are in a better position to succeed, other countries from the same era may also have precociously talented groups.

And that's where the golden generation tag stumbles over itself. It's very introspective and looks only at what that individual nation has at its disposal, not at what others had at the same time too.

'The golden generation tag was probably given rightly – when you consider some of the players in the England squad, there were world-class players – but it probably didn't help,' says Jamie Carragher, who played for England between 1999 and 2010. 'What you've got to remember is what other countries had at that time, like the French and the Spanish. You think how strong the competition was and they certainly had better squads. We didn't underachieve by not winning the World Cup if I'm being totally honest, if you look at those squads and countries, they had better players than we did.'

That's not how certain sections of the press remember it. And neither do regular memes on social media stoking the debate about how England didn't win a major trophy despite being stocked with so many big names.

Yet Carragher's assessment of the cold, hard facts of the situation, rather than the nostalgia-tinged narrative, is probably more accurate. That said, the former Liverpool defender does think a different manager other than Sven-Göran Eriksson might have done more with that generation of players.

'With us starting really well in terms of qualifying and getting to the quarter-finals, you can't say he [Eriksson] did a bad job, but with that group of players, a better manager could have got England to a final or definitely a semi-final,' he reasons. 'It could have been the case of the teams he was picking. He always picked the best players, but I don't think anyone thought, "What is he doing with that team?" and there's always debate over one or two positions in any team. At times he was criticised for always playing the big names and more often than not the big names are the best players, but do they make the best teams? Maybe substitutions in games or doing something different for a big game might just get you over the line.'

Perhaps the key ingredient England missed was similar to what Martínez identified at Belgium – a lack of killer instinct when the going gets tough. And it's that element that Eriksson needed to reverse to take his gifted squad to the next level.

'I don't know if it was a belief thing, where because something has happened so often before maybe that keeps getting passed down the generations, that this is what you're meant to do, that there's a belief there or a tough mentality,' says Carragher.

'I don't know how you put it into words. People criticised the golden generation for winning Champions Leagues [with their clubs] but not doing anything with England, but you can do that with any England team – lots of teams in the First Division won trophies in the 1970s but England weren't even qualifying for tournaments.

'It's unfair to pick out the Sven era and these players, because they got to quarter-finals of tournaments. The great players of the 70s didn't even qualify for tournaments and I'm sure they

It's unfair to pick out the Sven era and these players, because they got to quarter-finals of tournaments. The great players of the 70s didn't even qualify for tournaments.

were the golden generations of their clubs, so I'm not sure if there's a belief with England that you'll never get across the line or you'll always lose in these big situations.'

If decades of underachievement can hold back a gifted generation when their time comes around, then it should be easier for managers to instil a winning feeling when they're in charge of one of the perennial champions.

But before Joachim Löw led Germany to victory at the 2014 World Cup, their crop of players looked set to be another branded with the burden of one of the most talented never to win a major tournament. This was a new, modern Germany that emerged initially under Jürgen Klinsmann in 2006 – when Löw was an influential assistant – and broke the mould of previous sides. They'd evolved from the three-time World Cup champions of the past, built on an insatiable winning mentality, incisive attacking play and a sturdy backline.

Now the players were more technical and tactically fluid. But they kept falling at the final hurdle of major tournaments – losing two semi-finals and one final before the 2014 tournament came around. While the narrative at the time was about a side lacking what they needed to win, Löw said in a post-victory interview with FIFA that it was merely a case of development towards becoming champions that started under Klinsmann's reign.

'It has been a difficult journey, there were some difficult moments, there was a lot of criticism, but we kept going our way to reach our proclaimed objective, which was to win a major title,' Löw told FIFA. 'I think we worked meticulously on some aspects with the team in training and the staff, we weren't satisfied with just being good. I think we followed this path consistently because we never forgot about our objective.

'Of course, there were some key moments, we lost the final in 2008, we lost in the semi-final in 2010 and 2012. But I've always said our development from 2004 to now was always an upward path, and at some point we would be able to take the last step.'

That goes for Löw as much as the team and perhaps a portion of the credit for the manager finding a way for this generation to deliver was down to the German FA's faith in their man to reach his peak with the players.

Löw's role in the tactics and preparation under Klinsmann in 2006 earned him the job when the former striker stepped down, but Löw needed to grow, too. 'Initially, they thought Löw didn't have the force of personality to see this through, but he convinced the players with his ideas and they're always saying to me he grew as a personality into the role and kind of found his voice in that whole process,' explains leading German journalist, Raphael Honigstein.

'Löw was just very good for this generation of players and a lot of players describe it as a process. I'm talking about the 2014 winners, they started with him and it came to fruition in 2014, the likes of [Per] Mertesacker and [Philipp] Lahm, whose first big tournament was in 2006, then in 2014 they won it together. I think he had the respect of this team and developed this team.

He learned from his mistakes – he made mistakes – and changed to become more pragmatic.'

Context is also important. Just as Carragher points out with England, two of Germany's tournament defeats prior to 2014 came against an all-conquering Spain side, which was going through its own period of greatness. It's a line that keeps arising when it comes to golden generations. The Netherlands' Bolo Zenden also told me that it's not always a story of one team or one squad, it has to be set against others, when looking back at the great Dutch semi-finalists of 1998.

So then if there are so many golden generations, what can make the difference between them realising their potential and not? It seems to be having a manager who recognises the talent he has at his disposal, but who has the intuition to see how the tiniest changes of tactics and squad dynamics can make all the difference.

For Spain's World Cup winners, the catalyst came two years earlier, during Euro 2008 under Luis Aragonés, and was continued by Vicente del Bosque, when he picked up the reins after the tournament.

'With Aragonés, it was just that fit of putting all the jigsaw pieces together. If you can imagine that last piece going in and the satisfaction of the surface being flat, the picture being correct – that's what it was,' says Graham Hunter, the author of *Spain: The Inside Story of La Roja's Historic Treble*. 'When he said, "I'm not going to impose a coach's ideas on how a country should play on a set of talent like yours," he picked on merit. By removing what was considered to be an old hierarchy he brought together a group of people who played together at junior level and the majority of whom didn't have any club rivalries.

'So when Aragonés said, "I've assembled this group based on your individual talents. You all think the same way, you all play the same way, that's the way we're going to play," it was like saying he was making Spain into a mega club. It just fitted.

'It was an unleashing of some supernatural force by getting 23 players, plus six or seven who made it in and out depending on the tournament, who thought the same way, played the same way, who were similar in age, who worked their b****cks off for one another, for who the other guy matters as much as lifting the trophy. That's what Aragonés began and that's the winning mentality, the breakthrough moment, the shrugging off of history.'

It's a force that's been felt by some of the other great sides. If a manager can build an environment that balances out the more pragmatic side of the game without shackling the natural talents of his star players, the chemistry can be perfect.

'[Mario] Zagallo never curbed their abilities,' says Carlos Alberto Parreira, who was part of Zagallo's coaching team for Brazil's 1970 World Cup-winning team – a side considered the greatest ever. 'He was worried about organising them when they didn't have the ball, so there was 100 per cent organisation. But with the ball, he would give his permission for them to play. You see Jairzinho in the middle, Pelé going left, going right, Tostão in the middle.

'The players with the ball had the freedom to play to show their abilities, but without the ball he [Zagallo] demanded 100 per cent organisation. Brazil in 70, when we lost the ball, the players came back so there was no space for the opposition. He was very good at doing this.'

If those subtle managerial tweaks and messages can make a difference one way, then it stands to reason that it could work in the other direction, too. And some of the fabled golden generations of the past that ended up on the wrong side of success were sunk by crucial moments that transformed a great side into losers rather than winners.

For the most notable of these cherished runners-up, fine margins dictate their World Cup stories. From Ferenc Puskás's influence on Hungary manager Gustav Sebes to prematurely recall Puskás from injury for the 1954 World Cup Final, to the Dutch failing to hold their nerve when on top in the 74 final, or even the absence of Johan Cruyff in 78, who could have given the Dutch an extra dimension. Should the finger of fortune have pointed the other way, history would have remembered these sides differently.

'It shouldn't have happened, but it did happen,' says Cruyff's biographer Jaap de Groot, referring to the Netherlands' 2–1 defeat to West Germany in the 74 final. 'The players themselves, especially Johan Cruyff, he was a magician at turning the facts upside down. He was the one who, within the year created the narrative of, "OK, we didn't win, but after all these years, nobody really remembers the winner of 1974, but everyone still talks about the Oranje of 74. So at the end of the day, who's the winner?"'

* * *

The key to getting the most out of a golden generation, then, appears to be taking your chances. A World Cup comes every four years, so the opportunity to achieve a dream is rare even for the nations that frequently qualify. For countries with a smaller pool of players to choose from, the stakes are even higher when they have their own golden generation because the likelihood of getting enough players of the right standard at the same time again can create a now-or-never mentality. The side might not be expected to challenge for honours, but the pressure on a manager not to waste that talent could be even greater than with an elite nation that has the resources to produce another gifted batch soon afterwards.

The constant in many of these sides is their long-term development with each other, so the key for a manager is to recognise that bond and subtly add to it to become more successful at senior level. And some coaches have a distinct advantage with that.

'We had a group of six or seven players who played together at Steaua Bucharest, under the same coach [Anghel] Iordănescu,' explains Ilie Dumitrescu, who was part of the gifted Romania side in the 90s. 'Hagi, me, Popescu, Petrescu, Belodedici, we all used to work with Iordănescu at Steaua. We had a very good connection on the field and that was very important, then he put two or three players from Dinamo [Bucharest] in the right positions and he got the maximum from us in 1994. He knew us very well and knew how to get the maximum from us.'

The Romanians were a revelation in 94, with their team understanding in full swing – topping their group and beating Argentina in the last-16 to set up a quarter-final with Sweden, which they lost on penalties. Four years later, they were at it again, beating England on the way to reaching the knockouts.

Central to it all was how Iordănescu retained a camaraderie within the core of players who knew each other well, without creating a clique that ostracised the non-Steaua contingent.

'It was like a family and a fantastic atmosphere in the team in that period,' Dumitrescu says. 'We had known each other for many years, and we had a very good connection and relationship. We respected each other a lot.

'Iordănescu liked us to think together in the same way and have very good discipline in the match. This was the most important thing and we respected all the instructions he gave us.'

Once a spirit has been fostered within the camp, the next phase is to control the external environment outside of the group. Particularly with a smaller nation, the culture can be dictated by what's gone before and, for some, there can be a tendency to scale back expectations depending on people's traditional perception of what can realistically be achieved.

Similar to the way Carragher spoke about England's subconscious mindset, which led multiple generations of talented players to flatter to deceive in major tournaments, some nations can find themselves falling into stereotypes and repeating historic narratives. Heroic failure or consistently failing to get beyond certain stages of major tournaments can become the norm for a country, a presupposition that can only be overturned by finding a way to break the cycle.

We had a group of really ambitious players [coming through] and the older guys in the national team were really good characters, so it was a really good mixture...

'We didn't need to change the mindset of the players because they already had the ambition, that's for sure,' says Iceland's Heimir Hallgrímsson. 'We had a group of really ambitious players [coming through] and the older guys in the national team were really good characters, so it was a really good mixture and there was a lot of ambition there. It was just finding the right mix, then it was the FA, the people in the media and other things outside that needed to change their mindset.'

Iceland's emergence as an international force wasn't an overnight achievement. The Scandinavians would become the world's smallest nation to reach a World Cup finals in 2018, but it was the groundwork done in the years before that moment that led them to that peak.

Much of the same group of players had been together since Iceland reached the Under-21 European Championships in 2012, and several had gone on to forge successful careers with clubs across the continent. Yet while the talent was there to achieve something special, the ingredient they missed to realise their potential was a universal belief, which could create momentum within the country.

'In the qualification for the 2014 World Cup in Brazil we went all the way to a play-off with Croatia,' explains Hallgrímsson. 'A draw in Iceland, but a loss in Croatia meant they went to Brazil. Still, we realised how close we were to qualifying for the World Cup and that was likely the turning point for the Icelandic national team.'

It goes to show what role development still plays in senior national teams, even if their time together is relatively brief compared to club football. Sometimes a new manager can inherit a side that's ready to break new ground and lead them to success almost immediately, but often the coaching team needs to go on the same journey as the players before getting it right.

Hallgrímsson and Iceland needed the near miss in 2014 qualifying before finally reaching a first major tournament, while Belgium boss Roberto Martínez felt his golden generation's education was enhanced by falling narrowly to France in the 2018 World Cup semi-final.

This was two talented groups at slightly different stages of their development, but both on similar trajectories.

'The big thing about that semi-final, with hindsight, is that we got beaten by France because they got beaten by Portugal in the Euro 2016 final,' says Belgium assistant Jones. 'Didier Deschamps learned from his mistakes and the French national team's mistakes that day. When you've been that far in a big tournament the way France had, I think their experience shone through and they knew how to control certain moments in the semi-final of a World Cup – and that made a difference.

'I'd worked with Roberto [Martínez] for a long, long time. The England performance in Brussels in the Nations League in 2020, Belgium went 2–0 up early on and if you think about the tactics in the second half, they didn't go for the third, and [instead] sat back. It was very un-Roberto-like, but he told me he'd learned from his experiences in the semi-final of the World Cup against France.'

If it's possible for a golden coach to form alongside a group that already seems destined for success, the question remains if it's possible to do it the other way round. A lot of the coaches and players working with break-out groups talk about generations of players that are almost born into potential greatness. But is it possible to create a special group, or does a manager simply inherit one?

'When I started in 2000, I'd spent my whole career abroad in Belgium or Germany and people asked how it was possible that Denmark had educated so many technical players,' says long-serving former Denmark boss Morten Olsen, who managed De Rød-Hvide until 2015. 'But in maybe the last five, six, seven years [in the role], I didn't think the Danish players were playing so well. We of course had the Laudrup brothers, Peter Schmeichel and a few others [at first], but we didn't have so many good technical players. I was lucky in 2002–04, we had a good generation, but after that I saw how [the national team] worked in the youth teams and I didn't like it.'

Olsen set about changing that, realising that a country the size of Denmark, with a population of less than six million, couldn't simply rely on nature to produce players good enough to deliver sustained success.

Alongside his role as national team manager, the veteran coach became the Danish FA's technical director – a role Martínez took up with Belgium after the 2018 World Cup too – and began to use his experience to create a conveyor belt of new stars. The joined-up philosophy between senior and junior ranks created a clearer pathway to the first team, making the chances of another golden generation much greater.

'We started that, not only me, but I provided the inspiration and motivation, and we tried to inspire the clubs, and we now have coaches and youth teams for under-15s, 16s, 17s and so on,' Olsen explains. 'We said the team had to play a certain kind of football whatever the situation. It's not only about winning, it's about educating individual players. When you are 20 or 21, then football becomes about winning – and we have good technical players [to do that].

'But with education, it's a long journey, it's a marathon. If you see the team that has played in the past few years, half the players were playing in my last days. For instance, Pierre-Emile Højbjerg was in the national team in 2014 but he was only 18 then, Christian Eriksen was only 18, but now they are at the best age and they can compete on another level.

'It takes some years, but the national team mostly has talent. They must be very good players, technically, physically, mentally – and that's the name of the game nowadays.'

And as we're about to find out, every so often a truly special star is born.

CHAPTER 15

TACKLING THE ENIGMAS: STAR PLAYERS

Every team needs a hero. A talisman who basks in the world's attention, shows off his special talents and pushes his nation forwards on the biggest stage. The history of the World Cup is littered with them, the icons who can seemingly flick a switch and produce moments of brilliance that decide matches.

For an international manager, heading into a major tournament with their undisputed star in top form is like having a winning ticket. Take Diego Maradona in 1986, Johan Cruyff in 1974 and Zinedine Zidane in 1998: they are priceless assets to be used on the path to glory.

Yet, having a star in a team can also have a darker aspect, and has the potential to be as destructive for their own side, if things don't go their way, as they are for the opposition. Maradona's claim to fame was undoubtedly his imperious displays as Argentina galloped to victory in 86. And while he starred again to help the South Americans reach a second consecutive final in 90, his World Cup story was bookended with moments that showed his attraction to controversy.

In 1982, four years before his World Cup-winning summer, Maradona had been lambasted for letting his frustration boil over as he was sent off in La Albiceleste's defeat to rivals Brazil in the second round. By 94, that paled into insignificance, as El Diez was sent home in disgrace from the World Cup after testing positive for taking a banned substance.

Zidane was the same. An incredibly gifted player who peerlessly glided around the pitch in a way nobody else had, he was equally susceptible to suddenly losing the plot. Zizou's zenith in a French shirt was the 98 World Cup Final as he netted twice to help Les Bleus to their first title by trouncing Brazil. But he'd been absent from their final group game against Denmark, and the last-16 tie with Paraguay, after being sent off for needlessly lashing out in a routine victory over Saudi Arabia.

He repeated this behaviour in the 2006 final, scoring an impudent chipped penalty to give France the lead, before handing the initiative back to eventual-winners Italy after headbutting Marco Materazzi during the second half. It was to be Zidane's final-ever act as a professional player.

Finding a way to get the most from an effervescent star is one of the biggest achievements of many successful World Cup coaches. Give the player enough slack so as not to limit their natural creativity, but hold on to them enough to stop them from going astray. Because you can guarantee that the man in the opposite dugout is aiming to get your star man to do the latter.

* * *

It's the afternoon before England's Italia 90 quarter-final clash with Cameroon and Paul Gascoigne is missing. With the Sardinian sun beating down and the rest of Sir Bobby Robson's squad safely tucked up inside away from the energy-sapping heat, there's consternation among the coaching staff.

'Where the bloody hell is he?' Robson asked, peering around as though his midfield lynchpin would emerge, camouflaged, from the walls of England's training base. The truth is, Gazza wasn't too far away at all. The 23-year-old, whose never-ending source of vitality had played a key role in the Three Lions getting past Belgium in the previous round – winning a 119th-minute free-kick with a lung-busting forward run before delivering the set piece for David Platt to score the winner – was playing tennis. While the rest of his team-mates were shielding from the sun, Gascoigne was oblivious, simply hitting balls around as though he was on a summer retreat.

Gascoigne had so much energy, he was just bouncing around the place. It's like having a toddler around. In the nicest possible way, it was exhausting.

'He [Gascoigne] would just get away,' recalls author Pete Davies, who was granted behind-the-scenes access to the England squad during the 1990 World Cup for his book, *All Played Out*. 'Ending up playing tennis in the heat of the afternoon the day before a quarter-final was only one example of what Gascoigne would get up to, and you'd often find him wanting to play ping pong at midnight. He had so much energy, he was just bouncing around the place. It's like having a toddler around. In the nicest possible way, it was exhausting.'

England boss Robson knew what he was getting from Gascoigne, though. It was part of the playmaker's mystique, the reason he could produce a moment of magic as everyone else around him flagged. The challenge for the management team was keeping a lid on that energy and ensuring it wasn't spent elsewhere than on the pitch.

'They deliberately put him in [a room] with Chris Waddle,' says Davies. 'They're both from the north east and Waddle knew he'd basically been appointed babysitter.

'But you put up with the fact that Gazza could be tiresome because he can be incredibly funny and incredibly uplifting, and great to have around during a tournament. If your mood is dark, he'll walk into the room and cheer it up. He was more fun to have around than not, plus you knew when he got on the pitch, he could do something utterly magical at any moment.'

But as defender Paul Parker highlights, everything couldn't just be about Gazza and a few tweaks had to be made to the room pairings to ensure the entire squad remained happy. While the Spurs man was the carefree enigma of that side, loved by everyone and a character who could lift a dressing room, many of his team-mates needed some respite from his antics.

'Gazza, in that period of time, was always good to be around. I wouldn't have said I'd wanted to share lodgings with him, though – he'd have driven me mad,' Parker told the Vincerà! Italia 90 podcast. 'But, at that time, he was something different and there was something about him, you just had to laugh. Sometimes you'd want to strangle him, but you couldn't finish it off because he'd say something or pull a funny face and make you laugh.

'Trevor Steven was originally sharing a room with him [at Italia 90], but Trevor spent most of his time running away from him because he needed the breathing space. Gazza was always trying to find Chris Waddle and Chris was always trying to get away from him. People wanted breaks from him, but as a player and character, you couldn't find anybody better to be around, which could now be deemed a cliché.'

Gascoigne's story shows what the two aspects of a unique individual can bring to a group. Sometimes the mercurial character may not even be one of the star players, but instead brings a special ingredient to the group that others can't. Their sheer presence is enough to have a positive influence on the rest of the squad.

Gazza epitomises the challenge facing managers as they try to construct a winning squad. On the pitch, he could be a genius, but combined with the wrong team-mates, he could prove a hindrance. Robson appeared to understand what Gascoigne needed. Based on the midfielder's almost whimsical performances that drove England's Italia 90 charge, the manager appeared to restrict the player's boundless energy throughout the Three Lions' month-long stay in Sardinia and unleashed him at the right times to provide match-winning moments.

The potential riches for a manager if they can find their most-talented player's sweet spot is no better shown than by the special relationship between Argentina manager Carlos Bilardo and Diego Maradona in the 1986 and 1990 World Cups.

'The respect was mutual between the two of them and it was something sacred,' explains Nestor Clausen, who was part of the winning side in 86. 'I got the impression Bilardo asked for some things from the rest of the players that he wouldn't ask Maradona. Maradona had some sort of freedom the rest of the team didn't have, but that's something that had been agreed between the two of them.

'It was something Bilardo never gave any explanation for, but it was something agreed between the two – the rest of the team respected that without any questions. The important thing to us was that if Maradona was happy, that would be very positive for us as a team. We could see that when Maradona did well, the team did very well.'

The image of El Diez's stocky frame in Argentina's electric blue shirts is the one most people conjure up when they think of him at his peak. At Mexico 86, he was irresistible for La Albiceleste as they marched to the title with their star directly involved in 10 of their 14 goals during the tournament – scoring five and assisting five.

Yet Maradona didn't start the tournament as a universal favourite in his homeland. Bilardo's decision to build his team around a player viewed as uncontrollable and temperamental didn't go down well in Argentina.

The number 10 had been sent off in his last World Cup in 1982 for kicking out as Argentina lost to Brazil, and he then took a hiatus from the national team that only ended at Bilardo's insistence in 1985. An unconvincing qualifying campaign, paired with the manager's perceived pragmatism, had already caused many in Argentina to question if Bilardo was the right man to take the side to the finals, so his move to build his side around Maradona only heightened the mood of discontent.

But if backing Maradona against the advice of the naysayers was key, Bilardo's ability to leave his star turn to express himself enabled some of the World Cup's most famous moments. It was that understanding that arguably made all the difference.

'In that relationship, Bilardo had to find a way to adjust to Maradona,' Clausen continues. 'Bilardo was a coach whose approach was very tactical, but with Maradona you couldn't talk about tactics or technical aspects because he just created things on the spur of the moment in one second. If Maradona had accepted the tactical approach set out by Bilardo, he would never have scored the goal he did against the English [the mazy dribble from the half-way line past several players that was described as the Goal of the Century] in which he just went out on his own field to score.'

The Maradona–Bilardo World Cup story didn't end when the manager stepped down after losing in the final in Italia 90. They were reunited again for the 2010 World Cup when El Pibe de Oro was Argentina boss, with Bilardo as his general manager.

Their reunion wasn't always a smooth ride. There were heated exchanges between the two, but their understanding remained – Bilardo would advise on training and tactics, while Maradona came to the fore to motivate the side, just as the pair had worked in tandem more than two decades earlier. Only this time they had another special talent to get the most out of: Lionel Messi.

Maradona tried to share all his experience with Messi to make him a better player – it was something amazing to watch.

'Maradona loved Messi,' says Jonás Gutiérrez, who was part of Argentina's squad in 2010. 'He tried to teach him from his experience and make Messi a better player – Maradona was all about the Argentina national team and he wanted Messi to be his successor.

'He [Maradona] tried to get the best out of him and tried to speak in the best way to him. You have to treat Messi in a different way because there aren't many players like him, so Maradona tried to share all his experience with Messi to make him a better player – it was something amazing to watch.'

Maradona focused on areas of Messi's game where he thought he could make a difference, giving the Barcelona maestro special free-kick demonstrations and talking to him about how to handle the pressures of being the side's talisman.

Yet for all of El Diez's love and attention, it was Alejandro Sabella who got the most out of Messi in an Argentina shirt. Sabella wasn't as gregarious as Maradona and tried to let Messi's natural talent flow, even drawing criticism from the press for being too subservient to his star's whims, although Messi's performances during Argentina's run to the 2014 World Cup final dazzled, as he scored four goals and assisted one to win the prize for the tournament's best player.

'Messi is fine, but we must try to be the best possible team to help him. We have to get the team to be more compact, occupy the spaces,' Sabella said before the competition began. 'Messi has matured as a person, he has interior peace, but we have to create a climate to allow him to be happy. I think we have to allow him to be calm.'

There were reports that not only did Sabella set the team up to get the most from Messi, but he also allowed Little Flea to make tactical changes at half time of the tournament opener against Bosnia and Herzegovina. It spawned the idea that Sabella's control on the side was minimal, a claim he denied, and was just the figurehead for a team run by Messi.

For any criticism Sabella's relationship with Messi drew, it seemed to work. And as the former Sheffield United midfielder pointed out in an interview with FIFA before the tournament, the prospect of a fully functioning Messi is an asset no manager can ignore.

'We've played a few games without Leo, but the fact is that he's irreplaceable,' said Sabella. 'There's not a club or national team in the world that would play the same either with or without Messi. We rely on him so much that when he's not there, we notice it.'

Understanding what it takes to get the best out of your most gifted star is crucial if a manager is going to succeed at a World Cup when tight games can be decided by moments of genius, or by a stirring individual performance. For some, like Maradona and Messi, the answer could be to put them at the centre of everything a team does, although for others the solution isn't so obvious.

It was the intuitiveness of Sweden boss Tommy Svensson that sparked Tomas Brolin's mesmeric performances at USA 94, as he bravely shifted the then-Parma striker away from his favoured position and to the right wing.

While Svensson's call to move Brolin out wide ahead of the second group match against Russia may not have been popular with the player at first, it inspired performances that led to him being named in the tournament's all-star team as the Swedes finished third overall.

'Tommy told me, "We must try this, I hope it's OK for you",' Brolin remembers. 'I told him, "It's not OK for me, but of course we need to try because I know Kennet [Andersson] is in good shape, so let's try. But I've never done this for the national team before".'

As Brolin mentions, his new role allowed an in-form Andersson to partner Martin Dahlin up front, and created a three-pronged frontline that helped Sweden to become the tournament's top scorers.

'It was a good move from Tommy because Kennet scored in almost every game after that and we went to the semi-finals, so it was one of the key things that Tommy invented,' Brolin continues. 'I accepted it. I wasn't really happy about it, but I did it for the team and we needed to try it because everyone could see Kennet was in very good shape in training, so he needed to have his chance – and he took it. My new role was good for me too, because it went quite well for me as well.'

* * *

Not all stars are given special treatment, though. Sometimes their characters are so strong, they can find it within themselves to lead the way, even if the relationship with their coach is a bit strained.

That's exactly the situation Cameroon legend Roger Milla found himself in, as he arrived at Cameroon's training camp in

1990. The veteran forward says he and manager Valery Nepomnyashchy 'hardly had a relationship' even as his explosive impact from the bench made him one of the most-feared attackers in the tournament at the ripe old age of 38.

Milla, semi-retired and living on the island of Réunion, wasn't initially favoured by the coach who was strong-armed into including him in the squad by Cameroon's president, Paul Biya. That initial cynicism soon subsided when Milla's unorthodox talent caught Nepomnyashchy's eye in training, and while the Russian used his wildcard to great effect throughout the tournament, the level of instruction to hatch the masterplan was minimal.

'At first, many people didn't want me to be on the team because I was there thanks to the call of the President of the Republic [Biya]. It didn't appeal to everyone because some people thought I didn't deserve my place, but over time things got better,' Milla explains.

'I didn't expect to play a game at first, but when Nepomnyashchy saw me in training he knew I would be an offensive asset. He summoned me to his room with the interpreter and told me that I was technically skilled but physically it would be difficult. He added that I will therefore play the end of games to try to score when the defenders were already tired. I take my hat off to him because it worked out for us.'

When talented individuals have an ingrained determination to be successful, the manager can afford to apply a soft touch. While Bilardo left Maradona to his own devices away from training to get in the right frame of mind for matches, coaches elsewhere found they had to make allowances for Cristiano Ronaldo's astounding levels of professionalism.

The Portuguese forward was undoubtedly his side's focal point and all he asked was that he was left to prepare himself in the way he felt was necessary. For his coaches, that sometimes means relinquishing some control over schedules or drills in order to let Ronaldo get himself primed to his own high standards.

'It's like anything in life. If you have a salesperson in your company and he's the number one producer, generating a tremendous amount of sales, there might be a different space and different guidelines for that kind of superstar than for the rest of the employees,' explains Dan Gaspar, who was part of Carlos Queiroz's World Cup setup in 2010. 'Cristiano Ronaldo, in our case, happened to be an impeccable professional – first one in training, last one to leave. I remember days when Coach Queiroz gave the national team a day off and I walked in the camp in South Africa and I'd poke my head in the gym and who would be there? It'd be Cristiano Ronaldo.

'It wasn't rare that all the players would be on the bus [after training] and Cristiano was still taking free-kicks and we were waiting for him. Nobody was getting off the bus and telling him to hurry up because we all knew that one free-kick could change our lives.'

Gaspar's recollections are shared by Queiroz's predecessor, Luiz Felipe Scolari, who says managing Ronaldo was remarkably simple despite the public perception of the ex-Real Madrid and Manchester United forward.

'It was very easy,' Scolari tells me. 'He might have a reputation for being hard, but in reality, he is a very dedicated player that focused on what he does with a lot of determination and is a player who listens a lot to his manager.

'So for me to work with Cristiano Ronaldo was very easy and I believe he became the best in the world in a lot of elements because of how easy and calm he is as a person and because of the effort he puts into playing football.'

Ronaldo's discipline is an increasingly modern trait, with the demands of the game in the 21st century gradually phasing out the methods of the mavericks from past decades. Previously, it wasn't unusual for some of the most talented individuals to mirror their rock-and-roll performances on the pitch with similar behaviour off it.

Formerly, managers would be required to come up with a special plan to accommodate their star's characteristics and attitude, just as Bilardo did with Maradona. The likes of Bulgaria's Hristo Stoichkov, who was renowned for his temperamental character as much as his virtuoso displays, had to be handled with kid gloves. When things were going well, they were a priceless commodity; but as soon as things started to go wrong, they were like an unpinned grenade ready to go off.

Stoichkov's arrogance and volatile nature makes him the perfect juxtaposition. He regularly clashed with his club managers – most notably Johan Cruyff at Barcelona – but was capable of producing the goods in the big moments, as he did in Bulgaria's run to the semi-finals of the 1994 World Cup. Four years later and he was a non-entity on the pitch as the Bulgarians crashed out in the first round, with Stoichkov going AWOL on a 24-hour trip to Paris days before a decisive group game, which ended in a 6–1 thrashing at the hands of Spain.

On the face of it, the pendulum swung on the basis of Stoichkov's relationship with the national team manager. In 1994, The Dagger had enjoyed a strong bond with head coach Dimitar Penev and even went on strike when Penev was relieved of his position two years later. By 1998, the same strength of feeling didn't exist with Penev's replacement, Hristo Bonev. Now 32 and past his peak, Stoichkov couldn't replicate his heroics of the previous tournament and soon became disruptive.

'Stoichkov has been at the centre of every single crisis in the Bulgarian team here,' Bulgarian journalist Vassil Kolev told the *Independent* at the time. 'Whoever takes over from Bonev, I can't see how he can pick Stoichkov again.'

The difficulty for a manager is resisting the temptation to think they have the keys to unlock a star's potential. Perhaps compromise and bending to the whims of a capricious star can be the easiest option to bank some good will. Take Paraguay goalkeeper José Luis Chilavert, for instance, a dead-ball specialist who also happened to be the South Americans' top shot stopper and biggest personality. His record of more than 50 career goals – eight of them for Paraguay – shows his quality from free-kicks and penalties, but the idea of their goalkeeper charging up field to take them is enough to worry even the most trusting manager. Not that Chilavert says there was ever any doubt he'd be granted the privilege.

'When you're a leader and you have the respect of your team through a lot of work and effort, you are able to do free-kicks and penalties,' the larger-than-life keeper says. 'You need to work very hard to have that respect and that responsibility. We used to have a tactical system in place, so if the ball bounced or hit the goal frame, my team-mates had the instruction to clear the ball outside the field or make a foul.'

Having the sort of faith Chilavert talks about is sometimes all that a player needs to excel. With the knowledge that he's got the full backing of his boss to perform, even when he isn't producing, there's a foundation there to come good when it really matters. And in the intense competition of a World Cup, that can make all the difference.

'The fact that [manager, Enzo] Bearzot trusted me was fundamental,' said Italy's 1982 hero Paolo Rossi in an interview with Fifa.com. 'Without a coach like Bearzot, we probably wouldn't be having this interview about our victory and how I became top scorer.'

There's no exaggeration in Rossi's recollection. The Italian striker was the centre of a match-fixing scandal that was blighting the Azzurri ahead of the 1982 tournament in Spain and had only just completed a two-year ban.

The much-maligned Bearzot, believing in Rossi's ability, called up the striker despite his lack of

> *Without a coach like Bearzot, we probably wouldn't be having this interview about our victory and how I became top scorer.*

playing time and put him straight in his first XI. If criticism of the pick wasn't loud enough before the tournament, it only intensified as Rossi's rustiness meant he made very little impact in four goalless games as Italy made an unconvincing start.

But Bearzot stubbornly remained loyal to his man and was repaid in unbelievable fashion. Rossi burst into life with a hat-trick against favourites Brazil in the second phase and went on to score three more times in the remaining games as the Italians emerged victorious.

'When I started playing again after two years out, it was really, really tough – and Bearzot's trust was very important, as well as the support of my team-mates,' Rossi continued in his FIFA interview. 'Even when I failed to score, I knew they still had faith in me. This is fundamental for a player because if you find yourself in an atmosphere where you feel that your team-mates and coaching staff have lost faith in your abilities, it becomes difficult to perform.'

Rossi and Italy's story – which characterises the entire 1982 tournament – reflects the psychological impact a manager can have on even the most gifted player. With small moments making such a huge difference in elite sport, emotional support can sometimes play a bigger role in an individual's form than tactical instructions.

That's not always the case. And for all the countless examples of managers finding the way to get the most from their biggest stars, there are also times when their actions stifle their natural genius for the team's greater good.

Franz Beckenbauer did this when he asked Lothar Matthäus, West Germany's best player, to man-mark Maradona in the 1986 final – not only nullifying Matthäus's attacking thrust in the match, but also removing his all-round defensive awareness in favour of shadowing just one player.

Beckenbauer's decision created a strange synchronicity with what happened to him in his first World Cup final in 1966, as his manager Helmut Schön and opposite number, England boss Sir Alf Ramsey, hatched identical plans to counteract their two biggest talents.

'He [Ramsey] felt Franz Beckenbauer was the most dangerous German player who could change the game and he asked Bobby Charlton to mark him,' recalls England's Sir Geoff Hurst, who stole the show with a match-winning hat-trick.

'Now that's a fantastic example of one of the greatest players we've ever seen worldwide in Bobby Charlton, who scored two goals in the semi-final, whose record for England was one in two over 100 games, being asked [to man-mark Beckenbauer]. Bobby Charlton did that without a whimper and any resistance, and marked Beckenbauer.

'The strange thing about that was Helmut Schön, the German manager, quite rightly felt Bobby Charlton was the most dangerous English player and asked Franz Beckenbauer to mark Bobby Charlton. So here we had two of the greatest players in any era of the great footballing countries, virtually marking each other out of the greatest game we've had in this country.'

The willingness of two of the world's best players at the time to cancel each other out in the biggest game of their lives is testament to their relationships with their managers. It may have reduced their roles on the biggest stage, but they did what was needed for their nations.

But when a manager loses the respect of their stars it won't be long until they're hunting for a new job.

CHAPTER 16
FINDING AN EDGE: BIG GAMES

The big games come thick and fast at a World Cup. No sooner has a team negotiated one must-win clash than another arrives a few days later that's even more important than the last.

At the highest level, sometimes the narrowest margins can make all the difference between progressing to the next round or booking a flight home, so managers can't afford to leave any stone unturned when trying to gain an edge on the opposition. Down the years, coaches have tried all sorts of ploys to make sure they end up on the winning side when the final whistle is blown – and sometimes the lengths they go to seem more barmy than brilliant.

One of international football's earliest innovators was Sepp Herberger, who led West Germany to their first World Cup triumph in 1954. In an era when the subtleties of today's game weren't so rife, Herberger pioneered the idea of using video analysis of the opposition, studied the effects of pitch and weather conditions on performance, and helped to develop the first adjustable studs with Adidas founder, Adi Dassler, to make sure his players could adapt.

Other managers prefer not to have so many variables, though, and have long-held beliefs about how to get the most from their team when a big game is approaching and will stick steadfastly to their guns. Whether it's pinpointing an opponents' weakness by unleashing a secret weapon, accentuating their own strengths with a clever tactical tweak or by turning to the dark arts, there's normally plenty of subtle tricks at play at a World Cup.

International managers may appear to retain a certain nobility compared to their counterparts at club level, but don't be fooled that the lack of visible mind games means they're any softer.

When the world's most-coveted trophy is up for grabs, managers will resort to any strategy to come out on top.

* * *

Berti Vogts was dressed as a Coca-Cola vendor. Head to toe in the soft drinks giant's red-and-white garb, West Germany's assistant manager was on a clandestine mission to get the inside track on his next opponent. The former World Cup winner was lurking in the stands of the Estadio Le Corregidora in Mexico, keeping a beady eye on Scotland's training session down below.

He'd been sent there by manager Franz Beckenbauer to find out as much as he could ahead of their critical second group game at the 1986 World Cup. But after Vogts had been refused entry in the conventional way, he decided his only option was to enter incognito to spy on Scotland boss Alex Ferguson's pre-match session.

'Berti was refused permission because Alex [Ferguson] said it was a private training session,' coach Craig Brown says. 'But the World Cup was sponsored by Coca-Cola and Berti, being a resourceful wee guy, went to speak to a guy with a Coca-Cola barrel who was setting up a stall.

'Vogts said, "I've got a German jersey for you if you give me your hat and your white Coca-Cola top and I'll wheel your

Coca-Cola barrel in so I can watch this football going on". The guy wasn't to know, he was just a boy working for Coca-Cola, so Berti swapped a German jersey for a Coca-Cola outfit and watched the training session.'

Unknowingly, Ferguson had just played out his entire tactical plan right in front of Vogts, who took down notes on the session before disappearing into the stadium's shadows to inform Beckenbauer how Scotland would line up. The would-be Manchester United manager's entire line-up and game plan was laid bare in front of his opponents.

Alex Ferguson was beside himself, so he nicknamed Vogts the 'Coca-Cola man' from then on.

'We didn't know that at the time until Berti told us when we were talking after the game,' recalls Brown. 'He said, "I knew Gordon Strachan was playing and I knew your team," and he said he saw our training. Alex was beside himself, so he nicknamed Vogts the "Coca-Cola man" from then on.'

West Germany's methods may have seemed underhand, but Brown says 'everyone is at it at a World Cup'. He even remembers a time when he was Scotland manager when he double-bluffed watching scouts by practising a tactic in a pre-match training session that he had no intention of using in the game itself.

And he's not alone. While spies in the stands may make working extensively on certain tactics to get the better of another team almost impossible at times, it doesn't stop managers from hatching clever plots without the on-field practice.

In fact, one of the most famous goals from the 1994 World Cup was devised in just that way. Sweden manager Tommy Svensson had spotted attacker Tomas Brolin pull off a clever set-piece move while playing for his club Parma and wanted to recreate it for the national team in their quarter-final clash with

Romania. Only he didn't dare to try it out on the training field at risk of losing the element of surprise.

'Two days before the game, he [Svensson] told us to do it, but we couldn't practise it because we knew that at every training session, the Romanians had spies,' explains Brolin. 'So we didn't practise it and only did it in theory, so the match was the first time we did this, although we had talked a lot about it.'

By the time the game came round, Brolin and Co enacted it to perfection. The move was intended to drop the ball over the Romanian wall into Brolin's path where the Swede would peel away from the defenders and tee up a team-mate in the centre. But that's not quite how it went.

'It's an amazing story behind that goal because in the end I should pass the ball behind and not shoot, that's not the idea behind the free-kick,' Brolin picks up, thinking back to his moment of magic that saw him race into space behind the Romanian wall and fire a high effort into the roof of the net from a tight angle. 'At the last second I thought "wow, it's like I have an empty goal". I had the goalkeeper there, but being in the shape I was in, I felt that of course I should shoot and it went in.'

The goal proved crucial as Sweden forced a draw with Romania before winning on penalties to progress to the last four. It highlights how a sprinkle of managerial foresight – and individual ingenuity – can make all the difference in a big match.

That ability to find the sweet spot between providing tactical wisdom and allowing players the freedom to use their creativity is a managerial skill in itself. As a World Cup progresses and the games get bigger and the margin for victory even tighter, the subconscious temptation to overmanage grows.

Looking back over recent decades, the influence of top coaches taking the role of puppet master, orchestrating carefully devised phases of play to control a game has become greater.

And while that has transferred into the international game to an extent too, the difference in time coaches can spend with their squads means the effect isn't as great.

One theme that kept coming up during the interviews for this book was that players in the top international teams are of such a calibre that allowing them off the leash a little and giving them more responsibility can be beneficial – especially in the moments that matter most.

There's not so much a manager can do [during a match] and you hope you've got the players who can solve problems on the pitch.

'Guus Hiddink was very much a people manager and knew how to trigger the team,' the Netherlands' 1998 semi-finalist Bolo Zenden tells me. 'He knew when to let go a bit, but also knew when to get the group back together. If you talk about discipline, I remember in France having a certain level of freedom during the tournament. His tactics were also in order. It wasn't as though he didn't do anything about the tactics, but he was always good at getting everyone facing in the right direction and triggering people.

'Also if you allow the more experienced players to set the right example and take more responsibility, they're capable of adjusting things within the squad or on the pitch when things occur. If you have these players available to you and you're open-minded about letting them decide, and make them a little bit more important, they can do a lot more while a manager is on the sidelines. There's not so much a manager can do [during a match] and you hope you've got the players who can solve problems on the pitch.'

It was a philosophy that served the Dutch team well in the big moments. A 92nd-minute Edgar Davids winner helped them through to the quarter-finals, where another stoppage-time goal, courtesy of Dennis Bergkamp, saw off Argentina.

Hiddink's philosophy was far from unusual at the time. Of course, managers would always take different levels of control – and still do – but for some countries at the turn of the 21st century, player influence was an assumed culture within the national team.

One of the most extreme examples is Germany, where a strong player influence was a key factor in their success across several tournaments. And while a failure to adapt as the world's game became more sophisticated was part of the country's temporary fall from grace in the late 90s and early 2000s, the player-led approach was alive and well in 2002 as the four-time winners reached yet another final.

'In our era, the whole team talked all the time and thought about what we have to do if we want to win things,' explains full-back Christian Ziege. 'The team [sometimes] took the responsibility by selecting the players, doing things a little bit differently or [talking about] what we should have done, or once the manager named the team, we kind of reacted on the field the way we felt best to win the game.'

In 2002, former striker Rudi Völler was at the helm and took a lot of credit at the time for leading a side lacking in the quality of previous Germany sides to the final. Yet that perception began to change as stories of his time as manager emerged.

'Völler, because of his personality, was respected in the dressing room, but I don't think there was a lot going on,' says German journalist Raphael Hönigstein. 'Philip Lahm, in his autobiography, basically wrote – and Völler got very upset – that there was no real proper training going on. It was just a case of "let's do some five-a-side, let's do a few corners" and then you go out and play football.'

Several Germany bosses had done the same previously – and the same claims were made about Jürgen Klinsmann four years later – but it became more of a talking point as that approach changed at clubs and other national teams.

In 2002, the team won their three knockout matches 1–0 and Ziege says it was the group of senior players, not just Oliver Kahn and Michael Ballack – the team's two stand-out stars – that made all the difference in the pivotal moments.

'There was always a big group of seven or eight players who talked after games, during the week, before the next game was due, talked about players and what would be best,' the former Bayern Munich and Liverpool defender reveals. 'It's not just one person, it's a group of six to eight players who wanted to achieve the best possible result. So we discussed a lot between us, trying to find the right way to go as far as possible.

'Obviously he [Völler] would have conversations with some players, like the captain [Kahn] or Ballack, talking to them about what we were thinking because all of us – manager or players – who go to a tournament want to have the maximum success.'

Whichever way the internal politics within the camp work, there's no question a strong understanding between players and manager becomes increasingly important in the latter stages of a major tournament. By creating a trusting bond between the touchline and the pitch, messages and tactical shifts are conveyed seamlessly in the heat of battle and a freedom is created to provide the inspiration that can propel a team to victory.

'There is always that question of what does a manager do?' says *All Played Out* author Pete Davies about his time living in the England camp at Italia 90. 'If things aren't going well, the manager gets sacked and a different guy comes in. You look at it and say "how are we now playing so differently? What changed?" And in the same way at a World Cup – "how's the manager got them to this level?" Ultimately, they've done it together, but if Bobby Robson wasn't there [at the World Cup in 1990], it wouldn't happen.

'There's some magic that for those of us who haven't done it, we'll never know. People like to say it's the two per cent zone [where marginal gains are made to decide big matches], but it's more of a thing of spirit than that. If you look at how England performed in that semi-final [against West Germany], where did that come from? Whatever it is, they've got it innately – Robson brought it to a perfect pitch at exactly the right time.'

* * *

One of the most fascinating aspects of the way managers prepare for big games is their tactical approach. Two contrasting schools of thought exist: to either stick with what's served them well so far, or unleash a tactical surprise to catch their opponents on the hop.

Take the Republic of Ireland's manager in 2002, Mick McCarthy, for example, who is firmly in the "if it ain't broke, don't fix it" camp.

'Managers can make teams nervous with their behaviour and suddenly changing everything,' reasons McCarthy. 'You think, "Right, we're in this new position so let's do X instead of Y" and all the players go, "Hold on, we've done Y for so long, why are we doing X now?"

'When managers do that it creates doubt and apprehension, and nervousness among players and they wonder why, so stick to what you've been doing, how you've been playing, and your approach to games.'

On the other hand, France's World Cup-winning boss in 1998, Aimé Jacquet, picked a team based specifically on the opposition they were facing in the World Cup quarter-final and the backgrounds of his own players, too.

'I'd only played one game against Denmark before he [Jacquet] asked me to play against Italy – it surprised everyone,' midfielder Christian Karembeu recalls. 'But he chose me because I had played in Italy with Sampdoria. And you can see in that team there was Marcel Desailly from Milan, Zinedine [Zidane] and [Didier] Deschamps from Juve, Laurent Blanc and [Youri] Djorkaeff at Inter, [Alain] Boghossian and [Lilian] Thuram were in Parma.

'To play against Italy, he knew deep in our souls, we wanted to win against them. Why? Because we love Italy, had been in their championship, but also knew all the characters, we knew all the players – and I think that's why Jacquet put this team together. We knew the mindset of the Italian players and it was a more tactical game than any other, so Jacquet decided on that roster to play.'

It was a bold call, but as often happens when two teams know each other so well, they cancelled each other out, with France going through on penalties after a goalless draw.

Due to the nature of tournament football, managers need to have greater faith in their changes than at club level. Whereas a club boss gets a fixture list months in advance – or at least gets two weeks' notice in a cup competition – and so can hone a specific tactical approach for an opponent, the knockout phase of a World Cup is fast and furious, with only a matter of days between winning one round and taking the field for the next. The allowance for error is less – one loss and you're out – but the element of surprise also increases.

'We wanted to prepare the team to be flexible,' explains Belgium manager Roberto Martínez, whose tactical tweaks became a theme of the Red Devils' progress to the semi-finals in 2018. 'So the decision isn't to all of a sudden be flexible when you've been very structured. Our approach was to be able to use different systems, to be able to use players in different positions.'

Martínez's double substitution against Japan in the last-16 turned the tie on its head, with both Marouane Fellaini and Nacer Chadli coming on to score as Belgium overturned a 2–0 deficit in the last 25 minutes to win 3–2 – the first time that had happened in a World Cup knockout match since 1966.

Days later, a change of shape against Brazil saw striker Romelu Lukaku line up on the right flank and central midfielder Kevin de Bruyne wide on the

I did feel in the lead up to the game, there was too much comment about how good Maradona was and what Maradona could do to us.

left in a 2–1 victory. But despite the quick turnaround between matches, Martínez says it's not impossible to have match plans ready and waiting, despite the uncertainty of who they'll play next.

'You don't know who you're going to play, but there are four teams maximum, so you know more or less where your route is going,' he says. 'It's not that you have 31 teams you'll be facing, so you can narrow it down quite well.'

The prospect of a surprise run can throw some preparations into doubt, but sometimes that can be a blessing. As England found out to their cost in 1986, knowing their quarter-final opponent too well had a bad effect on their preparations to play Argentina. Naturally, thoughts turned to dealing with La Albiceleste's star man Diego Maradona. Keeping the stocky Argentinian quiet was crucial if Bobby Robson's side were going to have any chance of triumphing in Mexico City's Azteca Stadium, although hindsight suggests the manager paid too much lip service to the opposition number 10.

'I did feel in the lead up to the game, there was too much comment about how good Maradona was and what Maradona could do to us,' recalls England's Gary Stevens. 'I have huge respect for Bobby Robson, but I felt I heard him building up Maradona and what he could do a bit too much. Not that Maradona needed building up because his performances said it all. But to keep emphasising it… I kept hearing Bobby Robson talking about Maradona, how good he was, how dangerous he was, what he could to us if we didn't stop him, if he was on form.'

Stevens had been considered for a man-marking role on Maradona as the match approached, but Peter Reid was preferred when the day arrived. In the end, tactical musings made little difference, as Maradona turned in one of his most famous match-winning performances. His two-goal display shows Robson's assertions were right. But Stevens believes modern methods could have stopped Robson's tone from being too Maradona-centric.

'I have to say a sports psychologist would have helped,' says the former Tottenham defender. 'Not only will the sports psychologist be working with the players, but more importantly to some extent, he'd be in the ear of Bobby Robson.

'It's not a criticism but an observation, but I heard it too often from Bobby Robson that Maradona was a genius, that Maradona can hurt you, that Maradona can beat us almost on his own. I'm pretty sure a sports psychologist hearing that would have sat down with Bobby after breakfast and said, "I've been listening and here's something I'm hearing and maybe a better approach is…" and offer that advice.

'Some people possibly see it the other way – he's a great player, so therefore you've got to do something, so the motivating factor is he's a great player. For me, the motivating factor is that I can deal with anything Maradona does and I am fit, I am strong, I am quick, I am alert, I am intelligent.'

* * *

At times, opposition managers must have thought trying to come up with a plan to deal with El Diez in his pomp was a thankless task. Even if he was having a quiet game, he had the ability to conjure up a moment of inspiration from nothing to tip a game in Argentina's favour.

Managers tried all sorts to stop Maradona, but rarely did it work if he was in the groove. And the big stage only seemed to bring the best from him. So it's unsurprising that if there was no legal way of stopping him, coaches resorted to the dark arts instead.

One of the most notable examples was in 1982 when Italy boss Enzo Bearzot charged Claudio Gentile with the task of stopping Maradona by any means necessary. The Italian defender unleashed his own masterclass of skulduggery, not only marking the playmaker out of their second-round tie, but fouling him a scarcely believable 23 times throughout the 90 minutes without receiving a yellow card.

Rough receptions were the order of the day for many of the globe's biggest stars, though, until new rules were introduced to clamp down on some of the more agricultural treatment that was dished out. Before then, managers thought nothing of turning to physical measures when technique was failing.

Austria's Wunderteam of the 1930s were bullied out of the 1934 World Cup, while Pelé considered not playing in Brazil's 1970 side after being left battered and bruised in the 1962 and 1966 tournaments. It was also one of the ways teams tried to stop Hungary's Golden Team of the 1950s.

The Mighty Magyars were the dominant team of the decade, losing only one in 50 matches between 1950 and 1956. The tragedy was, that game was the 1954 World Cup final against West Germany, which became known as the Miracle of Bern.

But it was arguably the blow struck in a meeting between the two earlier in the competition that changed the course of history. Hungary trounced a much-changed West Germany 8–3, but it came at a cost as Herberger's side crocked the Magyars' main man, Ferenc Puskás.

'As the game continued, my opponent, finding his skill of no avail, resorted to roughness,' wrote Puskás in his autobiography, *Captain of Hungary*. 'It was inevitable that sooner or later, I'd be badly injured. We were attacking West Germany's goal. I dribbled the ball down the field without any challenge, put it across to Kocsis and ran forward to take up my new position. At this moment when I was no longer playing the ball, I received a vicious kick on the back of my ankle. The pain was bad, but I dared not think about it and kept moving.

'What does a man want? I asked myself. Does he want to cripple me completely and put me off the field? We were already leading by five goals to nil, so it could hardly be imagined that stopping me from playing would make any difference to the result. I just couldn't understand it. And then I was suddenly no longer concerned about my opponent's intentions. My ankle collapsed. I couldn't stand on my feet.'

Puskás was ruled out for the next two matches, before returning – some said prematurely – for the final. He struggled to make an impact and in a time before substitutes, the Galloping Major's non-performance was pivotal in their defeat.

While it might not be pleasing on the eyes, instilling a win-at-all-costs mentality is a legitimate way to give a team that edge in the biggest moments. A prime example of a manager doing this is Argentina's Carlos Bilardo, a cold-blooded winner who became renowned for his high standards and innate desire to come out on top however possible.

Although his 1986 World Cup winners are best remembered for Maradona's brilliance, the team were also fierce competitors and weren't averse to pushing the rules to the limit when matches were tight – a perception only added to by Maradona's Hand of God goal against England. That grit and determination was even in starker focus as a less-talented side than had lifted the trophy four years earlier, battled their way to the World Cup final in 1990.

When asked directly about that reputation in an interview for Simon Hart's book, *World in Motion*, about Italia 90, Bilardo was happy to justify pushing the boundaries.

'For me, it was wrong,' Bilardo told Hart when the author asked him about whether Argentina's notoriety for going against the spirit of the game was fair or not. 'If it's in the law, then you have to change the laws. If you steal, it's different to steal with a revolver than steal with your hand. It's a shame. We played well and we played within the laws of the game. We did nothing strange.'

It's not the only time the Argentinians have been accused of using underhand tactics in a World Cup. Their entire campaign in 1978 has been mired in suspicion ever since their six-goal victory over Peru saw them leapfrog Brazil with an improbable swing in goal difference to reach the final.

But while nothing has ever been definitively proved, there was little doubt about their intention to unsettle their Dutch opponents in the final itself. After arriving on the pitch late, the Argentinians then started complaining about the plaster cast winger René van de Kerkhof had on his arm, despite having played with it throughout the entire tournament. The Netherlands' wily manager, Ernst Happel, wasn't about to fall for the ruse, though.

'One of the Argentina players said to the referee, "Look at van de Kerkhof, he was a cast on his arm," and said because it was hard, he had to take it off, but van de Kerkhof said he wouldn't,' recalls defender Ernie Brandts.

'Then Happel said, "Come on, we won't play, we'll go home" so we went back into the dressing room and were waiting for 30 minutes until van de Kerkhof was allowed to put a bandage on the cast and allowed to play.

'It took half an hour, so the game started half an hour late. They [Argentina] were trying to find a way for van de Kerkhof not to play and Happel was very clever to say we wouldn't play. There were 120,000 people in the stadium, so there would have been a lot of damage if they'd said the game wasn't going ahead.'

Happel may have won that battle, but opposite number César Menotti was the man in control. A disruption had successfully been caused and it was La Albiceleste who started the brighter of the two sides – and eventually won the trophy their home crowd demanded.

It was one of the most remarkable games of brinksmanship to ever blight the World Cup. But when something so important is up for grabs, anything goes. After all, it's who gets their hands on the trophy that history remembers.

CHAPTER 17

MANAGERS ON THE SPOT: PENALTY SHOOT-OUTS

It's the ultimate test of nerve, skill and ability on the biggest stage of them all. Yet for some managers, the art of winning a World Cup penalty shoot-out remains as elusive as selecting the winning lottery numbers. Five players from each team stepping up to fire shots at goal from 12 yards until one team misses. How much can really be controlled from the dugout? It turns out, quite a lot.

If shoot-outs really were decided by something as random as dumb luck, then the trends we've seen develop since the first time penalties were used to decide tied World Cup knockout matches in 1982 would dissipate over time. Instead, almost four decades on and the same nations keep winning and the same formulas for success keep rising to the top.

England fans in particular have been brought up on a diet of shoot-out despair but they're not alone. Penalties have become a sensitive subject for several nations, with the Netherlands, Spain and Italy having recurring nightmares when it comes to shoot-outs. Or perhaps it's just down to that fact that, as England striker Gary Lineker once said, 'The Germans always win'. Or perhaps they just never lose.

As the tournaments roll by, managers seem to have developed two contrasting approaches to penalties. Some coaches embrace them, warts and all, with an increasingly scientific view on how to come out on top, or try to find innovative ways of gaining an edge on the opposition. For example, before the 2002 World Cup, Guus Hiddink insisted South Korea's players familarised themselves with the anticipation of taking a penalty in a shoot-out by holding practice sessions in an empty home stadium and asking takers to walk from the opposite penalty spot to create an even longer build up.

On the other hand, some managers appear to resent that four years of planning and hard work can be undone by something so simple, and seemingly leave everything to chance.

When Spain were dumped out of the 2018 World Cup by hosts Russia on penalties, caretaker boss Fernando Hierro showed his frustration at how much is left to fortune when a match goes to penalties. After the match, he barked at the gathered press, 'We are leaving this World Cup without losing a single match and that is a fact. A penalty shoot-out is basically a lottery and we weren't lucky. We're all suffering.'

Admittedly, after being installed as head coach just days before the tournament began, the former Real Madrid defender hadn't had much chance to drill his Spanish side until they were in the heat of battle. But history suggests there's something he could have done.

In a time of greater performance analysis, fewer penalties are being scored, suggesting coaches can tip the scales in their favour. In the nine World Cup shoot-outs before the turn of the 21st century, nearly 77 per cent of the 125 penalties were scored, which has since dropped to 69 per cent from 146 spot kicks.

And while the sample size for World Cup shoot-outs isn't huge, that downward trend in scored penalties has been mirrored in recent years in Europe's big five leagues and the Champions League. Perhaps managers have more control over shoot-outs than it initially appears.

* * *

Jasper Cillessen does a double-take at the fourth official's board. But his eyes aren't deceiving him, the digital display has a big red number one on it. The Netherlands goalkeeper, who just minutes earlier made a match-saving stop with his legs, is being substituted. Only seconds remain of extra time in the Oranje's 2014 World Cup quarter-final and the Dutch keeper looks shocked.

Pursing his lips, Cillessen begins the long jog to the touchline, where Tim Krul awaits. Every step feels like an eternity for the 25-year-old as he trots towards the bench, leaving the drama of the ensuing penalty shoot-out behind him.

As late tactical changes go, Louis van Gaal's decision to pull his top stopper in such a high-profile moment is one of the more unorthodox ones. In King Louis's defence, Krul is a spot-kick supremo and Cillessen's penalty-saving record is at the opposite end of the scale. But with underdogs Costa Rica's rearguard action already piling the pressure on his side, the swap only intensifies the mood. As all eyes move to his replacement, Cillessen's frustration boils over as he kicks a water bottle that nearly hits team-mate Bruno Martins Indi before slumping down into a seat on the bench.

'The coach [van Gaal] told Tim before but not me, so it was a big surprise,' Cillessen smiled wryly after the match, clearly still bemused by the situation. 'I was a bit angry. I wanted to play the penalty shoot-out… it's a pity I wasn't told.'

Despite tempers flaring around him, van Gaal remained calm. For him, the decision would make or break his second spell in the Netherlands hot seat – win and he's a genius, lose and he'd leave his post looking like a fool in front of the entire world.

Luckily for the boss, Krul is inspired. First, the then-Newcastle goalkeeper dives down low to his left to turn away Bryan Ruiz's penalty, before repeating the trick to deny Michael Umaña. Mission accomplished.

As the Dutch squad bursts on to the pitch to celebrate, Cillessen races straight to Krul, arms aloft in an emotional embrace.

'The manager and the goalie coach told me before the game that if we had another substitution left, they'd use me in the penalty shoot-out,' Krul explained post match. 'For the whole game, I was watching the action with a different feeling because I knew the possibility could be there. It definitely had an impact – when I started my warm-up, the whole bench was confused as to what was going on.

'If you see their [Costa Rica's] manager's face when I was coming on, he was looking over to see what was going on. His face was priceless. It's definitely one of those fantastic moves. To weigh up trying to psych them out, they were under massive pressure, I was under massive pressure because I had to deliver as well, so I used everything in my power to make it happen.'

Krul's saves not only helped his side make it to the final four of the 2014 World Cup, but helped the Dutch to achieve their first shoot-out victory in the history of the competition. The Netherlands has one of the worst spot-kick records in major tournament history, with only a 20 per cent success rate before going into the Costa Rica match.

So, while the weight of past failures can lay heavily on players' shoulders as they aim to reverse their nation's suffering from 12 yards, perhaps van Gaal's masterstroke wasn't simply having the gumption to swap his keepers so late, but to turn the spotlight away from the takers. Yet the boss says it was simply to get his best penalty stopper on the pitch.

'We thought it through,' he offered in his post-match press conference. 'Every player has certain skills and qualities, and they don't always coincide. We felt Tim would be the most appropriate keeper to save penalties. You'd have seen that Tim dived to the right corner twice. We're a tiny bit proud this trick has helped us through.'

'It was a mind game,' the author of van Gaal's biography, Robert Heukels explains. 'He [van Gaal] knows how Cillessen is: how he thinks, how he feels, how his reactions are. He knew that if Cillessen thinks he has to go out and face penalties that it will bring him down and make him not so sharp anymore. That was his analysis of the human being. Of course, Costa Rica were mentally ahead because 0–0 against the Netherlands is a win for them, so they have a good feeling about it. The Netherlands were very disappointed by 0–0.

'With the change of Krul for Cillessen, everything changes for Costa Rica. They were confused, "What's happening there?" and all the Dutch squad said, "We have Krul" and they get a boost. It was a gamechanger.'

Cillessen was back between the sticks for the semi-final against Argentina days later. And guess what? It went to penalties again. But this time, there was no goalkeeper swap and while van Gaal's ability to repeat the trick was limited by the need to make three substitutions earlier in the game due to fitness issues, Heukels says there was no guarantee van Gaal would have wanted to, anyway.

'He wasn't sure [whether to bring Krul on again] because you can do it once and there's an impact mentally also [so it might not work as well the second time],' Heukels says. 'But I'm pretty sure that if there were not so many injuries and not so many players with muscle problems, he would have brought Tim Krul on [anyway]. Jasper Cillessen never saved a penalty, which was a problem – not with club teams or anyone. That's something he's not so good at.'

* * *

While van Gaal's primary concern appeared to be about making sure he had the best goalkeeper available for a shoot-out, most coaches are solely focused on ensuring the line-up of takers is right. After all, it's the outfield players the pressure is really on.

Countless players have described the feeling of intense anxiety they experience while walking towards the penalty spot in a high-pressure shoot-out, knowing the glare of the world is on them. Even the most decorated superstars who appear ice cold during a match can melt when given the ball from 12 yards out in a World Cup. Just ask Roberto Baggio.

'I don't want to brag but I've only ever missed a couple of penalties in my career and they were because the goalkeeper saved them, not because I shot wide,' the Italian, who famously blazed over the bar in the 1994 final shoot-out, wrote in his 2002 autobiography, *Una porta nel cielo (A Door in the Sky)*.

'That's just so you understand that there's no easy explanation for what happened at Pasadena. When I went up to the spot, I was pretty lucid, as much as one can be in that kind of situation. I knew [Brazilian goalkeeper] Taffarel always dived so I decided to shoot for the middle, about halfway up, so he couldn't get it with his feet. It was an intelligent decision because Taffarel did go to his left and he would never have got to the shot I planned.

Unfortunately – and I don't know how – the ball went up three metres (10ft) and flew over the crossbar.'

The miss has become one of the World Cup's most iconic moments, in the tournament's first final shoot-out. If Italian manager Arrigo Sacchi had one man on his list of takers he would have had confidence in, it would be the Divine Ponytail, who'd almost single-handedly carried the Azzurri to the final.

Yet in the other dugout that day, Brazilian coach Carlos Alberto Parreira didn't have quite the same unerring faith as his own star player, Romario, stepped up. Parreira's side had been rehearsing spot kicks at least three times a week since arriving in the USA for the tournament, knowing it could be decisive in their quest to end Brazil's 24-year wait to win the World Cup – yet the striker was never expected to take one.

'We would get all the players, divide them into two groups as there were a lot of them and everyone was obliged to take a series of penalties,' Parreira tells me. 'From the results of the practice, we started to form our official list. Although on the day and time of the penalties, the list might change as we needed to check who was emotionally ready for it at the time. It changed so much so [in the final] that from the five we had on the official list, three got out of it.

'Romario doesn't like to take penalties. He would practise but didn't want to take them, but at the time we had lost Zinho, Raí and Jorginho and had to add other players who were not on that final list. I remember looking at Romario, I gave him a sign like "can you?" and he said "yes" and off he went – he was very brave.'

When and how to take that decision on the final five takers seems to differ from manager to manager. Of course, with most teams there are some obvious candidates to shoulder the responsibility when the moment arrives, whether that's your regular takers or senior players. The list is almost cast iron early in the tournament as long as those selected few are still on the pitch when the final whistle blows.

But when an unlikely player emerges during training penalty practice, is it worth shuffling the pack to make room for the man who is riding the crest of a wave? When England's manager in 2006, Sven-Göran Eriksson, was faced with that decision, his answer was 'yes'.

'The main penalty takers were set in stone and it was more of a practice [every day in training],' Three Lions defender Jamie Carragher explains. 'But when somebody comes out of the pack who you don't expect to be taking good penalties, it's something to maybe think about when you get to number six or seven. That's when somebody else gets involved and that was unfortunately me.'

As a shoot-out loomed in the dying moments of extra time in the 2006 World Cup quarter-final against Portugal, Eriksson turned to Carragher as his new penalty specialist. The Liverpool defender was fourth on the list that night and despite lashing in his first effort, he was forced to retake it because he'd taken it before the referee's whistle.

Carragher missed his second attempt and England went home.

'I used the same technique I'd used at Liverpool [when he'd taken two penalties for them in the past] and I just placed the ball down, ran up and took it,' Carragher says. 'I was just so focused on a routine that served me well but then unfortunately the referee made me take it again, which is right if he hadn't blown the whistle… it messed with my head whether I should go the same way or swap.'

Carragher wasn't the only England player to miss that night, though – Frank Lampard and Steven Gerrard also fired blanks.

But Eriksson's 2006 vintage weren't the first England side to crash out on penalties.

When it comes to handling those pressure shoot-outs, England are one of a select few countries – along with Italy and Spain – that have historically gone to pieces when asked to outscore their opponents from the spot. And the more the defeats stack up, the harder it becomes to find an answer to break that run.

'I was more than happy with the takers we had,' Terry Butcher recalls of England's first penalty defeat to West Germany in the 1990 semi-final. 'We just didn't take them as well as the Germans did. We [English players] have a feeling of "what if I miss?" and there's a negative feeling rather than a positive feeling. That's what differentiates us from the Germans and why they win the majority of their penalty shoot-outs.'

England bosses have tried to break the curse. Some have given penalty preparation short shrift, others – like Eriksson – simply practise every day and hope it works, then there's those with ingenious ideas to get it right.

'When Glenn Hoddle was England manager, I talked to him about it and he said they had a system of trying penalties,' legendary commentator Barry Davies says. 'For the players taking a penalty, they had a system that they had to take them from 14 yards and for the goalkeepers, penalties had to be taken from 10 yards. This meant the goalkeepers had to be at their extreme sharpest from that shorter distance, and vice-versa for the takers. If they knew what it was like to score from 14 yards, when they stepped up from 12 yards, it would look that much easier.'

Davies says that despite Hoddle's clever idea, the plan never made it on to the training ground when the former midfielder took England to France in 1998. Naturally, they were sent packing after losing to Argentina on penalties.

That elusive shoot-out win was finally achieved against Colombia in 2018 with yet another managerial brainwave, this time courtesy of Gareth Southgate. The England manager knew what it was like to miss a decisive penalty in a shoot-out after seeing his spot kick stopped by Germany goalkeeper Andreas Köpke in the Euro 96 semi-final, and became hellbent on not repeating that experience as manager.

Penalty practice after gruelling training sessions attempted to recreate the fatigue players would experience after 120 minutes of action to look after the physical side of a shoot-out, but it was meticulous planning and research that held the key.

'We've been practising and going through strategies on them since March,' Southgate said after England's final group game with Belgium. 'We've done various studies and had individual practice and we'll obviously go through that in a little more detail now.'

Within Southgate's penalty dossier, he attempted to unlock the secret of the shoot-out. He uncovered the trend that players taking more time over their spot kick were more likely to score and crunched the numbers so players could perfect the ideal penalty.

Goalkeeper Jordan Pickford was asked to take control of the process by handing the ball to each taker, who had been given his pre-determined place in the list thanks in part to psychometric tests revealing which players were most suited to the task. The methods aimed to prove it is possible to weight chance in your favour.

And from a sample size of one, it had the desired effect as England beat Colombia in 2018 to win their first ever World Cup shoot-out, and only their second in eight attempts in major competitions.

A year later, Southgate's charges beat Switzerland in a Nations League shoot-out, before succumbing to old habits to lose on penalties against Italy in the final of Euro 2020.

'Definitely, it's not about luck,' said Southgate. 'It's not about chance. It's about performing a skill under pressure. There are individual things you can work on within that. We have to know who is in charge, who needs to get out of the way, who can speak with clarity to the players. There's lots we can do to own the process and not be controlled by it.'

* * *

If it takes some nations such forensic attention to win one shoot-out, then surely the masters of a World Cup penalty, the Germans, must have been years ahead of their time as they took down their opposition, one spot kick at a time.

Since the first time penalties were used to decide a knockout match – West Germany's victory over France in the 82 semi-final – the Germans have proved unbeatable from 12 yards. They have a 100 per cent record in World Cup deciders and have incredibly only missed one penalty in all that time.

Their run also extends into the European Championships, where they've only ever lost one shoot-out – their first attempt against Czechoslovakia in the 1976 European Championships.

Pierre Littbarski was involved in three of West Germany's penalty successes, stepping up to score in two of them. But instead of pointing to any specific secret to guarantee players score, the German great says it's just the continuation of a cultural theme.

'We don't think much of the past and what happened before. We're maybe a little bit overconfident in ourselves in shooting penalties or handling situations,' Littbarski says. 'We just say, "OK, I can shoot the penalty. It's no big deal, I just put the ball where I like".'

Littbarski even says World Cup-winning manager Franz Beckenbauer was sceptical about the benefits of practising penalties in training – 'he was of the opinion there was a different pressure in training' – and only had cursory sessions before knockout matches. Even Jupp Derwall, the German coach in 82, didn't feel it was necessary to do anything special to address the topic of penalties after the 76 defeat.

We believe in ourselves and if somebody in the group misses, we tell ourselves 'yes, OK, he's not capable, but that can't happen to me'.

'I think it's not just about being strong, I think all Germans have this almost overconfidence a little bit,' Littbarski continues. 'If you asked 10 players, I'll tell you nine players would say they'll finish and they'd score the goal. To have that little bit of overconfidence in some situations is healthy.

'We believe in ourselves and if somebody in the group misses, we tell ourselves "yes, OK, he's not capable, but that can't happen to me". A little bit of bad German character comes through there.'

Based on the Germans' approach, it could be argued that the atmosphere and mindset instilled in players is much more important than the process of taking dozens of penalties before a knockout game.

It's a stance French manager Herve Renard agrees with. While his one appearance at the World Cup with Morocco in 2018 culminated in a group-stage exit, he has won two African Nations Cups – with Zambia in 2012 and Ivory Coast in 2015 – after winning the final on penalties.

'It's most important for the players who are taking the penalties to know we're together,' reasons Renard. 'We know we're going to win because we are together and everything in sport is about team spirit, especially in football. If you're thinking only about yourself, you don't achieve anything, even if you are the best.

'Football is not like tennis where Djokovic, Federer or Nadal are able to make the difference themselves. When you are playing football, you need to be united – this is the most important thing.'

That may have been the inspiration for Akira Nishino's novel approach to Japan's last-16 tie with Belgium in 2018. The Samurai Blue coach was asked about the prospect of penalties ahead of the clash, but shocked the roomful of journalists in his pre-match press conference by announcing his reluctance to even ask his players to take any in training.

'I don't think it's really useful to practise for a penalty shoot-out,' Nishino bravely announced. 'There are so many different aspects when it comes to a shoot-out and it's really tense, so we couldn't possibly recreate the scenarios. Therefore, it could do more harm than good to dwell on it in training before a big game.'

Nishino's policy to shun penalty practice came close to being given the ultimate litmus test 24 hours later as Japan succumbed to three quickfire Belgian goals to lose a two-goal lead and crash out 3–2.

For managers to decide not to place too much focus on penalties may not be that unusual, but Nishino's decision to broadcast it to the world was. The move was almost the antithesis of van Gaal's goalkeeper swap, placing extra focus on the takers.

But although there's no clear correlation between managers religiously practising penalties during a tournament and winning a shoot-out, there is one thing a lot of the coaches and players I spoke to agree on, and that's goalkeepers. For keepers, putting them in the nets after each training session can have a detrimental effect.

'Our goalkeeper didn't like the penalty-taking [practice],' Littbarski recalls. 'I can remember [Harald] Schumacher saying,

"Look, you don't shoot like in a game because you have no pressure, so it's quite different to train for penalties and shoot when it counts".'

It was a similar story with the Republic of Ireland. While their goalkeepers went to change at the end of training, striker Niall Quinn took the heat to don the gloves instead.

'The goalkeepers were precious and when they'd done their quota for the day, they went in,' says Quinn. 'In fairness, they don't like diving around with the ball in the net behind them too often, but I didn't mind it.'

Quinn was no slouch in goal, so much so that Jack Charlton named him as the number-three goalkeeper for Ireland's 1990 campaign. In fact, while playing at Manchester City, the 6ft 3in (190cm) frontman went in goal during a league game after regular stopper Tony Coton was sent off, and saved a penalty from Dean Saunders. It seemed he had quite the track record saving from the spot.

'I went in goal every day after training for the whole tournament [in 1990],' Quinn says. 'I was a good goalkeeper and I was of the view that I'd guess right one out of three times, so I had a bet with anyone who wanted to take three penalties and if they scored all three, they'd get a tenner. If they missed one, I got the tenner.

'I'd say in the three weeks I was out there, nobody scored the three penalties against me. I cleaned up, although getting paid was difficult.'

At least that's one guaranteed winner when it came to penalties. Well, apart from the Germans.

CHAPTER 18
BECOMING CHAMPIONS: THE FINAL

The biggest game in world football. The eyes of every fan on the globe gazing on the four-yearly showdown to crown the best team on the planet. For all the changing habits of modern society, the World Cup final has lost none of its sheen.

While the big bucks of the Champions League may grab huge TV audiences annually, the World Cup retains a special pureness in its competition. Chequebooks can't sway the path of victory that's the culmination of years of hard graft to create the best international side.

Mano-a-mano, country versus country, manager against manager.

But while many coaches and players can only dream of doing battle in the World Cup final, for those few who have earned the right, they know it could be their only chance to write their names in football history.

Only five managers have ever led a team in more than one World Cup final: West Germany's Helmut Schön and Franz Beckenbauer, Brazilian Mario Zagallo, Carlos Bilardo of Argentina and – the only coach to ever win the trophy twice – Italy's Vittorio Pozzo. Taking the chance when it arises is crucial.

The outliers to that rule are Beckenbauer and Zagallo, who appeared in two finals as players and then twice as managers – the Brazilian also working as an assistant to Carlos Alberto Parreira when the Seleção took the title in 1994. France's Didier Deschamps is the only other man to win as a player and manager.

When the curtain goes up and there's only one game between a coach and immortality, every decision they take could make the pivotal difference. So how does a manager prepare for the biggest game of his life?

There might not be as many passionate team talks as a Hollywood movie would have you believe, but there's still plenty of magic being sprinkled from the dugout as we step into the minds of World Cup finalists.

* * *

The world's media was going into overdrive, but Aimé Jacquet held his nerve. As news filtered out of the Brazil camp about Ronaldo's fitness, the France coach remained focused on what was happening in his own dressing room.

O Fenomeno had been the star of the 1998 World Cup, scoring four goals as he helped shoot Brazil to a second consecutive final. His pace, skill and incisive finishing had marked him out as the world's top player and the stage was set for him to strut his stuff in the most high profile of arenas.

Yet as kick-off moved closer, Ronaldo wasn't initially named on the Seleção's team sheet. Rumours began to circulate about Brazil's number nine suffering a seizure before the match, leaving him incapable of playing. But just as the news was being digested, it all changed again. Ronaldo was back in the team and would start.

It was the most dramatic build-up to a World Cup final ever. Brazil's preparation was in chaos and it could easily have seeped into opponent France's psyche too if it had been allowed to affect them.

'The manager, Mr Jacquet, had been aware of the information, but he didn't change anything tactically – he just told us to be focused on what we had prepared. And he was right,' says France's Christian Karembeu, who started the final. 'Before the final we had prepared something and did we need to change our game because of the other team? No. He was right not to change anything or to wear us out by focusing on another situation.'

Ronaldo's appearance was now under increased scrutiny and while Karembeu insists Jacquet didn't change because Brazil had 'lots of other talented players on the bench', the need to protect against the world's best if he did start would surely have been a factor.

France had the added pressure of being at home and trying to win their maiden World Cup, but outplayed their more-decorated opponents to win 3–0.

While Les Bleus managed to keep their eyes on the prize, it wasn't so easy for Brazil and their coach Mario Zagallo. More than two decades on, the exact details of what went on in the Brazilian camp still aren't entirely clear, although we now know Ronaldo's episode occurred shortly after lunch and he was sent to hospital for tests afterwards, with the assumption they'd rule him out of that evening's final. Yet the results came back clear.

Zagallo had already shuffled his pack to include Edmundo in the young striker's place, but as Ronaldo recalled in an exclusive interview for *FourFourTwo,* that was when the real uncertainty set in.

'I approached Zagallo at the stadium and said, "I'm fine. I'm not feeling anything. Here are the test results, they're fine. I want to play",' Ronaldo said. 'I didn't give him an alternative.

He had no choice and accepted my decision. Then I played and maybe I affected the whole team because that convulsion was certainly something very scary. It's not something you see every day.'

One version of events suggests there were two factions within the Brazilian squad, some campaigning for Ronaldo to start the final and others adamantly against it. It's something Zagallo's comments after the match half confirmed.

'The players had been upset that the first teamsheet didn't carry Ronaldo's name,' Zagallo said, after storming out of an earlier press conference. 'It was a traumatic shock. He was really not fit to play and it really affected us. I was wondering all the time if I should keep Ronaldo on the pitch or take him off.'

Ronaldo's story makes most other final preparations look tame by comparison, although an ability to read the mood of players before going into a match of that proportion has always been crucial. While some players thrive under the pressure, identifying how to leave them in the best frame of mind in the run up to football's biggest match is a key part of a manager's role.

So when Luiz Felipe Scolari led Brazil to yet another final in 2002, he needed to judge Ronaldo's disposition to decide if the Inter Milan kingpin needed any special treatment as the big day arrived again.

'The special work we had to do was to not talk about the episode of 98,' Scolari tells me. 'We gave no focus to that, we didn't talk about it so that situation wouldn't be reignited in Ronaldo's memories, so it was forgotten by us and him during that moment in the World Cup.'

The night before Brazil's showdown with Germany in 2002, Scolari admits to feeling the nerves of the occasion himself and it became just as much about handling his own emotions as that of the players.

'[I was a bit] fearful, anxious, scared, but trusting in our team,' he says. 'The night before the final, we saw the players were calm, tranquil and that would be put into practice the next day. We could see in their faces they were happy with what they had achieved and that they wanted to play a very good match the next day, so seeing that made me calmer that night.

'Before that you get really anxious, you worry about the opposite team, all the details you need to pay attention to, not to make mistakes. That's normal and after that, when the game starts, everything goes away and you feel normal.'

Holding their nerve is a big part of a manager's final preparation. By this point, it's the end of a long cycle and while there are still selection and tactical decisions to be made, the foundations for success are already in place.

From the outside, everyone romanticises about managers delivering stirring team talks to gee up players for the biggest match of their lives, but the reality is different. After all, it's a World Cup final and nobody needs telling what it means, so sometimes a coach says very little.

'Once you get to this stage, you don't need special motivation,' explains Zlatko Dalić, the manager of 2018 World Cup finalists Croatia. 'We tried to keep players on the ground and to relax them as much as possible. Media hype, ticket requests, seeing all the videos coming from Croatia with unreal celebrations – as well as playing so many extra-times [on the run to the final] – all of that can really influence your performance on the pitch. We tried to stay relaxed and focused on our task, which was the next game.'

The master at not overcomplicating things before a match was Franz Beckenbauer. Der Kaiser had been to two World Cup finals as a player – winning in 1974 after losing in 1966 – so was highly qualified to understand a player's mindset before such occasions.

His approach was almost the antithesis of the great coaches of the modern game in that he didn't want to fill his team's heads with instructions and would remain consistent in his approach – even when it came to West Germany's 1986 and 1990 final appearances.

'When he [Beckenbauer] put you in the starting XI, that was enough,' says forward Pierre Littbarski, who was in the squad for both of those finals. 'He wasn't the type of coach or manager who came to every player and had a man-to-man talk to boost your self-confidence.

'He was giving you just the formation. He put you in the formation and he said go out and perform. It wasn't the style that maybe I was expecting because from the club teams we had several coaches who did that, but Beckenbauer wasn't the type.

'He gave you confidence by putting you in his best XI. It wasn't different in 1990 either, even for the final, he said just go out and win the match, that's all. There was no attempt to provide performance-boosting confidence, extra character, nothing. That's not the way he coached the team.'

Scolari's approach with Ronaldo turned out to be similar to Beckenbauer's refusal to speak about the past in 1990. West Germany had lost the last two World Cup finals, including being beaten by Argentina in 1986, so when the same opponents stood between the Germans and a third World Cup crown four years later, some acknowledgement of the past might have been expected. But as Littbarski recalls, the time to worry about that was at the start of the tournament and by the time the final had come round, their minds were already firmly made up that this was West Germany's year.

'I never talked to the manager about that [losing in 82 and 86],' says Littbarski, who played in the 82 and 90 finals but was an unused sub in 86. 'It came into my mind before the World Cup that it was maybe my last, but it was really wiped away with the first match because I saw what sort of team-mates I had.

'Whereas in the 86 World Cup things didn't end well, I saw the 90 team and every match, beating the Netherlands [in the second round], the confidence was much higher than before the World Cup. Especially on the day of the final, the idea never crossed my mind that we could lose because we had so much confidence.'

As Littbarski explains, much of the magic that inspires a World Cup victory happens prior to the final itself. A confidence and momentum builds throughout the tournament and there's often a moment – a particular match, tactical change or incident – that stands out as a catalyst for the success.

That's not to say hindsight doesn't play a big role in the post-tournament narrative, so the key for a manager is recognising when something notable has occurred and ensuring that positive bounce remains unbroken.

Difficult decisions can be par for the course in order to do that, though. Take the situation England's 1966 World Cup winning manager Alf Ramsey was faced with ahead of the final against West Germany.

The Three Lions' first-choice striker, Jimmy Greaves, had an international goalscoring record of better than two goals for every three matches he played, but was ruled out of the quarter-final and semi-final through injury. His place had been awarded to Geoff Hurst, who'd scored the winner against Argentina in the last-eight and had been central to Ramsey's wingless wonders that took shape during the knockouts.

But when Greaves was reportedly passed fit to return for the final, Ramsey opted to stick with Hurst instead of rocking the boat – and the West Ham forward's hat-trick in the final vindicated that call.

'There must have been an enormous amount of pressure,' says Hurst. 'Even today, I'm not sure whether Jimmy [Greaves] was or wasn't fit, it wasn't something we ever discussed. I've met Jimmy over the years and it wasn't something we talked about, whether he should or shouldn't have played, or whether he was fit or not.

'If he was fit, then it was a hugely momentous decision to leave the great Jimmy Greaves out, one of the greatest goalscorers we've seen in any country – absolutely unbelievable. But what I did by coming in, I made it quite difficult for Alf because I scored the winner against Argentina in the quarter-final and made the winner in the semi-final, setting up Bobby Charlton. Although I'd been left out before the tournament started, I felt my form was coming back and nothing signifies that more than my first goal in the final.

'At that time, I just felt like I was back to my best. But that came through confidence, so in those two games I'm making a significant statement.'

Ramsey was a staunch believer in sticking with a winning side, so perhaps it wasn't a surprise Hurst was given the nod over Greaves. But he wasn't obstinate to the point of not changing things when it was necessary, such was his thinking when Alan Ball and Martin Peters were installed as wide midfielders to offer more balance than traditional wingers.

Ramsey's strength was his selection of players in roles that were similar to those they played in for their clubs, so Hurst remembers a familiarity to the build-up to the final that brought a sense of normality.

'The preparation for the final was much the same as throughout the rest of the tournament,' Hurst remembers. 'There was no need to change anything, so the preparation when we got together and when we trained was almost the same. The only thing he said to me occasionally was to remind me to play how I did for my club.

'He reminded me to do what I was picked for, getting to that near post and creating havoc in defence. Very simple things like that and just asking you to play the way he wanted you to play.'

* * *

The common theme running through most World Cup success stories is building and maintaining confidence. At the top level, the talent clearly exists in the ranks of several nations, so the difference can come down to psychology. Therefore, managers need to instil a belief in what they're doing and that this group of players has what it takes to the enter the pantheon of previous World Cup greats.

'There are only eight nations that have won a World Cup, so I think you can speak about every nation having a mental barrier before they become a World Cup winner,' says Belgium boss Roberto Martínez.

'You'll never find a national team that wins a World Cup by coincidence or by accident, and that's the work of a national team manager when you have a team that you can't relate to players that have won the World Cup before.

'When Brazil put the shirt on, they are favourites and the players feel as though they are almost expected to win the World Cup because they are the only nation to win it five times. Until you win that first one, it's not about how good you are, it's how prepared you are to face adversity when the doubts come in and say, "can you really win?" That's where the mental barrier filters the nations that can win a World Cup. That was the case for Spain.'

The Spanish were perennial underachievers before they won Euro 2008. It was a watershed moment for a side that had only won one major honour – the four-team European Championship in 1964 – although the nerves still existed when they arrived in South Africa in the 2010 World Cup.

They needed to experience the setback Martínez talks about by losing 1–0 to Switzerland in their opening group match before they could really take the next step. Once they had, there was no looking back.

'Immediately the press were on their backs, which I was disgusted about,' says journalist Graham Hunter. 'They were saying the system was wrong, [manager Vicente] del Bosque was wrong and there was a big clamour in the national press to drop [Sergio] Busquets.

'After the team got back [from the Switzerland match], they had a summit with Fernando Hierro, del Bosque, Iker Casillas, Pepe Reina, Xavi and Carlos Marchena and struck this deal. It was Chatham House Rule so it's free expression [but who said what remains confidential] and what emerged was one line: "Don't change".

'It took years to filter out, but what apparently happened was del Bosque said he didn't think the media's knee-jerk reaction was right, he'd been through the whole match but said to the players, "You're the guys who have to get through the next few games, are you behind this?"

'Apparently the verdict of the players was gritty and determined they weren't for knee-jerking, they weren't going to change. It [the defeat to Switzerland] was accidental and changing wouldn't affect anything.'

That unity made the side stronger. And once the side manoeuvred out of the corner the Switzerland defeat had left them in, wins against Honduras and Chile set Spain on a path that took them all the way to the final.

'I thought there was a change,' Hunter continues. 'Being around them was already quite intense but this became another level and the reason was they exuded confidence and certainty. The minute the final whistle went against Chile, I think that group thought they were going to win the World Cup. I don't think they thought that once they were in motion, and given they knew their next opponent [Portugal], and Iniesta was back fit, which was so crucial, that they could be beaten.

'On a day-to-day basis, there was a sense they were having fun and being given access to training sometimes twice a day, you can take that temperature. We'd see the first players come out from the dressing room sometimes 20 minutes before the rest of them because they couldn't resist being around the ball.'

There are instances of too much of a good thing, though. The Netherlands were bristling with confidence as they lined up to face West Germany in the 1974 World Cup Final, having beaten holders Brazil in the semi-final. The Oranje looked destined to take their first World Cup crown, especially after going 1–0 up. But West Germany fought back with two goals before half time that led them to victory.

German midfielder Rainer Bonhof put the victory down to 'more willpower' when we spoke, although the feeling in the Dutch camp was very different.

'[Johan] Cruyff said that game against Brazil felt like the final,' explains his ghostwriter Jaap de Groot. 'He said they thought they had no chance against the Brazilians, that was a step too far. Holland beating Brazil? No way.

'Then all of a sudden they could match them and outplay them, so mentally after that game we felt like we were becoming world champions, especially because of the level the game was played at and it's still considered one of the best games ever in a World Cup.

'It was just the effect of playing a good tournament and peaking against Brazil. The attitude against Germany was different and the first goal didn't help because they thought it was a done deal.'

For all of the credit that Netherlands side and their coach Rinus Michels deserved, perhaps the ingredient they missed most was experience. Just as there's a craft to seeing out individual matches, the tournament environment requires a certain level of nous in order to be successful. It's something that goes back to Martínez's point about nations calling upon past champions from previous campaigns to tap into the mindset of what's needed to jump the invisible hurdles that stand in a team's way. There's no better way of understanding what it takes to get over the line than having previously won the World Cup yourself. Several past winners have tried and failed to recreate former glories as a manager, so that experience is no silver bullet, but can be priceless when everything else falls into place.

It's telling, then, that Didier Deschamps hailed the psychological aspect of his team above some of their technical qualities as France took the crown in 2018 – 20 years after he'd done it as a player.

'France is the world champion, so it means we did things better than the others,' said Deschamps in the post-match press conference. 'I had a very, very young group and 14 of them were on a discovery journey in the World Cup, but the quality was there and that was it. My greatest source of pride with this group is that they managed to have the right state of mind for such a tournament – it's a word I'm repeating all the time, never give up.

'There are imperfections and today we didn't do everything right, but we do have those mental and psychological qualities, which were decisive for this World Cup. We saw that the teams with the best technical skills didn't have enough.'

Although France's win saw Deschamps graduate into an esteemed trio of Beckenbauer and Zagallo to have won the World Cup as a player and a manager, the Frenchman suggested it was more recent experience that gave the team the tools to be victorious.

'Two years ago, it was so, so painful to lose the opportunity to be European champions [when France lost to Portugal in the Euro 2016 final],' Deschamps added. 'But maybe if we were European champions, we wouldn't be world champions today. We learned a lot from that final. We did lower the importance for this match because we put too much emphasis on that [previous] match. The Euro final was different. We tried to stay relaxed this time. We had to get that star, that shining star. That is wonderful. I'm proud of them and also proud of myself.'

The idea of losing to gain the experience needed to win isn't one too many managers are likely to go for, so the next best option is to try to capture that experience from elsewhere. Sharing knowledge is something the Brazilians, in particular, do brilliantly. Of course, it helps when there are so many previous winners in their ranks, but their use of experience is an unheralded boon to their chances.

'I had experience of being at World Cups with Brazil in 1970 and 1974, one we won, the next we lost in Germany, so I knew the pressure,' says Carlos Alberto Parreira, who took charge for the 1994 World Cup, with previous boss Mario Zagallo as his assistant.

'I knew how big the challenge was and the pressure. You have to prepare mentally, characters, and personalities, it's not just football – you have to deal with the people, the spectators, the press, the players. In 94, Brazil hadn't won the World Cup for 24 years, which increased the pressure.'

A challenging qualification process proved the 94 side's mettle, but Parreira knew his charges would need something extra to become world champions. That came in the form of an engineer called Evandro, a friend of Parreira's who gave motivational talks and courses in several different industries. And it was across three sessions before leaving Brazil that the experienced boss believes the team developed the edge that made a difference in the USA.

'He left a lot of positive messages that we ended up using throughout the competition,' Parreira tells me. 'We also had 10 or 12 players who played in 1990, when we lost in Italy – Dunga, Ricardo Rocha, Ricardo Gomes, Romario, Bebeto – and they had the experience of losing at a World Cup and knew how to behave to avoid external pressure. Our solution was to shut everyone out, keep everything between the group, and nothing that came from outside would catch us.

'I think with all winning teams, not just with Brazil in 94 – other teams that won as well – everyone highlights the importance of the team. A group where everyone is working towards the same goal, to be a World Cup champion. 'There was no vanity or presumption, a player could play at team A, B, C or D, what mattered is that they were all playing together at the Seleção. That was perhaps the biggest secret [to our success].'

Whatever that special ingredient to guarantee success the first time is, repeating that trick can be even harder.

CHAPTER 19

THE WINNERS' CURSE: RETAINING THE TROPHY

Ruling the world comes at a price. While history readily remembers the string of great managers and players who have led their nations to World Cup glory, nobody talks about the come down. Dig a little deeper than the triumphant stories of national heroes and it's clear that reality bites them soon afterwards.

Since the World Cup's first edition in 1930, only two countries – and one manager – have successfully managed to retain their titles: Italy in 1938 and Brazil in 1962. Despite several countries looking as though they might be on the cusp of an era of glory after getting their hands on the trophy, dominating the World Cup doesn't come easy.

Aside from Italy's Vittorio Pozzo in the 1930s, there's only one direction of travel for a manager once they've won a World Cup. And the tournament's history is littered with past winners trying and failing to repeat their glory.

Some coaches do come closer than others, but there's a slew of former champions who follow up that all-time high from four years earlier by suffering early exits and humiliating defeats. The big surprise is there's no sign of that trend stopping, and if they haven't learned from each other's tales, can managers do anything to stop the winners' curse?

* * *

Vittorio Pozzo stands alone. The only manager to win consecutive World Cups, the Italian was a tactical trailblazer in an era when coaches weren't renowned for their ingenuity. Yet his achievements with Italy's 1934 and 1938 World Cup winners are rarely ranked among the greatest in the tournament's history. In fact, most football fans won't even be familiar with Pozzo's name at all.

But it's not just because Italy's back-to-back wins came during a time of scant coverage that means Pozzo's feats aren't as well celebrated as others. There's even some uncertainty about them in his own country.

'Those victories came under fascism, so they're all in some way tainted because they were used for propaganda by the regime,' explains Italian historian John Foot, who wrote *Calcio: A History of Italian Football.* 'It means there's this slight sort of smell, if you like, after the war and Pozzo isn't as famous or exulted as he might be because he won his trophies under a fascist regime. He wasn't forced to do that, he participated in that.

'His whole outlook was extremely nationalistic and he could probably argue he wasn't a fascist, but that's fine-line, grey-area kind of stuff. The players gave the fascist salute and there was a lot of rhetoric around them, so it's a problem in terms of Italy. Do those World Cups even count?'

As Foot points out, Pozzo's success was very much of its time. Looking back, the best part of a century on, it's hard to stomach a national team's glory being so well-funded by a figure so intertwined with fascism as Benito Mussolini. As with many world leaders, Mussolini understood the power of having a successful sports team to stir up nationalist feelings, so ploughed money into Italian football to give the Azzurri the best chance of success.

For all the rhetoric – including an unconfirmed story that Italy's side held fascist salutes in front of a baying anti-fascist crowd at the 1938 World Cup in France – there's no doubting that Pozzo's methods were effective. Even at a time when the idea of a World Cup wasn't universally supported by every nation, there's no doubting getting a second star in 1938 was a significant achievement.

'Pozzo's life is that he saw football as war and it was like the war had been transported onto the pitch. He used his nationalist rhetoric around international tournaments,' continues Foot. 'He was obviously a very good leader of men and very good at mobilising and motivating his teams over that four-year period. They were the best team in the world and you can't really argue with that.'

Italy had won four matches on home soil in 1934 to win the second edition of the World Cup and vanquished any lingering doubts about their status as the world's top side by beating hosts France, Brazil and Hungary away from home support four years later. Pozzo's side were well-drilled and spirited, willing to put their bodies on the line to beat the opposition in any way possible. But they weren't simply bullies. The coach embedded star players, such as Giuseppe Meazza, into his side, despite him not sharing some of the strict values of his team-mates.

For the time, *Il Vecchio Maestro* (The Old Master) was also tactically innovative, lining his side up to be more defensively minded than the gung-ho 2-3-5 formation that dominated the game at the time. Because of the outbreak of World War II, a question remains about what Pozzo and Italy could have achieved over an even more sustained period.

'The proof of the pudding is winning in 38,' says Foot. 'If it was just in 34, you could say it's a home tournament, dodgy things were going on probably, Mussolini wanted to win and maybe that's part of the explanation. But winning abroad in a hostile atmosphere shows they were a very good team and who knows what they would have done in 42? But then that World Cup never gets played and they don't play again until 1950.'

> But winning abroad in a hostile atmosphere shows they were a very good team and who knows what they would have done in 42?

Since Pozzo's double win, few managers have even come close to emulating him. The only nation to ever retain their World Cup crown were Brazil in 1962, although by then they were coached by Aymoré Moreira after Vicente Feola had stepped down shortly after leading the Seleção to glory in 1958.

Feola was back in 1966 but failed to progress past the group stage after the two-time world champions – and their star man Pelé in particular – were subjected to some brutal treatment at the hands of their opponents.

A long line of holders have struggled to hit the heights since and while there's an argument that bigger tournaments and a greater tactical focus make it harder in the modern game to win two in a row, so many former winners have failed spectacularly.

The closest anyone has come to retaining his title was Carlos Bilardo, as he took his 1986 winners all the way to the final in 1990 – only losing to a late penalty against West Germany. La Albiceleste didn't appear to be a patch on their 86 side as they edged towards another World Cup title, famously losing 1–0 to Cameroon in the opening game at Italia 90. But through a combination of Bilardo and Diego Maradona's bloody-mindedness, they continued to find a way to progress, even with El Diez not fully fit.

'Bilardo never changed the atmosphere, he kept being the same coach, asking for the same concentration and being as demanding as before,' says 1986 winner Nestor Clausen. 'He didn't relax after winning because, for him, winning the World Cup was history and after making history, you have to think about the present and the future.'

Making sure that hunger remains within the players is a tall order for any manager, but perhaps it was Bilardo's character that assured it wasn't an issue among his ranks. High standards were crucial, whatever the result.

Clausen, who wasn't part of the squad in 1990 but remained in the side until the year before, points to his manager's reaction on the touchline during the 1986 final as a prime example of what Bilardo demanded of his players.

A natural pragmatist, Bilardo was a stickler for defensive organisation and had spent hours on the training pitch to avoid conceding from set pieces. So when West Germany scored twice in quick succession from corners in the 86 final, his frustration almost concealed any joy at becoming world champions.

'Bilardo was very angry during the match and that was why he wasn't very accepted by the supporters because he was a person who was stressing out when things didn't go well,' Clausen remembers. 'He was a person who got angry quite easily – and very much. After we won, he forgot those two goals, but he had spent so much time telling us how to prevent goals coming from the opposition and telling us how to concentrate, he didn't like that we conceded the goals. He didn't like these mistakes because we lacked concentration.

'It's unfortunate, but sometimes goals happen because of mistakes we've made and it was an issue with Bilardo that he didn't accept mistakes.'

While that unbending acceptance of anything less than perfection might have been hard for Argentina's players – and sometimes their fans – to accept, Bilardo's role as a taskmaster undoubtedly played a significant part in the South Americans' run in 1990. After losing to Cameroon, Argentina conceded only twice in the following five games, squeaking past Brazil in the last-16, before penalty shoot-out wins against Yugoslavia and hosts Italy. Bilardo kept his foot on the gas pedal to get everything possible out of the side.

The subconscious lessening of desire to win again is probably the undoing of many returning champions. Whereas annual club competitions mean teams can carry on with the same winning momentum, the four-year gap means the beat of winning the previous tournament is nowhere near as strong, especially when automatic qualification is available to the holders.

When Carlos Alberto Parreira took over Brazil's 2002 champions for the cycle leading up to the 2006 World Cup, he sensed exactly that. Compared to when he won the 1994 title, a special ingredient was missing going into a tournament as holders.

'The pressure in 1994 was huge, much bigger than in 2006,' he tells me. 'In 2006, Brazil had won two World Cups recently in 1994 and 2002, so the pressure was not as big as it was in 1994.

'The team spirit was not the same because we'd won in 2002, it was a different feeling. Although the team in 2006 was so good with so many good players – Ronaldo, Adriano, Ronaldinho – the team spirit wasn't the same.

'Only Italy in 34 and 38, and Brazil in 58 and 62, succeeded in winning two World Cups in succession, after that no one.

It's so difficult because you relax a little bit and you're not as hungry as before. When we won in 94, it had been 24 years so it was something that was a big challenge for us.

'Once you win the World Cup and you go for the next one, believe me, it's different – not just for Brazilians but for most teams. You don't make real renovations... maybe you keep good players, you keep the name of your country, you have the history behind you, but in the moment during the competition, you lack something and you miss something. Maybe it's this enthusiasm and hunger, which is very difficult to keep.'

If repeating the feat with the same nation is a much harder task, then Luiz Felipe Scolari's decision to take over another country's side after leading Brazil to that 2002 success may have stood him in better stead to draw level with Pozzo.

Big Phil had brought the Seleção together to win the tournament in South Korea and Japan, but turned down the chance to renew his contract for another four years, citing 'some difficulties' and announced his intention to manage in Europe instead. So when he was named as Portugal boss in 2003, he had his sights set on another World Cup winners' medal.

Portugal were outsiders to win the tournament and although there wasn't as much focus on Scolari when the competition kicked off in Germany, that intensified as a team boasting talented players such as Cristiano Ronaldo marched into the semi-finals. The Brazilian coach was within touching distance of matching Pozzo's record, but this time with two different nations.

'Yes, it went through my head,' Scolari explains when I ask how it affected him. 'When we went through the first phase, the second and the third, then to play against France we could go to the final. We were alerted by people that if we won, we [Scolari and his coaching team] would be the first people to achieve that. We wanted it, we dreamed of it, we worked for it, but France were the better team and eliminated us.'

Had Brazil beaten France in the quarter-finals, then Portugal would have faced Scolari's native side in the semis. But while Parreira lamented the lack of competitive intensity for their defeat, a lack of pressure appears to have been a positive for Scolari at Portugal.

'One of the main differences is that Brazil had already won the World Cup four times and for us Brazilians, if you lose the World Cup it's one of the worst defeats a team can suffer,' he explains.

'With Portugal there was a different culture. The best they had achieved was a fourth place in 1966, so we could develop a more favourable situation with coming third or fourth as it was only achieved once before. The demand wasn't as big as the demand in Brazil.'

Whether or not the pressure of expectation was the deciding factor on Scolari's decision not to take Brazil to another World Cup isn't clear, but he's not the only manager to bow out at the top, and not defend his title.

Franz Beckenbauer and Aimé Jacquet called time on their international careers after winning the 1990 and 1998 World Cups with West Germany and France respectively. And history suggests it's not a bad idea.

Sometimes teams have naturally reached their peaks, but when a World Cup-winning manager stays on, it can accelerate that regression. It's human nature for them to lean more on the players who helped them climb the mountain previously and not introduce enough younger players to refresh their ranks.

Countless managers have fallen into that trap. Enzo Bearzot's faith in the 1982 Italian heroes saw them flop in 1986, Marcello Lippi – who left and returned between tournaments

– named an ageing Italy squad that failed to get out of their group in 2010, while Spain's Vicente del Bosque and Germany's Joachim Löw also fell at the first hurdle as holders.

'Beckenbauer was very smart when he won the World Cup and stopped,' says 1990 World Cup winner Pierre Littbarski. 'But Löw wanted different – he won the World Cup and then he wanted to win it again. German people are stubborn and have a lot of pride. If we get pressure from the media and they're telling you it's better to stop, we're then motivated to stay longer and that sometimes leads to success.'

Sadly for Löw, it didn't. Before 2014 was out, his mask had already started to slip as the newly crowned world champions showed signs of having dropped their level, although defeat to France in Euro 2016 had no shame.

But as seems to happen with startling regularity, it was on the completion of that four-year World Cup cycle that the cracks really began to show, with Germany losing to Mexico and South Korea, to suffer the ignominy of their first-ever group-stage exit.

'I think Löw mismanaged the World Cup,' says German football journalist Raphael Honigstein. 'He set the wrong tone, he made mistakes in the build-up and basically made it clear he was going to trust the World Cup winners, which had a real chilling effect on the new guys because they felt their wings were being clipped. Tactically they were all over the place and they couldn't quite react in time.'

Germany's defeat in their opening match against Mexico followed a long line of holders failing to win their first tournament game as holders, with eight of the past 13 winners doing the same since 1974.

Some, like Bilardo's Argentina in 1990, rally, but the struggles can be a symptom of a greater issue, so much so that four of the five defending champions between 2002 and 2018 have failed to even make it past the group stage. It can't be a coincidence, so what is causing the champions' curse? Based on Germany's experience, overconfidence may have played its part.

'[Löw] went into the tournament talking about the big games that would come in the latter stages rather than taking it game-by-game, which would have been a better approach,' Honigstein continues. 'I think he mismanaged the situation. Winning the World Cup is difficult, so when you don't win it twice in succession, it's easy to say it's because the team was lacking focus or whatever. In this specific case, Germany never found the right attitude towards the game and almost had a sense of entitlement, which came from the top.'

When a team has swept all before it in the run up to a World Cup, it's understandable that an overstated sense of belief can become a factor. Winning can feel like a pre-ordained right and, as so often happens with teams that go on long unbeaten streaks, one defeat can have a catastrophic effect.

France had followed up their 1998 World Cup success by winning Euro 2000, and went into the 2002 tournament as big favourites to add a third straight major trophy to their haul – especially after triumphing at the Confederations Cup the previous summer. But by the end of the group stage, Les Bleus were heading home without scoring a single goal.

'We didn't play as we should have, we must accept it as it is,' said France coach Roger Lemerre, who had also been on predecessor Jacquet's staff for their 98 success, upon being knocked out. 'There were lots of little injuries, which means we were never 100 per cent in good health. In a World Cup, we have to be ready from the first day. When you are in trouble the first day, it means something is wrong.

'I have to confess before coming here, we had a series of small problems. We have never been at 100 per cent of our full potential.'

While Lemerre's initial reaction seemed like he was looking for excuses, some of his players and French pundits were more outspoken, claiming the side were arrogant and lacked the 'power' they needed to be successful.

The truth is that France's steady decline had started in September the previous year when a friendly defeat to Chile sparked a run of only two wins in five, representing a significant drop in form by their own high standards. Afterwards, factors like the age of key players in the squad, a need to introduce new blood and dealing with hubris did become apparent, but Lemerre appears to have been too blinded by past glories to see the signals – even dismissing their shock 1–0 defeat to Senegal in the World Cup's opening match by saying 'that's football'.

'It's very difficult to analyse the situation right now,' Lemerre added after they were knocked out. 'It's very difficult for the world champions and European champions to be eliminated during the first round. It's difficult for the players first, for myself and for the French who probably were watching the game on television. This is definitely very difficult to take.'

Often when it's time for a post-mortem, the demise of great champions seems obvious – although it's only easy to see the writing on the wall after the fact. But just like the catalyst that propels a promising side to become World Cup winners in the first place, often it can be a moment in a match that can set a decline in motion.

'There are sometimes very fine margins in tournaments,' argues journalist Graham Hunter, looking back at his experiences following Spain's all-conquering side. 'Up until half time [in Spain's 5–1 defeat to Netherlands in 2014], Spain were dramatically outplaying the Netherlands and had a penalty to make it 2–0. If they had scored at that point, there wouldn't have been a Dutch blitzkrieg.

'It reminded me of when a great champion is caught with a big right hook to the jaw, such as when Buster Douglas knocked out Mike Tyson. By the end, the Netherlands were rampaging and Spain couldn't keep up.'

From there, the whole house of cards fell in on Spain manager del Bosque. Like World Cup-winning coaches before him, his loyalty towards players from previous tournaments led him to select players on past form rather than current ability, even talking Xavi out of retirement after La Roja's Euro 2012 success to play in 2014.

The spring in the step that Hunter had witnessed covering Spain during their 2010 World Cup triumph had gone. The energy on the training pitch had lessened and a lot of the Barcelona and Real Madrid players, who were mainstays of the side, were mentally and physically exhausted after long seasons, and coming to terms with the death of Barça boss Tito Vilanova.

Factions that hadn't existed previously had formed following the rivalry Pep Guardiola and José Mourinho had stoked in El Classico, exacerbated by a training ground scuffle between Xabi Alonso and Cesc Fàbregas.

Del Bosque didn't notice the signs of decline in time or perhaps was at the end of his own winning cycle, something a World Cup provides unlike any other competition with its four-yearly rhythm.

'By the end of Brazil [the 2014 World Cup hosts], it was death by a thousand cuts,' says Hunter. 'There were some players out of form, there were some players who were just physically and emotionally spent. I didn't think del Bosque took sufficient risks in introducing younger players who had been winning at under-19 and under-21 level with [Julen] Lopetegui, and I felt there was a clear case for including Isco and [Alvaro] Morata.

'When you've got a lot of players who have been to tournaments in 2008, 2010, 2012 and now 2014, they were like "here we go again". It wasn't p***ing it away, but a lot of them were reaching for a second gear – or even a third gear – that they didn't have.'

It's a story that will surely be repeated again in the future. And while it does, it leaves Pozzo as the only manager with two shining stars all of his own.

EPILOGUE

There's nothing quite like being an international manager – and it's not just the prospect of carrying a nation's dreams that makes the job so unique.

It's a specialism, there's no doubt. From the paucity of time to work with players on the training pitch to only having two or three opportunities in a four-year cycle to show the fruits of your labour, it's an intense, magnified test of ability in the full glare of a watching public.

Where a club manager has greater control of day-to-day matters, his international counterpart has a frenzied schedule of weeks pockmarking a football calendar. Deliver the expected results, and the gap between the next call-ups can feel much calmer than for a coach pining over the chance to correct the wrongs of previous matches and tournaments.

The fitful nature of the role is why when some of the current crop of supercoaches, such as Pep Guardiola and José Mourinho, indicate they'd be interested in an international job when their club careers have ended, it's no guarantee they'll flourish in that environment. Guardiola and Mourinho may be two of the most decorated coaches of recent decades, but club management has become so focused on each micro-factor a coach can control compared to its international counterpart that they'd have to adapt.

There'd be no time for them to work with players in anywhere near the detail coaches do at the world's top clubs and how easy is it to realise that new lonely existence of working without players? Where does the energy come from?

It was one of the most surprising aspects I discovered throughout my interviews that sometimes it's as much what happens when the attention isn't on international managers, as when it is, that can shape their success.

'An international coach probably has more pressure than a club coach because you can't repair [bad results quickly],' explains French boss Philippe Troussier, who has taken charge of seven national teams across his career.

As a club coach, you lose a match and you have a chance to repair in the next week, but if you're an international coach you have to wait one month or longer.

'As a club coach, you lose a match and you have a chance to repair in the next week, but if you're an international coach you have to wait one month or longer and automatically you feel the pressure a little bit more.'

So much about international football is about preparation for the next international window. Whether it's a short mid-season meet-up to play qualifiers or a month-long sojourn at a major tournament, the environment that's created is key to any potential success.

The coaches need to cherry-pick the messages and methods they can share for optimum effect. A sense of familiarity and camaraderie needs to be garnered within a camp of players who could be spread all over the globe or going toe-to-toe against each other domestically for the rest of the season.

The downfall of many managers has been to misunderstand quite how important enjoyment is in a national side's progress. Some become transfixed solely with on-pitch matters or maintaining the same reputation they developed as a club manager.

Fabio Capello's time as England manager immediately springs to mind. His hard-line, Italian disciplinarian style had made him one of the most-revered coaches in world football during the 90s and early 00s, but that same approach didn't translate to a happy camp during his time in charge of the Three Lions at the 2010 World Cup.

As his predecessor Bobby Robson realised a couple of decades earlier, there isn't the same allowance to be so strict on players while on international duty and if camps become less enjoyable, then problems can creep in. A balance needs to be found.

In the short term, the likelihood of players pulling out of camps becomes greater, but if problems are allowed to fester – such as factions within the group – the situation can become more explosive when everyone is living in close quarters during a major tournament. There's nothing else like it.

In a high-pressure environment when players have little time apart, any issues can escalate. While it might not always end up in some of the high-profile bust-ups seen in past World Cups, disjointed performances can often be a symptom that something isn't right behind the scenes.

That need for a strong holistic focus backs up so many decisions. Squad selections, captaincy appointments, handling egos can all start off a string of events that dealt with in the wrong way can end with a side failing to perform.

With such little player contact time over the course of a season, it's strange then that man management plays such an important role in a sport that is increasingly dominated by carefully choreographed sequences of play and in-depth tactics. That's not to say international football managers don't rely on a high level of tactical astuteness, it's just impossible for them to replicate club conditions.

Consistency is king and maintaining a message and ethos during international meets could make all the difference.

It's for that reason we see so many longer managerial reigns in the international game, such as Joachim Löw, Didier Deschamps and Morten Olsen. There's a need for a settled environment so returning players can quickly slip back into a camp just as a group of old friends meeting each other after time apart can do, and they're masters at creating that.

There's no silver bullet to make it click, though. Different eras and cultures dictate that what works for one manager and one nation won't necessarily work for another. Yet untangle the narrative spun around a World Cup and there are golden threads that weave together most tournament success stories.

For everything to come together, it takes a specialist at the helm. No longer is international management a trade that club managers can easily drop into as a semi-retirement choice. It takes honing and understanding of the skills needed to get anywhere near achieving a nation's dream on the world stage.

And the truth is, for most international managers, while they crave time more than anything else, four years just isn't enough to crack the World Cup's code.

ACKNOWLEDGEMENTS

Every football fan remembers their first World Cup. The moment they first experienced the wonder of the best national sides congregating together for a few weeks of competition.

There's just something so intoxicating about the prospect every four years and for everything that has changed in the world – and football – since the first tournament was held in 1930, it remains that way even now.

There's simply something about the World Cup that can't be matched by anything else the sport throws up, regardless of the riches on offer elsewhere in the game.

So, I guess in a way, I'm trying to unapologetically thank Jules Rimet for dreaming up the idea of a global football tournament every four years during his term as FIFA's third president.

Without Rimet, there'd be none of this. No World Cup memories, no moments of glory (and failure) and, well, this book wouldn't exist either. Ok, so somebody else would probably have come up with an idea of an international football tournament sooner or later, but Rimet takes the credit.

As a result, there's a treasure trove of stories from decades gone by that we still remember fondly. And there were plenty of managers and players from those past tournaments to speak to about their experiences.

A huge thank you must go to all of those figures who were willing to talk to me about their World Cup experiences. It's their insight and thoughts that form the backbone of this book and their generosity with their time to reminisce and explain what they do was incredibly valuable.

Tracking down some of the managers and players I spoke to was no mean feat, as I tried to find people from all four corners of the globe. I would also like to thank fellow journalists who were able to help me with finding contacts in some of the harder to reach locations and eras.

Similarly, too, to the trio of translators who helped me to conduct interviews with non-English speakers. Without the linguistic skills of Rafaela Aguiar-Hill, Dan Billingham and Sofia Valle, there would have been some very awkward bilingual conversations.

All of this would have been academic if it wasn't for Matthew Lowing at Bloomsbury, though. It was his belief in me that paved the way for any of this to happen. His time and patience were key to moulding an idea into something more and providing the platform for me to write *How to Win a World Cup*.

Matthew's support and thoughts throughout the process pushed me as I spent months pulling the book together and flanked by his talented colleagues – Zoë Blanc, Sarah Skipper and Conor Kilgallon – we've now got something that I'm proud of.

All I can hope is that the book provides a new and interesting perspective on the World Cup, and something that does justice to Jules Rimet's initial vision.

INDEX